HOW
TO
WEAR
EVERYTHING

A NO-NONSENSE GUIDE TO DRESSING

KAY BARRON

CHRONICLE PRISM

FOR THE
BARRONATHONS

THIS IS A BOOK ABOUT CLOTHES, NOT A BOOK ABOUT FASHION.

Clothes are important. Clothes can be the difference between a good day and a bad day. Clothes have the power to make the mood you woke up in ten times worse or one hundred times better. Clothes can change the way you walk and hold yourself. Clothes should give you confidence. Most importantly, clothes should be a source of joy and never a source of misery. Every. Single. Day.

I first understood what clothes could do when, as a nine-year-old, my oldest sister brought me back a bright-yellow sweater from abroad. In that little bit of German nylon sunshine, I felt sophisticated, older and, as I went to play at a friend's house, *European*, dammit. My friend just saw a plain yellow sweater, but I saw a whole world of transformation and potential.

As a teenager, I would lay out my clothes the night before. What I wore was my way of asserting who I was or, depending on the day—and the boy I fancied—who I wanted people to *think* I was. I achieved this almost exclusively through wide black trousers, striped tops or dresses, chokers (it was the nineties) or earrings (never both) and Doc Martens (again, it was the nineties).

Some thirty years later, I still lay my clothes out for the morning. Not always physically, but, without fail, mentally—I will prep my outfit, even planning day and evening looks for the week ahead. (This is not always successful. Sometimes the look in my head has not quite translated to the mirror reflection in front of me. Before you worry, there is, never fear, a fail-safe backup outfit that never lets me down.) For I know, through tried-and-tested methods, that the clothes I wear will help me have a good day, a great meeting, feel relaxed and confident for a presentation, or act as a perfect armor for a dinner that I feel nervous about attending. Clothes are a language and a way of communicating. Like any language, you need to understand it and respect it, then you can start breaking the rules to make it personal to you.

I want to make you feel confident and excited about what you wear. Ideally, if you are taking advice from this book, I want clothes to become something that makes you happy. And if not happy, then at least for clothes and getting dressed to be one less thing for you to worry about. For, my goodness, do people worry about what to wear. My WhatsApp chats contain hundreds of pictures of friends standing in front of their bedroom mirrors with piles of discarded clothing behind them, and the caption "What do you think of this?" Brilliant, smart friends with busy lives, important jobs, organizers of otherwise chaotic households, each with no clue what to put on their body. Be it a job interview, birthday party, wedding, vacation, or first/second/fiftieth date, honestly, there is nothing I like more than dressing a friend from my sofa as they prepare for an event in their life, significant or routine.

How to Wear Everything is your getting-dressed companion. When I started writing this book, I asked a friend's advice about tone. He said, "Use that school mistress manner you use with me when I ask you about my outfit." And when I was submitting chapters to my publisher, my agent described one as me "being at your bossiest best." I thought I was being quite nice . . . So no-nonsense, and occasionally slightly brutal, it is then.

My advice is always said with love, as I really, really want you to know How to Wear Everything. Wearing everything is not only for the innately stylish, or for those who can buy anything. It's about understanding what you want to put on your body, how, what with and when. There is no great mystery to it, and it should never be intimidating. No one should open their wardrobe doors with worry, panic or apprehension.

There will be some chapters that are more suited to your way of dressing than others; this is the case for me, too. I haven't been pregnant, and color and print are both slightly outside my black comfort zone. Which is why I invited other experts to be part of How to Wear Everything. Such as the incredible actor Jodie Turner-Smith, who wears color better than anyone I have ever seen. After speaking with her, I immediately put on a red dress. And all my brilliant friends and family who are moms and who pitched in on the pregnancy chapter. Law Roach, who has made Zendaya arguably the best-dressed star on every red carpet. And Sarah Jessica Parker, who revealed that I had been storing my beloved footwear incorrectly for years. Even after working decades in the world of clothes and fashion, I still have lessons to learn, new tricks to apply to how I get dressed. Which is the point. We can *all* get stuck in a style rut that is hard to get out of. *How to Wear Everything* invites and encourages you to try new things, step out of your comfort zones and experiment. It invites you to learn the rules so that you break them.

What is the worst that can happen? If you don't like something, you can take it off and try something new. But what if you love it? Surely that is worth the adventure.

CAPSULE WARDROBE

TYLYNN NGUYEN

Creative entrepreneur, designer, model and undoubtedly one of the chicest advocates for building a capsule wardrobe of essential clothing foundations. No one makes a white shirt and jeans look so damn desirable.

MAKING THE CAPSULE WARDROBE WORK FOR YOU

Just because you might rely on the tried-and-tested wardrobe foundations, it doesn't mean that you are going to look like everyone else. It is about making them work for you, with your own personal spin. Before you start, though, you need to know who you are as a woman, what you want to present to the world, and what pieces mean something to you. Which honestly isn't as daunting as it might sound.

For me, cowboy boots are one of my foundations. I am a horse rider, and my family is from South Dakota and South Carolina; they love animals, they love horses, and they love their cows, and so when I wear my boots, I am reminded that I come from America, and I feel grounded. They absolutely might not be one of your foundations, but you will find your own—it just has to be a certain thing in your wardrobe that brings you personal pride. It has nothing to do with anyone else, it's a sense of pride for *you*.

You might love a hunter-green bag, a pop of royal blue or platform shoes. Who cares if that color or piece goes in and out of style every couple of years, because it's something that means something to you. It becomes a part of your identity, and your personal capsule wardrobe. If you truly love something, then go for it! It might sound obvious, but you must be yourself while you're getting dressed. Clothes are there to amplify you; you don't want your clothes to wear you, you want to wear your clothes.

I think the trick is to keep it simple. Simple is the easiest way to feel elegant. When things are simpler you tend to shine through more. I love a white T-shirt, a great pair of vintage jeans, and some ballet flats, or a beautiful little black dress that works brilliantly with perfect, sexy pumps, or my cowboy boots (naturally). Women are naturally drawn to spend more on statement pieces, but you should invest in the actual pieces that you are going to wear again and again and again, not just a handful of times a year. Those are your investment pieces—an investment towards you, your well-being and how you present yourself.

And once you find your perfect foundations, please ensure that you take care of them so that they will last. Or, if you can, buy a couple of the basics. I have three kids and I can tell you that something is definitely going to happen to my white T-shirt . . .

CAPSULE WARDROBE

Recently a friend asked me if I could help her streamline her wardrobe. She was having a crisis of style confidence and needed a fresh pair of eyes to tell her what to keep, sell or buy. In exchange for a free dinner and a bottle of wine, I happily obliged. The week before, she messaged me to say she was nervous and had done a quick edit of the pieces she felt embarrassed by. We have been friends for a long time, so I naturally reassured her that it was just me, that it would be a very gentle process and there was nothing to fear. It turns out I was wrong, for I was brutal. BRUTAL.

As the pile of "what were you thinking?" grew, and the pieces I approved of started to look lonely on their hangers, her look of distress had me questioning why we had ever started this process in the first place. But I couldn't stop. "Was this a present?" I asked of a particularly depressing dress. Naturally it turned out that she had bought it herself and had worn it to countless weddings. I insisted that she try it on, look at herself in the mirror and tell me what was flattering about it. The silence that met her reflection relegated it to the loser pile.

Three hours later, with five bin bags of clothes for charity or resale (I know she rescued that sad dress after I left), a cold takeaway, a warm bottle of wine and a slightly frazzled friendship, we were left with a very curated closet—some might say bare—with large gaps to fill. And when I wrote her a list of what would fill those gaps, it was all the basics. My friend had a closet full of statement pieces, and some of those statements were great, but she lacked the pieces that should form the basis of almost everything she wears. Call them foundations or building blocks, but ultimately they are the essentials that most of us overlook in favor of something razzier.

Wardrobe foundations are not trend-led. They might not be the items that first draw your eye in a store, but that is precisely what makes them desirable. They are the best supporting character in your style arsenal. Simply by being there, they make everything else look good. Bought correctly, you will have them for a lifetime and should never again stand in front of a wardrobe and claim that you have nothing to wear.

So, what are they and how do you wear them?

WHITE COTTON BUTTON-DOWN SHIRT

I was going to write, "Let's start with the easiest one," but the four not-quite-right white shirts hanging in my closet as I type would suggest otherwise. One is too oversized, and when I try to roll the sleeves up to balance the proportions, it makes me look like a 1970s art teacher, which is not my desired goal. Another creases like the devil—to quote my mother—and only looks good for five minutes as long as I don't move. Of the other two, one has a collar that is too small, and the other has a hem that falls to the wrong place, namely straight across the hip bones, which makes you look both short-bodied and short-legged, even if you are neither. I have no idea why these four shirts are still demanding hanger space, as I have one that is just right.

The perfect everyday white shirt begins with the weight of the cotton—and it should always be 100 percent cotton. One that reveals a whisper of the lingerie beneath, but never gives the full story. The key is the fit—in fact, the key is always the fit. When it comes to the white shirt, the fit should be straight and narrow, but not tight. I will never forgive a white shirt with a nipped-in waist. The collar should have substance to it, allowing it to hold its own and not hang apologetically. It should command attention when layered over the neckline of a knit. Sleeves should be generously volumed (though not balloon) for freedom of movement, punctuated with a weighty cuff of no less than 6cm (2.5 inches), which will allow the sleeves to hang distinctly while also helping to engage a crisp fold when rolling the sleeves up. The rounded hemline should fall to, or slightly below, the crotch, which enables it to be tucked into waistbands without excess fabric causing unflattering bulk, but is also the perfect length when untucked and worn under a jacket, blazer or knitwear.

I have spent hours on TikTok watching women wear their white shirts upside down or back to front, folding, twisting and wrapping the hem corners, tucking them into the neckline, and awkwardly buttoning them up from behind, in order to prove that a white shirt is so versatile and anything but simple. But the true beauty of a white shirt is its simplicity. Undo the buttons from the neckline to your chest to reveal a hint of lingerie and it suddenly has sex appeal. Unbutton it from the bottom to reveal the midriff with pale blue denim and it is youthful clickbait. And when it comes to layered dressing, few pieces work harder.

In the colder months, layer it over a fitted turtleneck, unbuttoned to the chest bone, and tuck it into the waistband of a skirt or trousers. Layer a blazer over the top, but don't pull the collar over the jacket—it looks neater without. In the summer, layer the shirt over a white tank top, unbuttoned to the navel if tucked in, open completely if not. Treat it as a lightweight jacket, wrapped around the waist or over the shoulders until you need it. And finally, there is something irresistible, cool and sexy about a white shirt cover-up on the beach over a bikini and denim cutoffs. Very Amalfi Coast on any coast.

BLAZER

Blazers were invented for those days when you need to feel that little bit more put together. Their roots are in rowing, where they were considered informal items for sportsmen to warm up in, but once adopted by women, they assumed a much-needed glamor. For ironically, the blazer now serves to make the informal formal.

The way to approach buying or wearing a blazer is that you should not think of it exclusively as part of a workwear wardrobe, but instead as you would a denim jacket—a throw-on-and-go cover-up, albeit a more elevated one. It is the perfect trans-seasonal item that works with nearly everything in your wardrobe. It's the ideal between-season jacket, but it's also good for layering under generous coats instead of an extra knit in winter.

The classic shape to opt for—my personal favorite and probably the most versatile—is the oversized. Think masculine, but not as if you have borrowed a jacket that's three sizes too big. Straight cut, broad shoulders (though not 80s power shoulders for everyday) and a hem that falls to just below the bottom work best. A more structured one in a heavier wool is good for winter, and ideally a lighter-weight option for summer too, both single-breasted as that shape has ease and simplicity of line.

Traditionally the blazer favors brass buttons, but for an everyday essential, I would opt for those with tonal buttons that don't distract. Or, if the cut of the jacket is perfect for you, switch the bold buttons for something more subtle.

As casual wear, the oversized blazer worn over a white shirt and paired with straight-cut blue jeans is the influencer's uniform, and if it ain't broke . . . But it also looks chic worn over a loose knit and a miniskirt. Just ensure the skirt hem is slightly longer than the jacket. A blazer over a dress isn't my favorite look, but if it's your thing, make sure to get the proportions right. I'd avoid it if you're unsure.

Finally, never, ever shoulder robe. If that is a new phrase for you, lucky you; it simply means wearing the blazer over your shoulders but not putting your arms in the sleeves. It's as pointless as it sounds, and always looks more awkward than stylish. Don't do it and there are no exceptions to this rule. Unless your arm is in a cast, but *only* then.

TAILORED TROUSERS

I will bet that you already have a pair or two of these in your closet. I am also willing to bet that you hate them as they make you feel frumpy or schlumpy. Or they remind you of those occasions where jeans are inappropriate—job interviews, funerals and those weird parties where you had no idea what to wear, so you went with tailored trousers and a shirt, and even those drop earrings didn't save you from looking like you were about to broker a mortgage deal in the bathroom. But that's because you have the wrong trousers.

The right tailored trousers should make you look polished and together, even if you feel anything but. Such is the power of good trousers. They should sit somewhere between suit trousers and dressy trousers, ready to be dressed up or down as required. Styles in a medium-weight fabric with a waistband that sits below the belly button and just above the hips are the ideal, and a concealed zipper, single front pleats leading into pressed-crease generous legs (don't think wide, think comfort) and pockets are a must. You may have been told to stitch up pockets on trousers so as to not ruin the line, but that advice should only be applied to narrow coats and suit jackets. When it comes to trousers, there is often nothing better than standing with your hands in the pockets. I'm not sure why it is so comforting, but it relaxes the look, and if you are in a scenario that makes you feel nervous, hands in pockets is a fail-safe way to also appear relaxed.

As for the length, ideally you'd want shoe options: heels for evening or work, sneakers or loafers for day and casual. In which case keep the length right for your chosen heel height and almost too long for flats, as they look more pleasing if they slightly puddle around the shoe. But I will reiterate the word "slightly." It's not pleasing if you look like you are standing in a hole. Don't be afraid to have them altered if the length isn't quite right; just remember to bring the shoes you want to wear them with to the tailor so they can adjust the hemline accordingly.

It might go without saying but I'm going to say it anyway: make the trousers black. The right black tailored trouser will serve you over and over again, and will look as good with a neutral T-shirt as with a colored knit. Once you are confident you have the right style in black, then grey is your next ally, and only buy navy trousers if you are positive you will wear them regularly, as they can get nautical very quickly. For summer, a camel pair will be handy for workwear, styled with flat sandals, the tank, and a white shirt worn over and tucked into the waistband.

LEATHER JACKET

I once had a long leather jacket that I was very proud of. Until the day I was getting ready to leave the house and my then-housemate said, "You look like what's-their-name from *The Matrix*." At the same time as I suggested "Trinity?", he said, "Laurence Fishburne" and closed the front door behind him, leaving me questioning all my life decisions (and friendships). That jacket was promptly given away. On another occasion, my good friend sent her husband a picture of the leather blazer that she was considering buying, and he replied with a picture of Shaft. She never bought the jacket.

You see, a leather jacket can be tricky and not for everyone, and if in doubt, then maybe it isn't one of your key foundations, and that is fine. For those confident that they need a leather jacket in their armory, you need one with true staying power as the perfect leather jacket will only get better with age. Much like yourself, I'm sure. A classic motorcycle jacket in black leather with silver hardware is a personal favorite, and never, ever out of style. As is a sleek zip-up or button-up. In fact, sleek is the fit you are seeking—narrow and cut to the waist. Anything longer moves out of the everyday essential as it won't be the ideal complement to every shape of jeans, dresses or tailoring.

A good, 100 percent leather jacket is built to last, and if you want it to be something your grieving family are fighting over after you are gone, you need to take care of it. Before you wear it, spray or wax it with a leather protector. This should protect it from water and staining, but not a good soaking, so refrain from wearing it in heavy rain, if possible. And never, ever wash it. Once or twice a year, depending on how often you wear it, you should condition the leather to soften it. But for any stains along the way, a bit of soapy water and a cloth should be sufficient. I can tell that you zoned out there, but believe me when I tell you that you will be gutted if your favorite leather jacket bites the dust, so get that wax out.

TURTLENECK

As soon as autumn hits, out come the turtlenecks, and they are not retired until spring. I don't think any other item in my closet works as hard, for the once-humble turtleneck is now the backbone to my winter wardrobe. Worn under shirts, other knitwear, short-sleeved jumpsuits and tailoring, it turns pieces only suitable for warmer months into year-rounders. For the purposes of layering, ensure a fine knit and one that is not at all itchy or too tight in the neck. If it is either, it must be instantly relegated. Comfort is fundamental when layering, and ideally you should completely forget it is even there.

When it comes to the wardrobe foundations, I would recommend a starting palette of black, white, grey and navy or beige if they work for you. I look like a tea biscuit in beige, but you might have more luck. It may sound boring, but they are classic and called neutrals because their main purpose is to complement and not command attention. However, layered knitwear is where you can add your chosen colors—I love red—as they serve the purpose of adding a pop of color and difference, and will gently lift the more neutral pieces they are paired with.

BLACK DRESS

Ahh, the Little Black Dress, or Long Black Dress, or Midi Black Dress, or Knitted Black Dress or indeed any other black dress, for they are all faultless. You just need to choose the right one for you.

I love, love, love a Little Black Dress—or, more accurately, I love the idea of a Little Black Dress. But it is not the black-dress foundation that I turn to regularly. No, the favored black dress—at least in the cooler months—is one long black knitted turtleneck dress. Maybe not as overtly sexy, but let me tell you, that has been one lucky dress to the discerning eye. It's the dress that works for dates, work, dinner with friends, casual Sundays and travelling. It is a throw-on-and-go special, and it is simply the choice of footwear that makes it appropriate for each occasion. Heeled boots for work and dates, flat combat boots or sneakers for anything more casual.

While the minidress is the preference for some, I promise that everyone looks good and will feel good in a knitted dress, which is why they have been bestsellers throughout my retail career. Nothing too heavy as it gets too frumpy, but that sweet mid-weight spot, with a delicate rib. Long sleeves, a high-neck and a maxi length are instantly elongating, but I encourage a side or back slit for at least a tease at what lies beneath. Live a little. I like fitted, but if you are more comfortable with a looser silhouette, then choose a straight cut.

Other than shoes, it doesn't really need accessorizing, so please avoid belting it unless it is utterly shapeless. But in that case, I would rather you found it a new home and added a more flattering black dress to your capsule wardrobe.

For spring I recommend the silk slip dress. And for those of you who just rolled your eyes because you think a slip dress is just for slip-of-a-thing girls, you'd be wrong. The slip dress is universally flattering; just ensure the fabrication has a density to it and doesn't pucker at the seams. If you prefer to cover your arms, then a simple slip dress also looks great over a crisp white T-shirt, with long sleeves or short (which is perhaps the only 1990s styling tip that I would revive). You will live in the slip dress during the hot months; just add a flat sandal for day and a heeled sandal for evening.

JEANS

I bang on about denim details in the next chapter, where I will tell you exactly what makes the perfect jeans, well, perfect—so I will keep this brief . . . ish.

Everyone needs that one pair of jeans that you reach for on the days when you have nothing to wear, when you want to feel sexy, when you want to feel comfortable, when you want to stay home and when you want to go out. Finding the one magic pair that does all of that is very needle-in-a-haystack, or more specifically, a vintage haystack. For the likelihood is that the jeans you will want to reach for day in and day out are either a vintage discovery or a pair that you have had so long that they feel like a vintage discovery. The denim is soft but not too thin, the waistband sits below your waist and above your hips, and it permanently has a belt wrapped around it, even when tucked back into the wardrobe. And that stain on the upper right thigh has been there so long that it's been years since you've known where it came from. These beloved jeans are the most relied-upon item in your possession, and they make everything else on this list just that little bit cooler. No pressure.

TRENCH COAT

The trench really comes into its own when everything else is unpredictable. During the transitional months, when it could be warm and sunny, followed in an instant by a sudden temperature drop, gale-force winds and biblical rain, the trench not only supports you through sodden confusion but makes you look elegant while doing it.

The trench was designed to be lightweight but also protective and waterproof. While the design has moved on from its First World War beginnings, the beauty is still in the original details: double-breasted, large lapels, epaulettes and a storm flap are specifics that have stood the test of time. So, when it comes to choosing one to be a wardrobe staple . . . if it ain't broke, don't fix it.

Ever-so-slightly oversized is what to look for, as you will need generous room for layers in autumn, but you don't want it to look too big when wearing it with a dress or T-shirt and jeans in spring. The belt is key and defines the look and shape of the coat and body. You have options, so play with what you find most comfortable, whether that is tied at the back when the coat is open, knotted in front or fully buckled.

Finding the right shade of beige is integral: Are you a sand or buff, maybe a camel, caramel or tan? The answer is the one that doesn't wash you out when next to your face. Khaki is a great alternative to a beige shade, flattering on all skin tones and a neutral that works with every other item on this list.

It's an excellent flight companion too, regardless of whether you are flying from a warm country to cold, or cold to warm. It happily rolls into the overhead compartment and rolls out at your destination relatively crease-free, or acts as a mid-flight blanket, and it brilliantly elevates comfortable plane loungewear when you land.

The trench is rare in that it embraces both an English practicality and a Hollywood noir glamor, making it a truly versatile and universal investment.

T-SHIRTS

Much like the white shirt, I feel that there must be a kind of science or math involved in finding the ideal T-shirt. Sadly, those were my two worst subjects at school, so I will have to go with tried-and-tested life experience instead. And I assure you I have tried many, many T-shirts in my life to find the right fit.

You'd think it would be hard to go wrong with such a simple design, and yet I have physical evidence of T-shirts that are cut too close or too wide in the neck, sleeves that are too long or too short, and sleeves that make my arms look double the size simply in the way those sleeves are angled. Some T-shirts didn't survive a wash without losing all shape and support somewhere in the cycle, and others seemed to lose all shape while I was wearing them. I didn't take it personally.

But I have learned from every terrible T-shirt I have ever worn, and now sleep in. The trick is in the shoulders. It must fit perfectly across the shoulders with the sleeve seams hitting very slightly below the top of the arm. It should gently skim your body, but not hug it, and the hem should fall just below your hips so that it can be tucked in without too much excess fabric. Keep the sleeves loose and hitting just above the elbow. Natural fabrics are important, and I like a heavier cotton if I am layering on top of it, but something lighter and more transparent that teases a colored bra beneath in the summer.

I would advise you to have a neat little selection of black and grey T-shirts, but white T-shirts are your secret weapon. White T-shirts have the power to instantly lift your mood, your outfit and your face. They can make you look like you are both well-rested and have had a facial; a wardrobe savior if you have had a late night. But they can only do that if they are bright-white and pristine. Any deodorant crust, sad greying or irremovable makeup around the neckline, and it is time to turn that T-shirt into a duster.

SHOES

There is much to be said about shoes, and I do in their dedicated chapter, but they are an imperative part of the capsule wardrobe. They are the final punctuation to every outfit and are often the reason why a look falls apart. You get so close, and then you go and stick a loafer where a pump should be. Tut-tut.

While there are many other shoes that work with the capsule wardrobe, the following are the basic must-haves—the first steps of your shoe closet, if you'll allow me to say it.

Loafer

Androgynous, versatile, practical, comfortable and cool—what's not to like about loafers? While there are many delicate and quiet styles, it's ones that pack a bit of a punch with a chunky sole that feel that bit more confident. They work as well with opaque tights as they do with a bare ankle, or my personal favorite: a black loafer with a peek of fresh white sock under a blue denim hem.

Wear with: jeans, tailored trousers, black knitted dress

Pump

If you are comfortable in a heel, then the classic black pump is integral to your capsule wardrobe. It is the shoe equivalent of the LBD. A workwear necessity that takes you out after dark but also has the power to dress up jeans and uplift you both literally and mentally—or it does for me anyway. Personally, I like a sharp pointed toe, as it cleverly elongates the leg, but if it's not for you, then a gently rounded toe is always preferable to a square. When it comes to the vamp—the vamp is the front top line of the shoe where it hits the top of your foot—look for a style that doesn't come too far up. I know that the idea of toe cleavage freaks some people out, but even just a mere trace of it is seductive. However, if that's completely out of the question, allow the rounded vamp to sit 2.5cm (1 inch) above the base of your little toe. Heel height is up to you, and while being able to run in heels is unnecessary, please, please ensure that you can walk easily in them. Any wobbling at all at any elevation, and it's flats for you.

Wear with: jeans, tailored trousers

Sneaker

Sneakers have the ability to make you look relaxed, busy and contemporary. You are a woman with a place to be and need something easy to get you there. You are a woman who understands the need for some fashion high-low, and you know that the right pair of sneakers can transform something rigid and smart into something easy and approachable. To be clear, I am not talking about gym sneakers here, but the streamlined simpler ones. They are not for running a marathon in, but the right pair will take you much further than that in the long run. All white is more versatile than you think, and looks really smart and refined, though adding a pop of color will look very cool when worn with denim and a long coat. They add a little bit of fashion to a simple look. Adidas Sambas are a good place to start.

A pristine, box-fresh appearance is fine for some, but I like to see a bit of character in a pair of sneakers. A scuff on a white mudguard or a smudge on the leather upper is evidence that you are happy to live a little, and that is what the best clothes are for.

Wear with: jeans, tailored trousers, slip dress

Boot

I guarantee that you will never, ever regret adding a pair of black leather ankle boots to your go-to essentials. I used to swear everyone needed a pair of everyday knee-high heeled boots, but then I saw the comfortable game-changing light. Mine are black lug-soled Chelsea boots—you can opt for a narrower sole of course, in lace-up, zip-up or pull-on-and-go—and their weighty stomp awards me determination and certainty in every step, which reminds me how important the right shoes are. They are on my feet from October to April, battling through every weather eventuality better than I do, and by the time the temperature turns back up, they are largely unscathed. As faultless with a chunky sock and denim as they are with a long dress or miniskirt and opaque tights. But please keep them clean and polished—yes, those boots can take you almost everywhere and carry you through every adventure, but they don't need to wear the evidence forever.

Wear with: jeans, black knitted dress, tailored trousers

Ballet flat

A very well-dressed colleague of mine spends that time of year between boots and sandals in black leather ballet flats and grey socks. Her style is quite tomboy all year round, but that combination of the girly with the functional made me see ballet flats in a much cooler and more adaptable light. They are not just to be worn with bare legs and an A-line dress, after all. Thankfully.

The ballet flat is the more delicate alternative to the loafer, and while it does a similar job with similar pieces, it offers a gentler touch. Perfect when pairing with more refined dresses, so they complement and don't overwhelm.

Wear with: tailored trousers, slip dress, LBD, jeans

BELTS

We only need a little word on belts, but these often overlooked accessories are integral as they can literally keep a look together. You need two in your closet: matte leather in brown and black with a matte brass buckle. One that fits the waist and one that fits between the waist and the hips. For width, 3cm (just over an inch) is your friend. Wide enough to subtly draw the eye, but not so wide that it demands it. As for the length of the belt, try to avoid ones that jut out past the buckle but aren't long enough to meet another belt loop. Look for either overly long, with a soft enough leather that you can tuck into the belt itself and let it trail down, or short, so that you are left with a neat tail.

HAVE A CARE

Once you have curated your perfect capsule wardrobe, you need to look after it. For even though TyLynn swears by buying multiple T-shirts in case something happens to one of them, that's not always possible. These are the pieces that you will be reaching for again and again, so you need to know how to care for them.

Probably key in this chapter: you need to keep those whites white. I used to have my shirts dry-cleaned, but now I handwash them and my precious white T-shirts together on a silk handwash setting in the machine, using a specific whitening washing powder from Clothes Doctor. I have used in-wash sachets too, and they work well if your whites have started to grey, but economically the washing powder makes most sense for me. Then, get used to ironing, and then get great at ironing, because 100 percent cotton shirts and T-shirts will come out of that machine as scrunched-up balls. Make sure your iron is on the hottest setting, spray some water on the cotton, and then put your back into it. Nothing gives me more satisfaction than perfectly ironed shirts and T-shirts. Yeah, one day you are cool, the next you are thrilled with an ironed crease in the sleeve of a white shirt. Save yourselves!

The key to looking after your capsule wardrobe is maintenance. You must regularly check for loose threads and buttons, bobbling, unsecured hemlines and pulled fabric, and once you see it, you need to deal with it immediately as it will only get worse. If it is work you can do yourself, resew that button or secure that hemline, but if it is beyond your skill set, please do not wear the item until you have had it professionally mended.

CAPSULE WARDROBE IN BRIEF

1   Adapt the foundations to work for you and your lifestyle.

2   Basic doesn't mean boring.

3   If you try something on from your closet and it always depresses you, get rid of it immediately.

4   In front of a capsule wardrobe, you should never feel like you have nothing to wear.

5   Don't follow TikTok fashion trends. Sometimes a shirt is just a shirt. And that is fine.

6   Shoulder robing is not a thing.

7   Learn how to layer.

8   White T-shirts are a beauty treatment.

9   Fit is everything.

10   Never underestimate the power of quiet fashion.

DENIM

EMMA GREDE

British businesswoman, entrepreneur, co-founder of Good American with Khloe Kardashian, and one of the founders of SKIMS with Kim Kardashian. Board chair of the Fifteen Percent Pledge. Self-confessed "denim freak."

SHOPPING FOR JEANS

First, and this is very important: never go shopping for denim if you are in a bad mood. Or even in a potentially bad mood. Denim shopping is not for the faint of heart.

Second: before you start, you need to know exactly what you are looking for.

Are you looking for the perfect everyday jean, or are you looking for something more relaxed for the weekend? Do you want high-rise, low-rise, mid-rise, skinny, flared, cropped, boyfriend, tapered, blue, black, printed, colored? And this is just for starters. Horrifying, right? From the get-go you need to know what you are shopping for and be specific.

"I'm looking for a cropped jean that I can wear with a flat in the summer." GO. Then narrow it down on the inseam length, rise and fit. You must narrow your choices before you enter the shop. And know—as best you can—what suits you. There are some brands that are more forgiving and some that just aren't. Be prepared to do the research.

Online shopping has revolutionized denim shopping for me. I order a bunch of styles and try them on at home with my own lighting and my own things. I don't want to be in a shop in a small space with one pair of shoes. I want my own mirror and options.

When I try jeans on, I turn around and look at my butt first. I always do. I bet you don't immediately turn around to look at your ass in any other item of clothing, but it's a totally different experience when you put jeans on, and you need to take your time with it.

You also *have* to do it on your own, no friends allowed. They are too distracting. I don't want any interference or other opinions. After all, no one knows your body better than you do, or how you feel in jeans. That's why having your own stuff around helps you feel good.

I am never going to be that person who puts on a pair of jeans and waits until they give a little because they are a bit small. That is not my vibe. I never want to be uncomfortable. Ever. I need to breathe. And you will be surprised how many women walk around not able to breathe. Buy the jeans that are made for you and not the other way around. I can't be dealing with uncomfortable jeans that dig into me after I have washed them. Life is too short.

Finally, to answer that age-old question of "should I or should I not wash my jeans?", I don't say never wash them, but personally I wait until they are developing a life of their own before they hit the machine.

Honestly, there is very little I like more than a bloody good pair of jeans.

DENIM

Today I was on the phone to my mum for just shy of an hour trying to help her return a pair of jeans I'd ordered for her online. Miraculously, there just might be a pair of jeans winging their way to a post office in Scotland within forty-eight hours. As Emma points out above, my mum tried on those jeans, turned around in her bedroom mirror, looked at her butt and decided it appeared too flat. The jeans were quickly sent back to where they came from.

Even at the age of eighty-one, you will still be trying jeans on and hoping that your ass looks good in them. So, this chapter is key.

Thankfully, I love denim. Love it. It's my go-to for everything, and alongside finding the perfect denim jacket, skirt, jumpsuit, shorts and shirt, I completely understand and support the quest for that peachy-bottom-providing pair of jeans.

When it comes to jeans, I probably own more than I should, but honestly, I do wear every single pair. Or, more specifically, I have worn every single pair and it is very likely that I will again. I regularly pull them all out on to the bed, try them all on and see if there are any that are ready for charity. More often than not, every pair is meticulously folded and returned to the shelf. I once made the mistake of relegating certain styles to the "as if this will ever be in fashion again" pile, only to see low-rise boyfriends, flares and overly distressed pairs start to edge back into my subconscious and subsequently— and at expense—back into my wardrobe. So now I tend to keep them just in case and find it very difficult to let any go.

To give my denim collection context, and to justify the volume, I do wear denim all the time and for almost everything. My job doesn't require traditional workwear, so denim makes up a huge part of my 9 to 5. When out in the evening, I am partial to the jeans-and-a-nice-top uniform, and I don't own loungewear—instead I own slightly baggier jeans that I relax in and travel in. Yes, even long-haul. So other than sleeping or working out, I am to be found in some kind of denim all year round. I know the shapes that suit me and the ones that don't. I know the washes I like and the ones that can stay in 1995. I've made all the denim mistakes. I wore jeans with the waistband cut off, designed to showcase the bedazzled thong that rose above. My once-favorite pair had a crystal butterfly on the rear. Dear God. I used to wear a white pair so distressed that only when I looked at photographs years later did I realize I looked like a bedraggled mummy. And I have worn some way past their best, but more of that later. I really have put the legwork into this chapter, as denim can make or break an outfit, and finding the right denim can make or break you. For me, in my years of extensive trial and error, my go-to brands for the best denim are, at the top end of the market, Agolde, Citizens of Humanity and Khaite. Size down in Agolde and Citizens of Humanity, but I find that those three labels make the best denim in terms of wash, shape and longevity. For size, variety and value for money, of course it is Good American. Mango denim is a must-try, and a pair of wide-leg ones I have are always admired and subsequently also purchased by friends and colleagues. And you really can't go wrong with the original and best, Levi's.

While I urge you to try those brands, denim is personal to each of us, and what is right for me might be wrong for you. Some of you reading this will want to experiment with denim, and follow the trends of high waist/low waist/wide leg/skinny leg/flares, etc., while others have chosen their denim lane and are sticking to it. But to get to the latter, you will have to try the former. Body shapes change, and style preferences develop as we get older, so don't get stuck in one shape of denim because it suited you fifteen years ago. When you do your wardrobe edit, try on those long-term favorite jeans of yours and ask yourself honestly if they are still as flattering and confidence-building as they once were. If the answer is no, it is time to research what you could try instead. I think a good place to start is by looking at recent pictures of your favorite well-dressed celebrity to see what jeans they are wearing. The paparazzi might be a privacy-invading pain in the ass, but they do let us see how our favorite stars dress in their downtime, and that can prove very handy.

The right pieces of denim in your wardrobe should feel like the most reliable of friends. When you lean on them, you know you will feel more confident, together and pretty bloody great, regardless of the situation. They might be few and far between, but once you've found them you will rely on them for almost everything.

So, where to start . . .

JEANS

Know this: skinny jeans are not dead. They never have been and never will be, regardless of what headlines in Sunday newspaper supplements may tell you. One day at work, a colleague asked me if skinny jeans would ever be cool again. I was sitting in front of her, wearing skinny jeans. A high-waisted black pair that I love, looking pretty cool actually. That colleague is someone who believes the headlines. Super low-rise, stonewash or extreme flares aside, your favorite style of denim will never be "dead." Sure, they fall out of favor with the fashion crowd, but who cares?! If they are your go-to jeans, then please ignore sensationalist journalism.

When it comes to choosing jeans, Emma is right: it is a minefield. But one that is totally worth navigating. While I don't practice what I preach, you really do only need a couple of pairs of jeans in your life that you love and feel brilliant in. The more choice, the more complicated it gets. So, what are those perfect jeans?

It largely depends on what you want them for, but I will assume you want a pair of everyday jeans and a pair that are maybe more evening-with-a-nice-top appropriate. Am I right? Hope so. Let's start with the former. What constitutes "everyday" jeans differs for each person, but what will always remain true for all is the comfort factor. The most popular shapes are skinny leg or straight cut, and for good reason. Both are universally flattering, and both work with boots in winter (over skinny, under straight), flat sandals in summer and sneakers all year round. For both, the ideal rise is just below the belly button and sitting just slightly higher at the back. A concealed button or zipper is your choice, though if you have trouble with your hands or coordination, a zipper makes getting dressed a little easier.

If in doubt, keep it classic. Five-pocket jeans have remained popular since the late 1800s, so who are you to argue with that? That's three to the front, including the little watch pocket, and two patch pockets to the rear. Never deviate on the shape of the rear patch pockets: the traditional pentagon pockets are the most flattering when placed correctly. The bigger the pockets the better, though not comically so, and they're most flattering when the lowest point on the pocket sits just above the base of your bottom.

The fundamental thing when finding the right jeans for you is to ignore the size. Size is irrelevant and will vary depending on brand, shape, wash, density of the denim and fabrication, based on the amount of stretch. Try a few pairs and see what feels right. You are no bigger or smaller than when you stepped into those jeans, so hold your nerve.

When it comes to length, if you are not a heel-with-everything type of person, then ideally the jeans should hit the top of your foot, break once in front and fall 1cm (a third of an inch) from the floor. If you do wear them with heels, I am a believer that jeans should cover the foot and just reveal the shoe toe, though when it comes to skinny jeans, they should hit no further than your ankle bone. I am just under 5'5", which means I often have to have about a foot of denim removed from each pair of jeans. For sleeker pairs I take them to a local alterations place and ask them to color-match the thread on the rest of the jeans (always make that clear), but for everyday denim I take the kitchen scissors to them. I can feel you judging from here, but don't be horrified—if I can do it, anyone can. Try them on, fold the hem to the optimum length, pin or mark them with a pencil, take them off, measure from pin/pencil to hem, mark up both hems with a line to cut and, well, cut. Even if it is not perfect, the hems will fray in time to disguise your shaky technique. Trim excess threads as time goes on to keep them as neat as possible. If you are doubting me, Emma also uses the DIY approach. "Whatever pair of jeans I have, I cut the hems and fray them myself. I never like them to

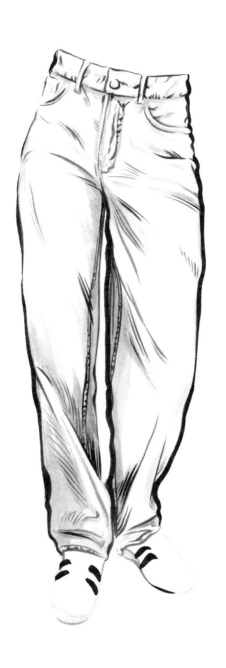

be a clean finish, I like them to be raw. There is no need to get them hemmed." If you don't trust me, trust her.

The wash is as important as the fit. For everyday, stay in the world of blue denim, particularly a mid-blue vintage wash. Think two shades lighter than indigo, and consistent throughout. Not faded on the thighs and backside. As you wear them the color will naturally fade slightly in the places you wear them hardest, and that way you give your jeans a unique character, rather than buying them with character already built in.

Black jeans are also classic, but opt for pure black rather than charcoal, and once they have started to fade, feel brave enough to dye them yourself. You did it as a kid, you can do it as an adult.

For your occasion jeans, everything above applies. But you can experiment a little more. Try a higher waist, but never too cinched as the following stomach pain is never worth the corseted illusion. Try low-rise, but ensure the back is raised as previously mentioned—exposing your underwear is something that will stay in the early 2000s. Break away from skinny, as a straight leg over a heel is the quickest way to elongate your legs, and let the hemline almost scrape the floor.

Belts are key for denim, worn on the waist or just below, but never fasten them tighter than they need to be as it will cause the waist to bunch and the seat to rise up and reveal far more than is required in the crotch. When it comes to low-slung denim, I prefer them worn without a belt so it looks as relaxed as low-rise is intended.

I know that is a lot to take in, but primarily, you should never dread pulling on your jeans—if you do, then you have the wrong pair. Great jeans should feel as comfortable as a tracksuit but look a hundred times better, and what is there to dread about that?

JACKET

I have had my go-to denim jacket for eighteen years. It is from a store's children's department, it's fitted (being meant for kids and all), and it's the ideal shade of blue, and has gotten better with age as the denim has softened. Since I found it, I have not so much as glanced in the direction of a potential competitor as they won't come close to its quiet perfection. And quiet perfection is the sweet spot of a denim jacket.

If you think of the Levi's jean jacket, its purity of design is to thank for its longevity. Born in 1880, it has remained the epitome of cool since and is largely unchanged. It is all you should look for in a denim jacket: cropped at the waist, straight fit, front button placket, single-button cuffs and chest patch pockets. Bells and whistles might be your thing when it comes to fashion, and that is of course fine, but if you are looking for a denim jacket that will stand the test of time, the no-frills approach of "the original" will ensure that you have a future fashion heirloom in your hands that will never go out of style. Blue should be your first point of call, but a white denim jacket always looks fresh.

In warmer weather it is the perfect throw-on-and-go cover-up, but it shouldn't be relegated in the winter. Treat it like a heavier shirt and use it as a styling layer over shirts or thinner knits—I think a fitted turtleneck looks particularly good under denim—and wear it under coats or blazers with generously cut sleeves so you don't feel constricted. The denim jacket was designed as a utility garment, so make that baby work.

DENIM

SHIRT

You only need one denim shirt, but you can go two ways with it. Look for either a narrow one which offers a slicker result, or an oversized one that's a more casual vibe.

For narrow, look for a little bit of detail, like a patch pocket or epaulettes, to stop it getting too basic. It will ideally have a rounded hem that hits below the hip bone, and small inconspicuous buttons on a narrow placket.

If the oversized silhouette is more your mood, buy (or borrow) a men's chambray shirt. Chambray has a plain weave instead of denim's twill weave, so it is softer and a bit less rigid when wearing a bigger shape. Roll up the sleeves to below the elbow, leave a couple of buttons undone at the neckline, layer over a white tank and tuck into jeans if not too bulky. Alternatively, you could do something that fashion folks are mocked for relentlessly, yet I stand by it: the "French tuck," which means tucking the front of a shirt or sweater into your waistband and leaving the rest out. It's flattering, I swear. If you prefer the shirt to fly free and untucked, then just ensure it doesn't swamp you. I also have an oversized denim shirt that is heavier than a chambray but lighter than a denim jacket, and I treat it as a layering piece in winter and as an alternative to a denim jacket in summer.

I do have a soft spot for a denim tuxedo—that's a denim shirt and jeans FYI—as it's a really easy and streamlined combination, but perhaps don't use early-2000s pop stars as a point of reference.

SKIRT

A denim skirt should be one of two lengths: mini or maxi. Nothing in between, as a knee-length denim skirt always seems to be stuck in a different time and doesn't have the kudos of a mini or the impact of a maxi. Prove me wrong if you so desire.

The trick with the miniskirt, as with any short hemline, is to wear it with pride. If you are constantly pulling at the hem, you will look as uncomfortable as you feel, and perhaps a maxi is more your speed. One that sits on the waist is favorable as it looks more precise, with a stitched hem and not cut-off, and while the length is up to you, hitting a hand span beneath the ass cheek is my choice. A denim mini with a tanned bare leg, ballet flats and white T-shirt is a summer uniform, but I think it comes into its own with matte opaque or 50+ denier black tights, boots and an oversized knit.

The maxi is more of a universal option and is a great year-rounder. A long A-line shape that drops from the waist is what to look for, but if you prefer a slender fit, look for those with a split hem to the rear, not the front, as they are easier to walk in. Pair with T-shirts and light knits and avoid blouses unless you are going for that 70s thing, otherwise it looks too retro. They look great with sneakers or chunky sandals, then switch up for block-heeled boots and a long coat as temperatures drop.

JUMPSUIT

When it comes to easy dressing there is nothing easier than a jumpsuit. Often there is also nothing cooler. We are not talking overalls here, as people tend to make that mistake. I am not advocating overalls. But the denim jumpsuit is timeless.

Contrary to reports, they are great on all body shapes, big boobs and little boobs. If you have a long torso, try a size bigger to avoid any potential wedgie; a slouchy fit looks good on everyone, but don't go too big if you are petite. A zip-up front fastening is less romper-suit-like than a button-down, and pull that zipper down to reveal some skin or the layers beneath. This is where your capsule pieces come into their own. Again. A turtleneck, T-shirt or even a lace-trimmed camisole, which is a cute contrast beneath the rigidity of the denim, will give the jumpsuit more depth and variety from season to season. White sneakers are a must.

But I will leave you with these wise words spotted on an Instagram meme: "Everyone compliments the jumpsuit when you wear it out—but when you get to the bathroom it's just you and your choices." Amen.

SHORTS

I have a pair of denim cutoff shorts that I love, but for the last three summers I have considered retiring them. Not for their sake, as they remain in perfect condition, but for mine, as they are very, very short. So short, in fact, that I used them as a very successful thirst trap on dating apps, which lured my boyfriend in, and for that I might have to get them framed. However, years of ridiculous articles questioning when a woman was too old to get her legs out clearly went to my head, as I ponder at the start of every summer, "Am I now too old?" But here I am in my mid-forties, and the older I get, the less I care, and therefore the shorts currently remain a summer and vacation essential.

Denim shorts or Daisy Dukes are a matter of personal taste, so I won't urge you to wear them if they are not for you. But if they are, I have only a little bit of advice. On or just below the waist is the best fit. I would suggest not to wear them with a knotted checked shirt—unless in an ironic way—and instead team them with a fitted tank or T-shirt with an open shirt over the top, or belted with a loved big T-shirt tucked in. Finally, and not to sound like your mother here, but if you can see the pocket linings hanging below the hem, then young lady, they are too short.

HAVE A CARE

DENIM REPAIR

Caring for my denim was once not my forte. I have worn a pair of beloved jeans even when one leg was literally falling off below the knee. It had a hole in the knee that got bigger and bigger over time, and when it stretched from seam to seam and gaped so much that it made the left leg of the jeans longer than the right, I still wore them. When friends asked me, nicely at first, when I was going to give them up, I still wore them. When friends threatened to stop hanging out with me when I was wearing them, I still wore them. When an elderly lady on the street gave me and my bare knee such a stink eye that I still wonder if I am cursed, I finally cut those jeans into shorts. I have also worn a pair so often that they got very thin in the seat. So much so that after a romantic stroll around a park on a date, I got home to realize that the seat had given up and my ass had been out for the duration. Good times.

I have learned my lesson from both those experiences, as I grieved the jeans that could have been saved and now know the difference between denim with character and denim that's past it. A little light fraying or small rips do give denim a loved quality, but don't let it go beyond that. Sadly, most denim production is environmentally damaging, due in part to the huge amount of water used and the energy consumption. While some brands are making massive steps to change that, what *you* can do is ensure that your jeans last rather than regularly replacing them.

Usually, the first places to see wear and tear on jeans are the knees, inner thighs and seat, but all those can be salvaged with a little professional (or DIY if you are more skilled than me) TLC when caught in time. A great local alterations place can work miracles with invisible mending on all denim, and color-matched patches hide a multitude of chafing, staining or neglect sins.

DENIM

TO WASH OR NOT TO WASH

I won't say this often in this book, but when it comes to washing denim . . . to each their own. However, there are levels of common decency that must be adhered to, so allow me to offer a little hygienic advice.

A quick survey of female friends suggested they wash their jeans after about four wears; male friends seem much more relaxed about the idea of washing them at all. One friend spot-cleans and airs them on a radiator. Another relies on freezing his jeans to kill bacteria without damaging the fibers. Sadly, scientists have repeatedly shattered this theory and reiterate time and time again that household freezers don't kill bacteria. I'm sure he will ignore that expertise though.

Personally, I am also in the four-times-then-laundry-basket camp, but the following washing routine is definitive and applies to all denim pieces. Though as I write this, I realize that I have never washed a denim jacket in all my days . . . Anyway, turn the jeans inside out as this helps retain color and shape. If there is a zipper, pull it up to avoid the teeth chewing anything else in the drum. Wash them cold, so 60°F (20°C) should be fine, and I prefer the handwash setting and a light spin rather than a heavy-duty one. Some brands make specific detergents for denim—I think that is a nice-to-have rather than a necessity, but opt for liquid over powder. One expert recommended mixing a cup of vinegar with a tablespoon of salt, but that seems an anal step beyond unless you get your denim imported from Japan at huge cost. Finally, and most importantly, never, ever tumble-dry denim. Ever. Air-dry and warm iron instead, for the dryer will destroy those peachy-butt-enhancing fibers in an instant.

DENIM IN BRIEF

1   Only shop for denim when you are in a very good mood.

2   Jeans are all about the ass.

3   Don't buy jeans that are too small assuming they will give, as even if they do, the first wear post-wash is too traumatic to be worth it.

4   Skinny jeans will never die.

5   No-frills denim will always triumph over bells-and-whistles denim.

6   Don't think you know better than Levi Strauss.

7   Care for your denim—it is not as tough as you think it is.

8   Understand the difference between distressed denim and plain distressing.

9   No one is too old for denim.

10   Wash your goddamn jeans.

WORKWEAR

JO ELLISON

Editor of HTSI *and Deputy Editor of the* Financial Times Weekend, *known for her distinguished and much-imitated personal style of oversized tailoring and classic, clean lines. Jo knows how to make a work uniform work well beyond the office.*

WHAT YOUR WORKWEAR SAYS ABOUT YOU

Traditional workwear still exists. If for instance you live in London and go to the pub on a Friday night in the City, every single bloke has a suit on—even if the tie is less common—and a considerable number of professional women will be wearing a fitted dress of some description and a low heel. Definitely, there's been a casualization in the wardrobe, but there is still a uniform. I think most people in offices, wherever they live, do still follow a basic code.

I have a uniform because I hate, hate changing for different occasions throughout the day. A typical day usually starts at 8 a.m. at the gym, and then is followed by office meetings, meetings, meetings, followed by a tea with someone around 4 p.m., and very often a formal dinner that starts at 8 p.m., so I need an outfit that I can wear for everything. This usually means wearing a suit, or at least a suit jacket, because a blazer dresses anything up. A black blazer does everything a favor, even a pair of leggings (although, to be clear, I do change after the gym). My professional uniform therefore is a kind of variation on the same theme: either jeans or black trousers and a black, brown or tweed jacket. I switch between a sweater or shirt according to the weather forecast.

I try not to look shabby, although I'll never look like the most dressed-up person anywhere. I have a distinctly "low-key" approach to style. (In fact, I went home the other night to change before going out again, and then realized I had substituted one black jacket for another, and no one would notice the difference anyway.) Despite the best intentions, I'll always opt for the more comfortable option—and I think it looks more elegant to slouch around in a simple, oversized silhouette than pour oneself into an outfit which will give you VPL anxiety all night.

I prefer to be underdressed rather than overdressed. And so the idea of rushing home from work in order to rip off all my incredibly uncomfortable work clothes is a bit anathema to me. Most of my clothes are at least three sizes too big for me. Comfort is king—although I have never technically worn slippers to work . . .

The women who work at the *FT Weekend* are pretty stylish. I would call it modern bluestocking style: lots of high-waisted chinos, button-downs, and a flat brogue. Quite serious. With flashes of deep pretty. There are no big visible designer labels, but there's definitely a fashionability, and people tend to make an effort while allowing for an individual flair. A young colleague wore a T-shirt that said "I'd rather be 40 than pregnant," which made me chuckle. Youth, eh?! But it surprises me how many women are still so uncomfortable with their sartorial choices. Recently a really senior member of staff asked me what they should wear to a conference. It baffles me that people are still so unsure of their tastes and choices, that the act of getting dressed should still provoke such basic neuroses. People feel so vulnerable about clothes, and for some reason, there still exists in the UK a snobbery that intelligent people shouldn't be seen to enjoy fashion: it isn't considered a "smart" thing to do. Which is nonsense. Without wanting to get too *Cosmo* about empowerment, there's nothing shameful about wanting to look and feel your best.

Clothes convey different things in your work environment. They can empower, they can soften, they can feminize or they can toughen one's impression. I'm a huge believer in putting on a heel when you want to feel a bit bigger in the room. And tailoring is such an easy shorthand for "I understand how this works." I was working at *Vogue* when I first interviewed for the *Financial Times*, and I wore an outfit that I imagined those interviewing me would think someone from *Vogue* would wear: a Saint Laurent blazer, jeans and a high-heeled pump—I rarely wear a pump which is why I remember this so vividly. It was a little bit casual, and a little bit disrespectful of the business dress code that I imagined might prevail at an institution such as the *FT*, hence the jeans. I wanted to look insouciant I guess, like I didn't need the job. Although, to be clear, I badly wanted it.

In interviews I totally notice people's tastes. I'm intrigued by individual choices. And sometimes mystified. If someone came in, in let's say a Tropicana-print kaftan, it would grab my attention (and not necessarily in a good way), but I don't expect people to reflect my personal taste. I like diversity in the office. I don't want to see everyone looking the same.

Is there a fail-safe work look? I hate to be prescriptive, and there's nothing wrong with a pair of trousers and a good shirt, but I still want to see some disruption in the codes around me. And I quite enjoy being around people with diametrically opposed taste. My colleague wears scarlet lipstick, circle skirts and heels, and she looks like a fabulously 50s-era bombshell. And sometimes, you can come around to things that you thought you hated. I have, for example, finally been persuaded as to the wisdom of the vest. Although I'll never wear velvet. Or purple. And I do remember, during one interview, I decided I wouldn't be able to work with the candidate on the basis that they were wearing loads of really loud jangly bangles. The noise was too annoying.

WORKWEAR

For my first proper job, a coveted Monday to Friday position on a very cool style magazine, I dressed up every day in a "look." A "look" for me meant skinny jeans or a fitted maxi dress, a totally insane coat that swamped me, and incredibly high heels that I had bought on discount at the Saturday and Sunday shop job I still had to supplement my terrible magazine salary. One day on the way to work I had to go home to change, as one of my heels had snapped. Quality footwear. When I arrived late and apologetic, harping on about my broken shoe, I hadn't realized the subdued atmosphere in the office, and then someone showed me that day's *Guardian* newspaper, which announced the imminent closure of the very cool style magazine. Three weeks later and my weekend job was also my new Monday to Friday job. It was a brutal first employment experience, but I have never lost that appreciation for dressing up for a day in the office.

On any normal day, from my desk at NET-A-PORTER I can see someone dressed in a three-piece suit and heels, another in a battered old band T-shirt with denim cutoffs and massive boots, a senior member of the team wafting past in a flowing floral dress complete with voluminous ruffled sleeves, and a sea of very sleek-looking women in the unofficial office uniform of blue jeans, white T-shirt, blazer and sneakers. There is no expected dress code, *almost* anything goes (in my time there I've seen some things that shouldn't go for anything or anyone), and individuality is celebrated.

But I know that this is sadly rarely the case, which is why "what to wear to work" content, created by those in an office similar to mine, often features outfits or suggestions that aren't corporate-job appropriate, or relevant anymore. A quick Google Images search suggests that street-style pictures of influencers at fashion shows are your inspiration, and that tailored suits or colorful midi dresses with high leg splits are your essentials. After sitting at London's Liverpool Street station at rush hour, which serves as the City's thoroughfare, I can assure you that most people pay no heed to Google. At Liverpool Street early one bright Tuesday morning, the uniform consisted of tailored trousers, identical but nondescript shirting, ballet flats, the odd fitted midi dress—all seemingly in a palette of grey. Blame it on my love of 80s films, but when I was a kid I thought we'd all be dressing like Sigourney Weaver in *Working Girl*. Realizing that isn't the case is almost as heartbreaking as actually having to take the Underground and not having a chauffeur-driven car. Damn you, Sigourney.

"There are no suits in sight, and the pencil skirt seems to have evaporated," reveals a friend with a very corporate job in one of the country's biggest insurance companies. As most of us now work in a home/office hybrid, the go-to uniform there she says is cropped tailored trousers and any type of smart top, with a blazer when meetings present themselves. Flat shoes over heels, but now and again a pair of heels is added by some colleagues ahead of big meetings.

That particular company, and others I have heard of, have a "dress for your day" policy, which means you are entitled to dress down if you have no external meetings. However, the general consensus is that people largely dress the same regardless of what their working day looks like.

But if the suit is dead and casual has been incorporated, where does that leave workwear dress codes? Well, thankfully it means that they have loosened up a little, and work is less about a work uniform and more about making it work for you.

THE MODERN
WORKWEAR DRESS CODES

Even when there isn't an official applied dress code, you will usually find that one is naturally implemented by the employees anyway. It makes dressing for the office easier. There will still be businesses that insist on formal, and others that imply that you can wear what you like. But neither is quite straightforward.

BUSINESS FORMAL

This is where your capsule wardrobe really comes into its own, and a blazer is essential. As Jo Ellison said, "A black blazer does everything a favor." But don't mistake a blazer with power dressing. Traditional power dressing is something slightly stuck in the 1980s, when women wore shoulder pads, suits and tailoring in order to be treated like men in the workplace. Today power dressing is more about attitude than shoulder pads. That said, smartness and good tailoring are still relevant, and there is something to be learned from the boys here: invest in it. If you are expected to look smart on a daily basis, it is worth putting some of your hard-earned cash towards it. Where some men might fork out for bespoke suits, think about what you like to spend your days in, and get quality items that will stand the test of time. If it is dresses that make you feel your best, buy three variations in a shape you look great in, choosing two neutral colors and one in your favorite color for the days you need to bring something a little extra. If tailoring is your thing, look for a few pairs of tailored trousers, and once you find them in the shape and weight that make you feel and look positive and fearless, buy three pairs in neutral colors—black, navy and grey are good bets, though there is always space for chocolate brown. Then add a couple of blazers, ideally one in black to match the trousers if you need a suit, and a black blazer works with the other neutrals too.

Blouses and shirts are your allies, and while you can't go wrong with a white shirt, here is where you can add some individualism. Block bold color, stripes or polka dots, oversized collars or cuffs, feature buttons—not all at once, I hasten to add, but take the opportunities, however small they may seem, to allow your personality to emanate. Same applies to tops. A sleeveless silk or twill tank with a round neckline will sit easily under a blazer but also look smart enough to hold its own without. It's more appropriate than a camisole as it is slightly more covered up. Personally, I also love a vest worn with nothing underneath and paired with the tailored trousers. But if that feels slightly too naked or risqué for your office, pair it with a close-cut white or black shirt with narrow sleeves underneath. What you choose to reveal or conceal in a work environment is up to you, but let me just leave this story here. Several years ago, I realized mid-meeting that the person chairing wasn't wearing a bra beneath her white silk shirt. My concentration vanished, as did that of everyone else in the meeting as they also were drawn to her very exposed nipples. Christ knows what any of us agreed to in that meeting, as we just wanted it over as soon as possible. In which case, maybe it was an excellent tactic.

Anyway, enough nipples and on to dresses. Dresses are the easiest way to dress for work with very little thought. Midi length is the most universally flattering, and also a good length that works if you feel the need to add a blazer. A long-sleeved, single-color shift dress is difficult to get wrong, and lighter-weight shirt dresses will see you through the summer.

Then there are the shoes. From my morning spent watching the corporate professionals rush through a busy London station, I have to assume—or hope—that most of the shoes were "commute shoes." Now I am guilty of this myself from time to time, when I want to wear a particular shoe for work that day but the idea of actually getting to work in them is out of the question due to comfort or weather, and so they are replaced by the "commute shoe" for the journey. When they are not on the journey, they lie under my desk at work or are kicked off by the front door when I get home. The commute is their only purpose: they are a comfortable shoe, *not* a fashion shoe. But I understand that sometimes the role they play becomes confusing—since they are so comfortable why would you change out of them and into something that might blister your feet? Before you know it, they have become your work shoes, and while your feet are ecstatic, the rest of your look, well, it's been let down. Don't fall at the final hurdle. A great shoe will complete a great look; a bad shoe will destroy the whole thing. Whether you carry them in a bag or wear them, a smart work shoe can be a flat brogue, a ballet flat, a heeled pump or a great boot, but please keep them immaculate, polish them and have them resoled when required, and they will work as hard as you do.

When it comes to bags, you need a tote. Not one that you also use to carry your gym stuff, and still contains kids' paraphernalia from when it doubled as a nappy bag. Not that one. I mean a slim two-strap leather or canvas shoulder bag that is strong enough to carry a laptop and essentials, but not so big that you will be tempted to add more stuff.

BUSINESS CASUAL

You'd think that this would mean wear anything you like. But don't fall into that trap. In some businesses, usually in the creative and tech worlds, you can often wear anything you like, and you can dress up or down as much as you like and no one will bat an eyelid. But for the majority, business casual still secretly means formal.

Jeans are universally still a no-no in most corporate headquarters, though they do creep into satellite offices where what you wear above the waist is more relevant for virtual calls with the bosses at HQ. In casual offices they are appropriate, but dress them up rather than letting weekend casual seep into business. Avoid denim that is overly distressed and sneakers—or anything actually—that are on their last legs. Loungewear should remain in the lounge. Dresses that are ideal in a club at 2 a.m. on a Sunday morning are less so at 8:30 a.m. on a Wednesday under strip lighting.

Most importantly, avoid anything that you don't feel good in. You have been hired to do a job that probably has nothing to do with the way you dress, and is all about your talent, ability and attitude; however, you do owe it to yourself, and the company paying you, to look like you have made a bit of an effort. And psychologically it will help with your output. Honestly.

Finally, and this applies to both formal and casual, in most office environments I have worked in, the temperature is controlled by the climate Illuminati. Having no control over the thermostat or AC means that dressing in layers is the only power you have. Think fabric, weight, fit and how they all work together in terms of shape and silhouette. Wide-leg trousers are always a good idea, ideally in a light wool, paired with a fluid silk or soft cotton shirt. Either wear tucked in or out, whichever you are more comfortable with. Or if you prefer a skirt, consider how you feel in the office with bare legs if it is usually warm, or with tights if cooler. I think the days of no tights and certain hemlines being inappropriate in the workplace are long gone, so long as you are comfortable, and depending on how long your hemline is.

If you struggle for ideas of what to wear each day, look to your colleagues for inspiration. Select someone who you always think looks good, and consider what she wears. Then take that information and insight back to your wardrobe, and on one Sunday afternoon, choose outfit combinations for the week. There is nothing worse than trying to pull an outfit together when you are trying to get your family fed and out the door. Be prepared.

DRESSING FOR AN INTERVIEW

I once interviewed someone who grew more and more nervous and flustered as we chatted, and she proceeded to sweat through her entire dress. Now I promise I am not a scary interviewer. At all. I felt dreadful for her. I offered to stop the interview, and we fetched her a glass of water, concerned that she was now clearly dangerously dehydrated. We continued at her request, but once she squelched—I am afraid there is no other word for it, poor woman—out of the office, I never saw her again. I often think of her and wonder where she is, but I also think of her before I have any big presentations or meetings. For she reminds me to never wear man-made fibers in an environment where I am potentially already going to be slightly nervous. For that I thank her. If you have an interview, big meeting or presentation, plan your

outfit accordingly. Always opt for natural fabrics, nothing too tight or restricting, and never, ever something that you have never worn before. Nothing is worse than realizing a top is itchy as hell before you are due to appear confident, collected and commanding.

Before an interview, research how formal or casual your potential new office is, and dress for the job you want. If the dream job is casual and you turn up in a suit, it's unlikely that the interviewer will see you fitting in with their culture. If it is a formal environment and you arrive in jeans and sneakers, then ditto. However, dressing as yourself is key, not how you think they want you to dress. If you are someone else on the day of your interview, it is hard to sustain that persona if you actually get hired. And if only for the interview, maybe lay off the bangles.

My final piece of interview advice is this, and it is key: if you are dressing for an interview on a day that you are in the office in your current job, think about how it compares to your average everyday look. Saying that you have been at the dentist and arriving at the office dressed smarter than you have been since your first day is an instant giveaway that you are exploring new jobs elsewhere. Just take the whole day off.

INTEGRATE WORKWEAR

Many people think that their work persona is very different from their true self, but if so, how do you present yourself authentically? I have friends who have one section in their closet for workwear and the rest is "them." For one thing, this isn't sustainable, and it could also suggest that if you aren't dressing like yourself at work, then you aren't acting like yourself.

I understand that early in your career, you might want to blend in at work until you figure out who you are in the professional world. It is easier to assimilate than to stand out. But don't be afraid to show a little personality at work. Express yourself. You are the same person in the office as you are outside of it.

On an average day at work, I like to dress up. Sure, it is the nature of my job—with a title like Fashion Director, I feel like I need to lead by example—but regardless of title or position, I have always dressed like myself. I don't have a separate part of my closet that is only for work, and I like to wear pieces to the office that put me in a good mood. If you treat workwear separately, and associate it with a stressful 9 to 5 job, then of course it isn't going to bring you any joy and you won't invest in it. If you start your day dressing in something you don't like or particularly care about, how does that set you up for the day? Even when I am working from home I still dress up, and I have to put shoes on, otherwise I can't fully concentrate. That might be quite singular, but wearing something I like, that makes me feel good, helps me focus.

Your workwear uniform should complement everything else that you own, and be sustainable in a timeless way. That doesn't mean that your workwear should be boring, and if color is your thing, please inject some color into your professional life. This could be as small as a scarf or a bag, or as bold as a coat. If it is something you feel unsure of, try it initially with one of the pieces you take off as you arrive. If it gets the desired attention, then add that color in dresses or tops. The world of work can of course be the equivalent of a grey day, we all have those moments, so all the more reason to bring a bit of your own style cheer into your working life. And if not just for you, then for the people around you.

"It's nice to dress up for work," says Oscar-winning costume designer Ruth E. Carter. "I promote this with my staff. I feel it instills a lot of confidence and a sense of pride. We encounter each other every day, and what we wear has a direct effect on our relationships with our colleagues. It's nice when someone surprises you and to see their closet, and mine, at play."

As you get older, your style evolves with you, so ensure that you are evolving your work wardrobe at the same time. That is how some people lose sight and confidence in their work style. If on-duty and off-duty are integrated, it makes it easier. A lot of us are guilty of saving clothing for particular moments or events, but other than a ball gown, gym wear and bikinis, everything should be mixed and mingled. Clothes are there to be worn, and not just for the highlights in life, as they really come into their own when they make the everyday monotony feel a bit more special. So, open your wardrobe and assess what pieces from your non-working wardrobe can be integrated into your working one.

HAVE A CARE

If, despite all my advice, you still insist on keeping your work uniform separate from the rest of the clothes in your life, then fine, but please, please look after them. If you have been rotating the same pair of trousers, several times every week for longer than you can remember, have a look at them and see if they need replacing or a bit of TLC. If the fabric is shiny, or thinning, perhaps it is time to replace them and pop them in your local clothing donation bin for recycling. Check for wear and tear on your go-to shirts and tops—are there unknown stains that have been your constant companions for years? If you can't get them out yourself or professionally, it may also be time to replace.

If you do wear the same pieces over and over again, of course there will be a little damage, but you can make those pieces last longer if you consider the fabric in the first place: a wool blend with a synthetic partner should hold up nicely in a blazer, skirt or trouser (as it will help them keep their shape), a heavier cotton shirt will outlast anything synthetic, and when it comes to silks, make sure you don't need to wash them after every wear—and when you do, be a fanatic about the washing instructions. It may not bring you joy to buy a pair of tailored trousers and a jacket for your day job, but you will be spending most of your week wearing them, so unless you want to replace them regularly, invest in what you buy.

WORKWEAR IN BRIEF

1   A blazer does everything a favor.

2   Learn from (some of) the boys and invest in great workwear.

3   Business casual doesn't actually mean casual.

4   Layers are the only defence against the office climate Illuminati.

5   Knowing that your work persona and off-duty persona are the same will make getting dressed on a Monday easier.

6   Find inspiration in a stylish colleague's wardrobe.

7   Dress up! Work can be depressing enough without feeling depressed about what you have on.

8   Don't be afraid to show some personality.

9   Avoid man-made fabrics in stressful environments.

10   When planning for an interview, get to know the business and get to know their uniform.

SHOES

SARAH JESSICA PARKER

Award-winning actor, producer and founder of the eponymous shoe brand SJP Collection, she became a shoe icon thanks to the footwear-obsessed character, Carrie Bradshaw, she played in Sex and the City, *but it is a love affair that continues off-screen too.*

FOR THE LOVE OF SHOES

When I was growing up the shoe store was an "occasion." I was one of eight kids and while we were often given hand-me-downs, shoes were harder to pass on than clothes. We were allowed to go to the shoe store twice a year: right before school started and then again at the end of the year when school broke up. To me, the shoe store was not unlike a library: air-conditioned in summer, warm and cozy in the winter.

This was back when shoes were made solely from leather—there were no plastic shoes, no pleather shoes, *just* leather. While my siblings were busy getting their feet measured I would wander around, taking in the distinct smell and marvelling at the stitching. You might know what I mean—the bottom soles were layers of leather and proper, beautiful, waxed-cotton stitching. We would get saddle Oxfords for the start of the school year and in spring we were allowed a T-strap shoe that was perforated. And even though they weren't the more trendy shoes that my classmates had, I thought they were beautiful. We also always had a Mary Jane, though my mother didn't call them that; she referred to them as our "patent leather shoes" and every girl in the family wore them for all dress-up occasions. And even though none of those would have been my shoe of choice, I treasured each pair. Every Sunday we got the newspaper and the Kiwi polish out and we polished and buffed our shoes, by ourselves, as we were taught by our parents.

I remember being very young and putting a shoe on, and the salesperson—who knew every local family, and who had worked there for years—asked me to wiggle my big toe up and down so that they could check the size while they squeezed the sides of my feet. Sometimes I still catch myself wiggling my big toe when I try on a new pair of shoes.

Personally, I think people have a more heightened and emotional relationship to shoes than they do to clothes. Shoes make you walk differently—they literally change the pitch of your body—and they can give you height, but they can also change how you present yourself to the outside world. As an actor, only when I have slipped on my character's shoes do I feel complete. It's akin to being on set, ready to start, when the prop person hands you the pen you're going to use in the scene. All the various pieces come together to make you feel whole.

I have several pairs of shoes that I adore and, even though I don't wear them all now, I would never part with them. I have a pair of Calvin Klein short boots—a press sample from the early 90s. The softly rounded-off square toe is outdated, and the buttons on the side look as though they need a button hook to close, but I wore those boots to *everything*, including my best friend's wedding (which at the time looked kind of bananas). I love them.

I also have a pair of shoes my husband gave me around the time my son was born. I wouldn't dare call them a push gift (which I've never asked for, nor received), and I don't think the two were related. But they did appear around the same time. The shoes are a true bubble-gum pink Manolo Blahnik pump. Very simple, very pretty, they're also embossed to give the impression of animal skin. Stunning.

I have one more amazing pair that I've had forever and which I don't wear. Years and years and years ago, long before I even met my husband, I met [actress and model] Kelly LeBrock. She was working with my boyfriend at the time, and we became friends. She'd been a model and she was very worldly (especially to my provincial, less-travelled eyes). Kelly had an old pair of Charles Jourdan black suede pumps that were probably

110s. They'd been so worn in that you could bend them in half, like a pointe shoe with no shank. I don't know why but for some reason she gave them to me. I worshipped them then and I worship them now—they even helped inspire my shoe collection, because when I started my brand shoe colors were mainly neutrals. But in the 70s, Charles Jourdan was famous for their perfect suede pumps in multiple colors. And so with the Fawn, which is an evergreen pump for my brand, we always bring out a couple new colors each season. They're handmade in Italy, a lot of them are suede, a huge number of them are satin, and they are the perfect shoe. Thank you, Kelly.

Nowadays, I'm not really inclined to be running around cobblestone streets—as I was for twenty years—wearing 100 or 110 heels. It doesn't feel practical for my life today. I will wear heels for an evening out and not complain (there are bigger things to complain about in the world), but the ball of a woman's foot takes so much punishment and needs extra padding! And, having spent so much time in pain, I was determined to create something different. I know that I may be biased, but, for me, our SJP shoes are the most comfortable shoes I have ever worn, the sort of shoes that you *don't* have to secretly take off under the table. This means a lot to me—when you take painful shoes off, you really don't want to put them back on. Life is too short for painful shoes!

SHOES

My love of shoes is absolutely my dad's fault, and I take no responsibility for it, or for the stupid money I have spent over the years trying to satisfy that love. Nope, I am completely blameless. Because when I was a kid, my dad owned shoe shops. Like Sarah Jessica Parker (I've always wanted to say that), I remember the thrill of going to get new school shoes—though never the ones with the key in the sole that I wanted—and having my feet measured. I remember climbing the stairs in the stock room that had boxes piled high and I remember wiggling my big toe as requested so my dad could see if the shoes were too big, too small or just right.

In my early teens I almost ruined a family vacation trying to find a pair of purple Doc Martens that I had seen in a magazine. I researched the locations of all the shoe shops in the area and dragged my parents and siblings with me, leaving a string of stores in a teenage fit when they didn't have the particular shade I was after. How dare they. Naturally, I found them in the very last place we visited, which was lucky as my family was quite ready to disown me by that point. God, I loved those boots. When I returned home to Scotland, I recall the excitement of wearing them that first day back at school, and the disappointment that none of my school friends cared a damn about my new boots. More fool them. I did something similar a few years later trying to track down a pair of carmine-red Chuck Taylor Converse, probably because I had seen them worn by someone I idolized on MTV. I wore those sneakers until they could practically walk away on their own.

The first time I had a relatively significant amount of my own money to spend, I bought a pair of short block-heeled loafers and felt elevated in every sense of the word. And so began my obsession with heels, which remains as I type. I had a closet built in my house to exclusively store my shoes, 40 percent of which I don't really wear but all of which I love. Like SJP, my days of regularly running around in super-high heels are limited, but I'm not ready to give them up just yet. Occasionally I open that closet just to look at them, now and again trying on the ones that haven't stepped foot off their shelf for several years, just so they know I haven't forgotten about them.

In the closet I have my shoes arranged by heel height, style and occasion. Summer sandals at the top, winter boots at the bottom and an array of taxi heels, walkable heels, kitten heels, evening flats, day flats and sneakers in between. I am not suggesting that everyone should have a shoe closet—I understand that I am a certifiable anomaly who should probably have a savings account instead. But a capsule shoe wardrobe is as important as a capsule clothing wardrobe, and everyone should have a selection of go-to shoes to allow them to confidently step into any occasion. You don't need many, but they should be tailored to your life and priorities.

Shoes are the quickest way to update an outfit, and if you can, it is where you should put your money. I say the same in the Bags chapter, as accessories have the capacity to elevate clothing, but unlike bags, bad shoes can ruin your feet. Though be aware that bad doesn't necessarily mean cheap, as you can have poorly made expensive shoes that trash your feet too. You only get one pair of feet, and I know women who suffered in bad shoes in their youth and have been paying for it in podiatrists since. So whichever shoes you decide to spend most of your time in, ensure that you choose comfort over crippling, or your only future shoes of choice will be orthotic.

ANATOMY OF A SHOE

I am shortly going to be talking about uppers and vamps, and rather than you skim-reading it pretending you kind of know what I am saying, I'd like you to fully understand what they are. Understanding the anatomy of a shoe should lead to more comfortable shoes, so it is worth taking the time.

I am going to assume that you know where and what the heel, toe and insole are, but we are going to start at the toe. Or the toe box, which does exactly what it says and is the frontmost of the shoe that contains your toes. It is imperative that the toe box does not feel too tight when you try the shoes on, as your toes need and deserve the space, otherwise the shoes will be too painful to wear. You should always be able to wiggle your big toe up and down easily. Then we have the upper, which is the top part of the shoe that holds the rest of the foot. It is edged by the topline, and where the topline falls on pumps is where you are most likely to suffer rubbing and blisters, especially on the inside of your foot by your big toe joint, and on the outside by your little toe joint, so again, ensure it isn't unbearably tight even if you think it will stretch. Good shoes will a little, but not significantly. Then there is the vamp, often confused with the upper, but the vamp is the part of the upper that extends from the tip of the toe box to where the shoe ends on your foot.

Still with me? Good, it's important.

Next up we have the counter, which supports the back of the heel. Ah, the bloody counter, as for some of us this part is often covered in our own blood thanks to the blisters the counter can cause. Now I wish I could give you a quick fix on how to prevent this, but I can't, as expensive shoes will do it just as much as cheaper ones, and sometimes shoes you thought you had worn in long ago will also decide to punish you for no reason. If a shoe is slightly too big and slips a little when you walk, that is territory for a blister, so never opt for half a size up even if you love them and they don't have your actual size. Those shoes will be the devil. Blister plasters work short term, but I find that they tend to roll down your heel and create an even bigger mess, so call me old-school but I prefer normal fabric plasters. Further down the counter is the seat, which should beautifully merge with the shape of your heel for maximal comfort. The seat is supported by the heel, which I am assuming you know, and then there is the outsole. Now the outsole is the part that touches the ground, and keeps you safe—or not—on slippy ground. For the shoes I love and know I will be wearing regularly, if they have delicate leather outsoles on them on arrival, I will stroke them, admire how buttery soft they are, and then march them down to my trustiest cobbler to attach rubber soles. Don't judge: better safe than sorry. Finally, mirroring the outsole is the insole, and the part to focus on here is where the ball of your foot will be sitting. In a heel, it is the ball of your foot that takes all the weight, so do as SJP does and make sure there is significant cushioning in that area as that is truly the sweet spot.

CAPSULE SHOE WARDROBE

Just to be clear, I'm not saying that you must own all of the following shoes. Instead, consider this a shoe pick 'n' mix that should suit your needs, lifestyle and desires (for they are significant too).

HEELS

It has taken me to my mid-forties to accept my actual height. I always felt that I should have been taller than my 5'4" (and a half), so I created extra inches at every opportunity. And I know that I am not the only one. "Because I'm short, I don't feel people take me as seriously when I'm wearing flats," stylist Kate Young, who is 5'3", told me. "I mean maybe this is just my own craziness, but I feel I look more like an adult when I wear heels. So, I wear incredibly high heels. The higher the better."

I would wear walkable heels for the commute to work, then change into higher heels once at my desk and keep them on if I was going out that evening. Every single weekday. At the weekends I wasn't a sneakers and comfort person, but I would have more everyday heels in which to do life errands or meet with friends. In winter, safety came first, as I didn't fancy my chances in the heels-and-ice battle (I had some sense), but the boots I would opt for instead would still have a chunky sole to lend me a couple of inches.

Then came 2020. During the initial lockdown, I wrote a feature about the importance of dressing up at home to raise your spirits, even if you weren't going anywhere. For me that included heels. I sat at my kitchen table, in front of my laptop, working from home, wearing heels. I must wear shoes while working in order to concentrate, but—spoiler alert—as I write this chapter, I am wearing flat boots. For during those months locked in, aside from one walk a day, I discovered the beauty of flat shoes and how fast I could move in them. When lockdown lifted and we slowly went back about our lives, like many, many other people it took me a while to get used to walking in heels once more. Me, a seasoned veteran. There were sensationalist headlines announcing that the heel was dead, as the comfort we discovered in our own homes spilled on to the streets. But fear not, for while heels did take the brunt of the retail downturn, the only way was up for a good 4-inch heel. It was just, ironically, about the balance. Flats have their place, of course they do, and I am now quite happy to see people in real life while wearing a flat-as-a-pancake ballet flat, but for me, heels took on a greater transformative power. If I am having a big work meeting, I change into a heel for extra confidence (it works every time for me, and for many people I know). Dressing up for a night out in towering heels now signifies that it is an important night to me, and I want to make an effort, rather than a run-of-the-mill dinner.

If you love high heels, flats will never replace them or how you feel when wearing them. They can raise you up in every sense of the word, give you the courage to boss a meeting or the poise to feel like a star as you walk from restaurant door to table, and they can even help—just a little—with your own self-esteem. But please, please make sure you can walk in them.

I never thought that you could teach someone to walk in high heels, but one designer I interviewed many years ago assured me that you can. "I think that as human beings it's remarkable that we can adapt to almost anything," Edgardo Osorio, founder of luxury Italian shoe brand Aquazzura, once told me. "My sister would always ask me how to walk in heels, and I would tell her to put some music on at home, slip on some mid-heels and do her chores—and once she's comfortable in those, change to higher heels. If you trip, then at least you're in your own home so it's not embarrassing. If you do it every day, it becomes a habit. I've obviously met women who have had surgery and back problems and need to wear lower heels, but if you talk to a doctor, they actually say that very flat shoes can be bad for your back too, so even a little height is important."

Despite what Kate Young wears, there is such a thing as a heel that is too high. Most designers say that 10.5cm (4 inches) is the highest a shoe can be without it distorting the foot too much and knocking your balance off. I have worn higher, and I can attest that it is correct. If you do go over 10.5cm, either do so for a very short period—they look good in a photograph—or with the assistance of a small platform sole to help redistribute the weight.

OK, my love of a heel is clear, and while I have collected quite a number over the years, I would recommend three styles which I reach for time and time again.

Heeled pumps

I mention these in detail in the Capsule Wardrobe chapter on page 27 and in the Black chapter on page 245, and I point you to them on many other pages too—that is how much I believe in them. In a stiletto, kitten or block heel, with a pointed or rounded toe—for all are excellent and work for almost everything—and a vamp that brushes the very base of your little toe, you can't go wrong with a pump. I also love a Mary Jane strap detail to hug the bridge of the foot, not the ankle. Matte or patent leather would be my guidance, in a neutral shade for a more classic take, a brighter shade that you love for an easy way to wear color, or—a favorite of mine—in white to wear with blue denim.

Strappy evening sandal

In all my years, I have only owned two of these, both of which I still have and still wear, for they sadly don't come out as much as the pumps. But there are some outfits and occasions for which a strappy evening sandal is the best and only choice. Usually summer weddings or parties, and over-the-top holiday soirées. Yes, I said soirée. If your outfit is light in both weight and color, a solid pump tends to overwhelm, whereas a strappy heeled sandal is impactful but subtle. How strappy is up to you, depending on if you like a complicated gladiator lacing around the foot and up the leg, or maybe something simpler. A strap around the base of the toes and ball of the foot, combined with rear heel support and an ankle strap, can often be all you need.

This is where I break my self-imposed color rule too. In the Color + Print chapter, I warn you against pairing a flash of bright color with a black outfit canvas; however, I have worn, and will continue to wear, a 10.5cm (4 inch) scarlet-red suede strappy sandal with a black silk dress. I know, I know, but hear me out. The delicacy of the sandal means that the red is inconspicuous and serves to lift the black with just a flash. Consider it the bright nail polish of the look—suggestive, but not substantial. The other pair I have are black, naturally, with a shorter 9cm (3.5 inch) heel, which means they are practically the sneakers of the strappy sandal world. Metallics of silver, gold and bronze are other excellent choices, as they catch the light as you move and dazzle like jewels.

Evening boots

As I wrote "evening boots" I imagined a dashing highwayman, or a tenth-century well-to-do Persian gent. That isn't quite the look we are going for, though I would encourage you to google the latter as the boots are quite fabulous. By evening boots, I simply mean boots with a higher heel that aren't designed for stomping around wet pavements and office corridors, and instead seductively suggest they need to be worn on a chilly evening to a cozy candlelit bar. Now I don't want to propose that men are basic, but I will say that these babies are guaranteed to help you get what you want. Fitted on the leg to just below or just over the knee, in a suede or soft leather, with a side zipper, a heel as high as you can comfortably manage, and a pointed or rounded toe once again, as they are more gently provocative than square. They look great with a cropped wider-leg trouser, like a culotte, or with a midi skirt or dress hemline in a fluid fabric, so no one is quite sure how far up the leg those bad boy boots go . . . Sigh. If you have a lucky LBD, consider these your lucky LEBs—Long Evening Boots. You're welcome.

Platforms and wedges

Both platforms and wedges are quite niche footwear choices, and a very personal choice, so I don't feel I need to go into too much detail. I used to wear platform shoes myself, as I wanted higher and higher heels, and the platform aids that. I think done correctly they can look quite sexy and vampy in the best way, but done badly, well . . . I once interviewed the inimitable Manolo Blahnik, a man who has designed some of the most iconic shoes in recent fashion history, and who is never short of an opinion. "I hate platforms," he told me. "I always say that if you want them, you can find the best ones in Frederick's of Hollywood, who sell the best porn shoes in plastic. They aren't my thing, they totally distort the body. When I see a tiny girl wearing huge platforms, I think it is terrible. It shouldn't be about distorting the figure but enhancing it." I mean, that is quite a strong reaction, but we can all picture the very shoes that he is talking about, and I know that not all platforms fall under that umbrella.

But sticking with opinions for a moment longer . . . I hate wedges. Hate them. They are big and bulky, and they really aren't much comfier than a normal heel, regardless of what wedge fans claim. And the only thing I hate more than a wedge is an espadrille wedge, for there is no need. It's like a vacation heel when heels are totally unnecessary on vacation. If you want to wear them, you do you, but I can't and won't support with outfit suggestions!

FLATS

Parking my love affair with heels for a moment, I turn to flats: while they are more of your everyday essentials, that doesn't make them any less special. Honest. Firstly—and I say this because there are possibly people reading this who are where I used to be when it came to my attitude towards flat shoes—never, ever apologize for wearing flats. I understand that that might sound like crazy talk for many of you, but for the few, I mean it: don't apologize.

I think it is unanimous that flat shoes are considered to be cooler, and I say this as a devoted heel wearer, but hey, I have chosen height over hip (yes, I said hip). They make you feel freer, quicker and more relaxed, and they work as well for day as they do for evening. As they are less expected for an evening event, they can look much chicer and more elegant than heels. But don't tell my heels I said that.

Loafers

When I got my first pair of loafers, I wondered what on earth I had been doing before them. I chose a more delicate classic pair—soft black leather, gold hardware, thin leather sole—and wore them day and night, all year round, with bare feet, socks, stockings and tights, and I watched as they slowly gave up the shoe ghost. I have since had them repaired, but I learned my lesson. Loafers may bring to mind school shoes that could take a battering, but adult loafers need to be treated slightly more gently. If

you want to live your life in loafers (and why wouldn't you?), then think of them more as you would your winter boots, as they need to be resilient. Look for a pair in a tougher leather, with a heavier sole that has been designed to carry the weight of your day, for you will want to wear them all the time. With mini hemlines and bare legs, socks or tights. With trouser suits and a complementary sock or 10 denier hosiery knee-highs. And, of course, with all kinds of denim, though they look best with a straight-cut, slightly cropped jean and worst with a baggy, wide-leg oversized pair.

Ballet flats

One day in late spring, a friend of mine arrived at work wearing a pair of pale blue jeans that hit just above her ankle bone, a pair of slate-grey socks and simple black ballet flats. Gun to my head I couldn't tell you what she was wearing above the waist that day, as I was fixated on the combination below. I had personally relegated ballet flats in favor of a loafer, but in one morning dressing choice my friend had swung me back to ballets. With the weight of the sock, they looked less cute and more contemporary, more hot French girl and less schoolgirl. Incidentally, as a grown adult, you never want to look in the mirror and think "schoolgirl," unless you are focusing on your skin routine. With the combination of the sock and the pump, my clever friend also solved the problem of blisters, for ballet flats are well known for causing many in the very painful early breaking-in days. Sadly, blisters caused by ballet flats on bare skin are inevitable; it has to do with where the collar (back) of the shoe hits the back of your ankle, but you can avoid the worst by selecting a softer leather or suede, and making sure the fit is perfect. Too tight and you will know about it, too loose and the movement of the shoe as you walk will shred your skin. Other than that, I promise that ballet flats are a good spring and summer alternative to loafers and are flattering on the foot if you look for a pair with a shorter vamp (the upper that covers the front of the foot) that runs across the toe line and exposes more of the bridge of your foot, resulting in the illusion of a longer leg.

Obviously, they are great with socks, as above. But they are also a soft punctuation to a shorter hemline and 15 denier tights, or with bare legs (or just the flash of ankle) if you can bear it.

A reminder from Edgardo earlier: just as too high a heel can create knee, back and balance issues, so too can a shoe that is too flat. If you spend a lot of time in shoes without substantial arch support, it can result in plantar fasciitis, which causes burning pain in your heels. While I don't expect you to pirouette down the street on your tippy toes in ballet flats, ensure there's a bit of density in the sole so your feet aren't flat as a pancake with no support, as the agony of feeling every single tiny stone through a paper-thin sole is never worth it, regardless of how pretty the shoe is.

Evening flats

In theory you can dress up day flats and dress down evening flats, and either can be worn at any time, but some shoes are so special that you want to save them for oh-so-special occasions. I once wore a pair of dainty velvet Mary Janes when my weather app swore to me that it wouldn't rain. As I ran through flooded streets later that day, cursing that lying app, I almost sobbed as my shoes began to swell with water. But lesson learned as beautiful flats made of satin or velvet should not be your everyday basics, nor should those embellished in crystals and gems, nor those so dainty they would make the Fairy Godmother proud. Evening flats look really elegant with three-quarter-length hemlines in dresses or skirts, or with cropped wide-leg or slightly flared trousers.

BOOTS

Maybe it is the Scot in me, but even though I often say I am never happier than when I am in a bikini on a beach, I almost look forward to the weather turning cold so I can turn to my favorite boots. I like the support of boots and the illusions they can create—elongating your legs, or making them look narrower; transforming a casual look into something more elevated, or making something elevated look more casual and cool. I'm here for it all.

Ankle boots

Let's start with the classics, shall we? From mid-autumn to early spring, these are imperative to getting dressed and leaving the house. They can range from practical stompers to those with a heel, as day boots don't have to mean that you are ready to hike up a mountain at a moment's notice. But, and not to sound like your mom, they do have to be comfortable, well-structured and supportive.

What is key is where they hit on your leg. Too low and they appear squashed; too high and they will be really unflattering. No one needs a boot that hits mid-calf. There is a very good reason that they aren't called mid-calf boots. The sweet spot is about three finger widths from the top of your ankle bone. The circumference of the top of the boot should allow enough room for your finger to easily slip in, even if wearing a thick sock. If a slip-on Chelsea-style boot is too tight for your legs, then opt for a lace-up variation instead, or a pair that zips on the inside of the foot, as they allow more give at the top if you tie them loosely, or don't tie or zip them all the way up. If the boot leaves any indentation in the skin, they are too tight.

Wearing them with a chunky sock that is scrunched up above the top of the boot will narrow the calf if you are pairing the boots with a tighter trouser. I would never recommend tucking a trouser leg into ankle boots, as it can get very 90s talent-show contestant very quickly. Always wear over, or if you can, roll the hem up to hit the top of the boot if narrower, or to just below the top of the boot if a wider or straight leg. Showing a flash of bare ankle, or a strip of sock, in between boot and trouser is totally fine too. I also love the weight of an ankle boot with a midi-length (or longer) shirt dress in spring, with bare legs if you can bear it, or a lighter denier tight.

Flat knee-high boots

Full disclosure, I don't own these. But I used to, and wore them all the time. Then I became loyal to heeled knee-high boots, though I do think I will revisit the flats in the future now that I have made peace with my actual height. I have always loved them on other people though, especially when worn with black leggings and oversized blazers. There is a French influencer who wore that very outfit when she was the chicest pregnant woman of all time, and the boots and the bump balanced out the proportions in an excellent manner. I would avoid with dresses, especially those with knee-length hemlines, as they create a bulky silhouette. Lean into their riding origins and try those with a slimmer profile and defined ankle, rather than shapeless ones that lean more towards Wellington boots.

Heeled knee-high boots

Not to be mistaken for the evening boot, though they can certainly be worn in the evening, consider these to be your slightly loftier day boot. Block heel, not stiletto, is preferred for a more refined practicality, and go as high as you can realistically walk in for a long time without the ball of your foot burning from the pressure. An 8.5cm (3.3 inch) height allows you to confidently strut day-to-day and shouldn't throw your weight off-balance after wearing for long periods of time, but I would reserve anything higher than that to short bursts, and transport by car.

They lend a substantial and contemporary spirit to midi dresses, and regardless of what you think of skinny jeans, a black pair of heeled knee-high boots look great when pulled on over pale blue denim.

SNEAKERS

I am not talking about sports shoes here, which you actually need support from for activities—this is about your everyday sneakers. The ones you want to spend your commute and weekends wearing. But even if you are not a sneaker-head who obsessively follows all cool collaborations and limited-edition releases, you will still know the importance of the right sneakers. It was ingrained in us all from a very early age, thanks to middle school. God help those kids who weren't wearing the right sneakers. I can say that, as I was that kid in the wrong sneakers. Regardless of the pleading, often followed by hysterical tears, as I tried to explain to my parents why I needed to have a new pair of Nikes or Adidas or whatever was "trendy," they never budged, as they tried to instill in me that the right sneakers didn't matter. Well, Mum and Dad, that lesson failed miserably: the right sneakers bloody do matter. They did then and they still do now. But it's not about them being designer or the hottest brand of the moment; the right sneakers applies to what is right for you.

I found my right sneakers in Adidas Gazelles. And while I have tried a pair of oddly (for me) colorful Nikes, it is to my Gazelles that I return. Comfy and streamlined, classic without the need for design bells and whistles, and they aren't overly sporty so they work well with denim and tailoring. A slouchy but excellently tailored trouser suit worn with sneakers is one of my favorite looks on women. The right sneakers turning up with an unexpected outfit will always be worn by the coolest woman in the room. So there, Mum and Dad, learn that lesson.

SANDALS

Let's be realistic here: if you don't live in a warm climate, you only need two pairs of sandals. One for day, which also works for the beach, and one that is a little bit fancier. The day pair needs to have the practicality of your comfiest boots, but also needs to be able to work with denim, light summer day dresses and swimwear. Every summer we are offered up a new style of sandal—from the big and bulky with Velcro straps and dense soles that promise to take you from the beach to the apocalypse, to the delicate strappy ones that bafflingly seem to reveal more of your foot than if you were wearing nothing at all. But never listen to trends when it comes to sandals. If you have found the ones that work for you, stick with them, as these shoes work so hard, you don't need to add fashion peer pressure into the mix.

City sandals

I also talk about these in the Summer chapter, as these can require a bit of a journey to get right. An overwhelmingly hot day in the city can be made even more unbearable with painful shoes, as there is no sock or stocking to help the poor bare skin of your feet. The main thing is to ensure that they aren't too tight, as a shoe that fits just OK first thing in the morning will be hell by lunchtime when your foot swells. Personally,

I always think the answer is a slide, and certainly a shoe that doesn't involve an ankle strap. The beauty of a slide is that your ankle and heel remain free, and the front of your foot is offered some gentle security by an adjustable strap or two. Look for soft leather and suede as they are breathable and allow moisture to pass through them. They also mold to the shape of your foot, encasing yet not constricting. As for the sole, if you are commuting and walking around town, you will need a heavier tread that can take a little hot pavement beating.

Elevated sandals

Think of these sandals as the ones you would wear to a dinner on vacation at the hotel you can't afford to stay at, but you like to spend an evening there to people-watch and eat the snacks that come with the drinks. These sandals suggest that you too belong at that hotel, as does the dress you packed for this very evening and location. These sandals suggest that you arrived at the hotel by car, and that they have seen very little walking. They only come out for special occasions, and when they do it takes you a minute to remember how to tie them. These are the sandals that perfectly expose your tanned feet and pedicure, as they are made of little more than a thin leather sole and even thinner straps that secure the big toe and criss-cross up your foot to your ankle, where you tie them loosely so as not to dent your skin. You love them, and they are the perfect companion to the special fly-away dress you have on, as your city sandals would be too heavy with them. You love these elevated sandals, and they have their specific job to do a couple of times a year before they are returned to the closet. Because they really are shoes meant for a car, and not for trekking back to your hotel down the hill.

HAVE A CARE

My dad did his national service so he knew the importance of having perfectly polished footwear, and he had the technique mastered. Literal spit and polish, and a large basket of numerous brushes and cloths. He would use scraps of old clothes, ensuring they were completely smooth and soft, pour a little water in the lid of the polish pot, and dip the cloth (wrapped around the tip of his index finger) first into the water and then the polish.

He would work in small circles around and around one area of the shoe, build that to a shine, then move on to the next. Our shoes all gleamed, and even when I left home, I would ensure that my shoes were polished before I returned to visit, and I now have my own basket of Kiwi polishes, brushes and rags (old T-shirts).

He used to say to us, "If you are down in the heel, you are down in life," which repeats in my mind as I head to a cobbler to replace worn-down heels and soles on my most beloved shoes. I once worked with a very glamorous woman who was totally immaculate in every way except one: she wore each of her stiletto-heeled shoes right down to the metal pin, and until the surrounding leather peeled up like a banana skin. If you allow a heel to get to that state, and continue to wear them, it is very hard to then rescue the shoe, so please always keep an eye on the rubber tips and have them changed before they are worn to nothing. If one does fall off, as they sometimes do, take off the shoes as soon as you can and don't walk in them, as that will make the problem worse.

Find yourself a good local cobbler, and make sure you read the reviews before you commit, as they can make mistakes. Don't be afraid to ask about the work they plan to do on your shoes—for instance, if you are having a pair resoled, be careful that they don't select a sole that is too thick, as it can tear the upper away.

As for storing shoes and keeping them looking pristine, Sarah Jessica Parker had tips for me that I immediately implemented. You know that tissue that comes in the toes of new shoes when you buy them? Do not throw it away. "I always tell our customers to stuff their shoes after they wear them and when they're still warm," she said. "Stuff them with force because that's how a shoe keeps its shape. Leather likes to expand and then it shrinks back, and sometimes it shrinks back further than it was initially built. I'm pretty meticulous about stuffing my shoes, and that is what the tissue is for. It's really helpful, as it's already in the shape of the toe of the shoe." If, like me, this is something that you shamefully did not know—even though you were brought up to look after your shoes— and you threw all the toe tissue away as soon as you got the new shoes home, all is not lost. "You can also take an old sock and do the same thing."

SHOES IN BRIEF

1   You are allowed to have an emotional relationship with shoes.

2   Life is too short for uncomfortable shoes.

3   If you can't walk in high heels, you don't need to wear them.

4   Invest in your feet. You only get one pair.

5   A heel can be too high, and a flat can be too flat.

6   Learn how to properly polish your shoes.

7   A great cobbler is worth travelling for.

8   You do not need espadrille wedges.

9   The right sneakers matter.

10 Do not throw away the toe tissue in new shoes.

EVENTS

LAW ROACH

As a stylist and image architect, working with Zendaya, Celine Dion and Anya Taylor-Joy, Law transformed celebrity red-carpet expectations. The now author, presenter and one of the best-dressed men at any event explains how to get dressed UP for anything.

WHAT DRESS CODES MEAN NOW

Confidence is the most important dress code. When a woman walks into a room—no matter what age, race or size—and she walks in with confidence, you, and everyone else in the room, will want to know who she is. That confidence is coming from within, but it feeds on what she has chosen to wear. It's that extra little bounce in the walk or the flip of the hair; it's knowing, without even talking to her, that she was excited to get dressed and that she loves how she looks in her clothes. Confidence will make me think "wow," and I will cross the room to say, "Oh my God, you look so beautiful."

When I dressed Celine [Dion], I always knew when she loved a look because her walk would change into more of a strut. It is as thrilling now as it was then, to see how clothes can turn on something different inside someone. It is powerful. If you love what you're wearing, if you are confident about it, people will pick up on your enthusiasm. This is the big secret to dressing for a special occasion or event. It's not about what you're wearing, it is about how you wear it.

You also don't need to care what anyone else thinks. With some clients that I work with, I want outfits to be polarizing—I want people to love it or hate it, because at least people are talking about it. Fashion is one of the things that brings people together, even if we disagree. I have never really cared critically about what people have thought of my styling; instead, I am driven by the idea that people will go into work and say to their colleagues, "Did you see what such and such wore last night?" So even if they say, "Oh God, it was a mess. I hated it," someone else somewhere will say, "Oh, I loved it so much." I like that fashion entertains in this way.

If I am given a dress code for an event, I always want to make sure that my client is comfortable. But dress codes mean less now than they once did, and when I am dressing people, I like to push buttons. Many of us saw Timothée Chalamet with no shirt on at the Oscars, and he was rightly celebrated for it. It is very cool to see, this toppling of the old guard, because it shows that fashion has become more about individuality.

Those who break the rules a bit will always stand out, though some rules still apply. Black tie still means a tuxedo or tailoring, or a long and formal gown. Cocktail is a little more fun. I still have no idea what white tie means. But for me, business casual is the most confusing code, because it can almost mean anything to anyone. For those people who are more eccentric, a gown might be casual, and to others it is denim. But it also means that there is no way you can get it wrong.

If I had a party, my dress code would be "glamorous and chic," so that you can interpret chic however you like. I like the idea of giving people the freedom to figure out what it means to them.

Actually, shit, this isn't true. I *always* think about the dress code—and rules—for my funeral. I want people to dress *UP*. I want women in hats, and everyone in black tailored suits with nipped waists. I've told Zendaya that she has to be in a big hat with a veil. I know I won't physically be there to see it, but I want to have the most glamorous funeral ever. I want everyone to be impeccably dressed. I want drama!

EVENTS

I had been living in London for just under a year when my cousin got married. It was the first Scottish wedding I'd be attending as just a guest, not part of the bridal party, and so could wear exactly what I wanted. I was studying fashion at Central Saint Martins, and I was damn well going to look the part. Or so I thought. My memory of how I managed to buy a dress from Harvey Nichols and a hat from Fenwick is rather hazy, but I assume my student loan was involved. Anyway, the dress was knitted and fitted, with an oversized turtleneck, and the hat was more of a headband with adornments. Honestly, it was a thing then. Well, it was a thing then in London. In Aberdeenshire, maybe not so much. But I felt delighted with myself. Alas, that feeling was short-lived, as when we arrived at the hotel venue, it became apparent that the print on my dress was an exact match for the wallpaper in the event space, and later a man asked me if I had shot my hat or bought it. I was crushed. However, the excitement of dressing up and wearing something I loved was such an endorphin buzz that—despite the wallpaper and opinions of others—I was hooked.

As a teenager, I used to stay up really late and watch the Oscars red carpet so I could see the outfits. Now, I am less likely to watch TV until 4 a.m., but the morning after the awards, as soon as I wake, I reach for my phone and scroll through every look. And I mean every single one. By the time I have reached image number 245, I have no idea who the pretty lady is, but I think her dress is a lovely color on her and that maybe less jewellery would have been better. I then exchange my best-dressed selection with equally gripped friends, and when I arrive in the office, I want to gather the team to discuss again. Sounding pretty cool again, aren't I? Obviously my team really don't care as much as I do, so this is not top of their priority lists on a Monday morning. You may not care that much either, but my favorites of all time include Martha Plimpton in a vintage 1930s dress at the 1989 Oscars, as it was pared back and minimal, and Zendaya at the 2021 Oscars in a blindingly bright yellow Valentino gown with a large Bulgari diamond necklace. They were at either end of the red-carpet minimal to maximal spectrum, but both answered the brief perfectly and were true to their own personal style. Which is essential. Speaking to Law was a book highlight for me, as he constantly pushed the boundaries and expectations of what red-carpet dressing could be. If Zendaya is on a promotional campaign for a movie, you can bet I will be poring over every single look, as she is undoubtedly—thanks in part to Law—the best-dressed star of her generation. And some generations before too.

"One of the biggest compliments I ever got is that none of my clients ever look the same," Law says. "Sometimes a stylist can have a certain aesthetic, and that can bleed into all of their clients. But for me, everyone I worked with had to have their own story. Especially when working with Zendaya, as there is a thread through every single look that we have done together that links to the ones before and after. It's an ongoing story, and it may change, depending on what she's promoting, but it is always her story and hers alone. I just use clothes as the words."

OK, so we aren't all Zendaya, and we don't all have Law dressing us for the events we attend, but there is a lesson here. For the majority of us, big events, from weddings to black-tie or cocktail events, are probably few and far between. Which means that we can get a little, well, overly excited when it comes to choosing what we are going to wear. I've been to elaborate dinners where other guests appear so uncomfortable in what they are wearing, and even sometimes apologize for feeling over- or underdressed. Then there are the panic last-minute purchases, as you simply have nothing appropriate for whatever dress code is demanded of you. Last-minute clothing purchases are a terrible idea 87 percent of the time (I have guesstimated this, but I am pretty sure it is true), for you never feel like yourself. Special occasions are already loaded with social anxiety, so why make it worse by wearing something so not you? It is also very easy to fall into a costumey hole, as if we don't often attend events, we can tend to dress like a character attending the event, and not our actual selves. This is where a trusty LBD comes into play, as discussed in the Black and Capsule Wardrobe chapters. It eliminates moments of panic, and you can build it up with accessories and jewellery. Like Law and Zendaya, you need to tell your own clothing story and be the best-dressed version of yourself—

not the person you think is expected of you based on the invitation dress code. I have been invited to events with dress codes ranging from "summer glamor" (I wore a nice dress) to "chic cocktail" (short dress), "dress from the feet up" (shoes), "La Dolce Vita" (nice dress again) and "festive fun" (I didn't go). Most are just unnecessary, nonsensical interpretations of the classics, which include "business casual," "cocktail" and "black tie." So let me break them down for you.

THE DRESS CODES

BUSINESS CASUAL

I always think a business-casual dress code is a trap and a cop-out. Why have a dress code at all if it is this one, which is unclear and unleashes hundreds of text messages between guests all asking, "What are you wearing, and do you think I can wear jeans?" The answer to that question depends on the actual event itself. If it is a business-casual wedding, then probably not, but out of courtesy rather than following strict rules.

To me, business casual means make a bit of an effort. Pull a brush through your hair, maybe top up this morning's makeup, wear a nice top with some jeans or trousers, and opt for shoes that aren't sneakers. By all means wear a nice dress, but not too nice, and if you can only pop in for one drink on your way to or from somewhere else, then whatever you are wearing for the other thing is correct too.

If the dress code is business casual, then you can be formal or casual about your outfit and attendance.

COCKTAIL

A cocktail dress code usually suggests that the event has the potential to be fun rather than too formal, so get dressed with the idea of enjoying yourself in mind. You don't need to wear a long dress—midi and mini are completely acceptable, and more relevant, as long can be too formal. Trousers are also acceptable, which feels unnecessary to be writing in this day and age, but just so you know, women are allowed to wear trousers to anything. My go-to for a cocktail dress code is black trousers, a black camisole and an evening jacket. More on what defines an evening jacket later, but wearing one can make you feel a little protected, especially if you are entering a room where you don't know many people, and it can also help you avoid feeling over- or underdressed. Any color and print goes, but sidestep the summery prints if the cocktail party isn't taking place in the sunshine by a pool. While cocktail is not as formal as black tie, it isn't exactly casual either. So, avoid denim, sneakers, loungewear and sportswear.

BLACK TIE

For many of us, this dress code doesn't come up very often, which is why we need help. In layman's terms, it means go all out. This is your Oscars (even if it is just someone's very formal wedding); this is what you would wear on the red carpet, prepared for someone to stick a microphone in your face and ask you, "Who are you wearing tonight?" Again, I have revealed too much of myself here, so if that doesn't resonate, instead think of this as your moment to shine.

We are talking gowns here, and by gowns I mean a floor-length dress. It can be narrow and slick, full and dramatic, or anything and everything in between. A tuxedo was also made for these invitations, and like the gown, whether you go tightly tailored with a wide trouser, gently oversized, or nipped and streamlined is up to you. I love a tuxedo with nothing underneath but bare skin, but there is an androgynous strength in wearing a shirt beneath, buttoned right to the top, teamed with large drop cocktail earrings.

Speaking of jewellery, go big or go home. I don't mean you should be dripping in it—instead choose one area and go large, whether that is rings, a necklace, bracelets or earrings. It is better to focus on one area rather than pulling attention elsewhere. Also, contrary to what you may believe, black tie doesn't mean you need to reach for your high heels, for a very wise and very famous Italian fashion designer once told me, "It's not always about heels; a long gown worn with flat shoes creates a more fluid stride." He wasn't the only one either, as another said, "I think one of the best red-carpet looks

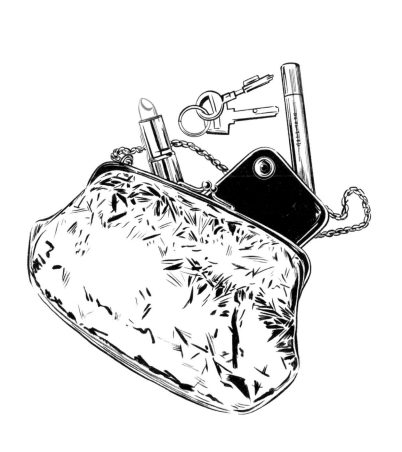

ever was when Elle Macpherson arrived at the Met Gala in 2005 in a beautiful Calvin Klein gown and flat gold sandals. It's incredibly chic to wear flats in the evening with a long dress." Just ensure you have your hem tailored to that length, so you aren't tripping over it all evening. That is less chic.

When searching for your black-tie look, consider the fabric. The reason you see images of celebrities lying down in the backs of cars on their way to the Oscars is because they are trying not to crease their dresses. A heavy silk won't crease quickly, and fabrics with a mix of wool, or a synthetic, are low-wrinkle, which is great if you are sitting for a long period of time. Sequins (vintage please) and dark-colored lace both disguise wrinkles and any rogue wine or food spills. Also, never size down with black-tie outfits, even if you love it so much but they don't have it in your size, as standing in a dress or suit that is on the slightly tight side is OK for half an hour or so, but think about sitting in it for hours, and imagine how cramped and torturous that will feel. If you can't find your dream dress in your size and you must have it, always size up and get it tailored to fit.

WHAT TO WEAR TO A WEDDING

I love weddings. Love them. I love a celebration of people, and I love a room full of people who have really made an effort, who are wearing their most special clothes and are having a marvellous time in them. What is not to love about that? And while I learned a lesson from my cousin's wedding (including not to spend my student loan on an extortionate headband with a feather on it), it did not diminish the thrill of getting dressed for the wedding of someone I love. Weddings encourage you to push the envelope a little, so take this as your opportunity to truly make yourself (and the central couple, of course) proud.

Unless there is a specific dress code—and I do judge wedding invites that demand a particular color palette of the guests; let people live, for God's sake!—there are only a few rules for dressing for a wedding, and even these can be treated with your own discretion based on how well you know the nature of the wedding. For a start I would say no jeans. Even if the whole day is a casual affair, it is still a special occasion, so please treat it as such. The other is please don't wear a long white dress, or even a short one. Or a white suit. Or anything that could be considered bridal. It may feel like a daring style choice, but you will end up looking like you are about to start screaming, "It should have been me!" Also be careful about very pale pastels and grey, as they can look white in certain lighting. Finally, there is the whole "Can I wear black to a wedding?" debacle. I talk about this in the Color + Print chapter and the Black chapter, and I will repeat here that unless someone specifies that you *can't* wear black to their wedding, I think the general rule is that you *can* wear black to a wedding. I have worn a backless black dress four times, a long black skirt and top combo twice, a black suit three times and many other black iterations. The only comment I have ever received about it—compliments aside, of course—was from a mother of the bride who said, "You must be the one who works in fashion," which I also added to my praise pile regardless of the tone in which it was said.

Permission aside, for those of us who wear a lot of black, a wedding is an opportunity to try something new—after all, you will never see many of these people ever again, so what is the worst that can happen? I wore a bright-pink dress that I had only worn once before and had been thinking about selling to a countryside wedding. It was a last-minute decision to take it with me in case it was too cold for the other choice, and thankfully it was. For I had the best time in that dress. I felt like a Barbie doll, in the greatest way, and while the whole wedding made me feel happy, that dress served to amplify it. That pink joy is now classed as one of my favorite things I own; I just need more invitations to bring it out. Bright colors and bold and cheery prints ooze positivity, and that should be the aim at a wedding.

I helped a friend of mine select a dress for the plethora of weddings she had one summer. When I asked if she felt OK to repeat the same look at each, she said, "Oh, it is fine. None of the bridal parties know each other, and only one of the weddings is Instagram-worthy." Slightly harsh, but I admired the thought process. Because of course you can repeat the same look to a number of different weddings, whether in the same year or years apart. Mainly because, no offence, no one will remember what you were wearing. Think of the last three weddings you went to, and without looking at photographs, try to recall the outfits worn by your closest friends at each of them. I'd put money on you struggling. If it wasn't your own wedding, then you weren't the center of attention, and if you loved what you were wearing, then please do the outfit, and yourself, a favor and wear it again. "It should be completely unremarkable, the idea of re-wearing [clothes], because we do it in our daily lives," award-winning actress Cate Blanchett said after wearing an Oscars dress to the Cannes Film Festival. "We do it out of habit, we do it out of choice, we do it out of necessity." If Cate Blanchett can repeat couture outfits that she has previously worn on red carpets and been photographed in for the world's media, I think you can re-wear your favorite dress to another wedding.

HAT OR NO HAT?

Since the "buy it or shot it" incident, I have never worn another hat to a wedding. That's a lie, I vaguely remember a mini hat somewhere in my past, but the less said about that the better. Other than mothers of the brides or grooms, and possibly some older relatives, I can't think of a wedding I have been to over the last five years when someone younger has worn a hat. But that is not to say we should dismiss them as old-fashioned. I love a royal wedding or event with hats galore, for they can be dramatic and cinematic, and perhaps it is something we should bring back to those more low-key weddings that aren't televised. However, it is difficult to know where to start with hats—like glasses, they suit us differently depending on our face and head shapes. What I will say, though, is this: hats that are wider win over hats that are taller. Wide-brim hats, worn on an angle, are usually more elegant and refined if you keep them simple and avoid an explosion of taffeta, feathers and bows that they all seem to be offered with.

WHAT TO WEAR TO A FUNERAL

I deliberated over writing this section, as I don't believe there is a right or wrong way to dress for a funeral. However, it was brought to my attention that in March 2022 the top occasion-wear search term was "what to wear to a funeral." So here we are.

At the time of writing, I have only been to a handful of funerals, and while I know that number will sadly but inevitably increase, currently all the services I have attended were either Christian or mentioned nothing of religion. My knowledge here is limited to my own experience.

At my dad's funeral, everyone wore black except my mum, who wore a pale blue dress that my dad loved to see her wear. A friend who attended told me years later that she often thought of that, as my mum had stood out in a blanket of black and she radiated. My dad would have loved that. The different attires expected of different funerals globally never occurred to me (I try not to think much of funerals day-to-day), but I know that in some cultures funerals are quieter affairs, where people dress for comfort, while in others people dress up—but both are a mark of respect in their own way. In some cultures, black is considered traditional, while in others white is often the color of mourning. For those who want the ceremony to be one of pronounced celebration, friends or family often ask those attending to wear something specific, be it a color or adornment, that reflects the life of the person being honored.

As I said, there is no right or wrong way to dress for a funeral, though I would probably ask you to rethink something overtly sexy, unless specifically requested. Of course, if you are attending Law Roach's funeral long, long, long in the future, if you don't follow the dress code, you aren't getting in.

EVENTS

THE EVENT PIECES

LONG DRESS

I would call this a "gown," but I think that sounds more intimidating than what it is: simply a long dress. But the long dress has many guises, appropriate for different occasions. There is the vacation long dress, which doubles as a beach cover-up and a breathable summer evening dress. There is the day long dress that is office-appropriate all year round and feels right with boots in winter. And then there is the events long dress. The one that is that little bit—or a lot more—special.

This is the dress that might only make it out of the closet a handful of times every year, if that, but every time it does, you wish you would wear it more. This is the feel-fantastic long dress. The item you own that gives you confidence as soon as you pull it on, and the item that reduces the anxiety of attending a function where you know few people, or where you will see people that you haven't seen in years. It is the dress that perfectly answers and fulfils dress codes for weddings and black-tie events alike. So, you better make it a bloody good dress.

It does not need to be OTT, unless that is your personal style. If you are not OTT in any other aspect of your dressing, do not end up with a ruched, poofy, bow-festooned gown with a train. You've gone awry. The long dress needs to fit your aesthetic. If you are minimal in your day-to-day, then minimal is your LD go-to too. If you are more flamboyant and like elaborate silhouettes, go maximal. There is something for the social butterflies and for the social wallflowers, and the sweet spot in between. A long, simple slip dress in your favorite shade can be black-tie appropriate with the right accessories. Just add statement earrings to draw attention up the dress, or a statement necklace if the neckline is low. Large cuff bracelets enhance too, but rings alone won't do a lot to help. Rings do, however, come into their own with a more modest dress with long sleeves, as sparkly digits at the end of a cuff are a gloriously elevated punctuation. Feel free to add several cocktail rings, if you have them, to both hands. If you go simple with the gown, go OTT (or as much as you can bear) with the jewels.

With a more extravagant dress that needs little in the way of "dressing up," you can let the dress do most of the talking and add simpler pieces of jewellery. Personally (after studying every Oscar dress ever) I love a bare décolletage with a big dress, and just subtle earrings and rings. It looks fresher and more modern.

Whether you opt for understated or excess, the most important thing is how you feel in your long dress. If it doesn't give you the confidence that Law talked about earlier, if it doesn't give you an extra bounce in your walk, or make you want to flip your hair, or make you feel excited to put it on, it isn't the dress for you. Keep looking for the one that you can't stop admiring yourself in when wearing.

SUIT

There is nothing sexier than a woman wearing a suit to a black-tie event. I know it isn't revolutionary, a woman in a suit in the twenty-first century, but it still turns heads. Perhaps it is the rule-breaking connotation of it, which projects that the wearer doesn't give a damn about what is expected. Or maybe she is simply a trouser person. Either way, I love it. I mentioned that both strictly tailored and oversized work for the occasion, but whichever you choose, it must be the perfect fit. Too tight and you will feel awkward and uncomfortable; too big and you will look like you have borrowed someone else's suit, and not in the I-just-borrowed-my-boyfriend's-blazer sexy way you are imagining.

If strict tailoring is your preference, try sitting down in the trousers before you buy, or try to hug someone while wearing the jacket. You want to be able to move freely, and not feel restricted or constricted. You also want to easily slip your hands in your trouser pockets, just as the women wearing Yves Saint Laurent's Le Smoking suits do in Helmut Newton's 1975 portraits. Dress shapes may come and go, but those images prove that a great tuxedo never dates.

If you prefer your suits a little looser, focus on the word little. I love an oversized silhouette, but not one that overwhelms and drowns the wearer. Big shoulders with structure are better than those with a softer line, and if the sleeves are too long, have them tailored to hit your thumb knuckle. Rolling up a tuxedo sleeve is too casual for black tie, but appropriate for weddings. Ensure that the trousers fit on the waist, and I still think those that sit higher are more flattering than those that sit on the hips, but ultimately it comes down to what you prefer. The hem length, however, is non-negotiable. If you wear the suit with heels, the hem should cover the heel and graze the floor. If you wear it with flats, the hem should break once for tailored and once and a half for oversized. Any longer than that and you will look like you are standing in a hole.

A risqué bare chest under a buttoned tuxedo jacket is a red-carpet classic, mainly because it looks so good. But if that feels too exposed, then the white shirt will never let you down. The shirt should be as sharp as the tailoring, and narrow-fitting to avoid bulk under the jacket. The neater the shirt's fit, the easier it is to unbutton from the top without the shirt immediately looking like it is trying to escape down a jacket sleeve. If it looks untidy, then button up to the top and embrace the contours.

The tuxedo benefits from subtle feminine touches like a small clutch bag and then big old drop earrings to frame your gorgeous face and skim your shoulder pads. Or—and I swear this is my last mention of her, for now—do as Zendaya (and Law) did at the 2022 *Vanity Fair* Oscar party and swap the earrings for a matching brooch and rings. After all, if anyone can bring back brooches, it is Zendaya.

COCKTAIL DRESS

I am going to focus on the cocktail dress rather than cocktail outfits, as a lot of that is covered in the Parties chapter, for cocktail dressing and party dressing are one and the same. Or they should be, but the cocktail dress is harder to get right. I just typed "cocktail dress" into Google Images, and dear God, no wonder people are so confused. According to Google you could be in an emerald crushed-velvet midi dress, a crystal circle-skirt minidress, or a minidress that is almost completely cloaked by a colossal bow.

You also need to have huge blown-out hair and stand with one hand on your hip all night. While all those examples are horrific, there is a sliver of truth in that search, as the cocktail dress can be many things. Though being nice is a good place to start.

Short, knee-length, midi and even ankle-length (but not long dress/gown territory) count for cocktail, so select what you are comfortable with. Long sleeves, short sleeves, no sleeves, bustier and off-the-shoulder are also all approved by the cocktail committee. Take a similar approach here as you would to buying any other item of clothing for yourself: try what you like, and what you like yourself in, and not what you think is expected of you. You want to get years and years of wear out of this dress, you want to feel true to yourself every time you put it on and you want to feel like you are going to have a really good time.

If you have no idea what that might look like, start an online search to give yourself ideas. When you have some time and are not distracted, log on to your favorite multi-brand retailer's site and select dresses. Then begins the filtering. Select the length you like to wear (I think two is better than one), then if there is an option, select the style. But if there are too many styles, rule out the ones that are a no from the start—for example, discount open back if you need to wear a bra, or day dresses if you need cocktail. Then hit the color filter, but keep an open mind, and select the colors that you wear a little of and like, as you might just surprise yourself. Ignore the size filter for now, as your size could have sold out on that site and you don't want to limit yourself. Once you are happy with your filters, start scrolling. Now this isn't a fool-proof solution, but it will give you an idea of what you like (and what you hate) and will reduce a world of dresses into a more digestible edit just for you. Once you have found a few that you like, see if they have your size, and either buy or search for a similar style on vintage or pre-loved websites, and of course rental apps.

When it comes to accessories, a lot depends on the dress, but I believe this rule works. If the dress is maximal, the accessories should be minimal. If the dress is minimal, have more fun with the accessories.

EVENING JACKET

This is not a regular jacket. This is not the jacket that you pull on as an extra layer, nor is it the jacket that you take with you "just in case" on a summer's day. Instead, this is the jacket that can turn something casual into something cocktail.

I have two. One is a simple, perfectly tailored black blazer—as Jo Ellison says in the Workwear chapter, there is nothing a black blazer can't dress up. That black jacket, a pair of earrings, another layer of mascara and some lipstick, and I feel ready for a cocktail or business-casual invite, even when all I am wearing under that jacket is a white T-shirt or camisole and some tailored trousers I wear to work. But the other jacket is next level up: more of a cape than a jacket, it swings over my shoulders and the hem drops to my waist. It is black with gold, silver and white embroidery, and when I wear it I feel like a key character from *Game of Thrones*, which is always an outfit win in my book. When I am faced with an event that I have no idea what to wear to, and I'm running low on energy, that is the jacket I reach for. I've worn it to a brilliant wedding in a castle over a long black dress I have had for twenty years, and I have worn it with jeans and a T-shirt for a drinks party that had a dress code I couldn't decipher. It saved me at a small wedding where I knew no one, as after not speaking to anyone for hours (I swear I tried), someone swept across the hall floor to ask me where my jacket was from, and she then pulled me under her wing for the rest of the evening. A conversation piece: that is what this jacket should be.

It is easy to go elaborate with this piece too, as it serves to elevate the simplest of outfits. Think of this as a statement piece of jewellery in clothing form. Embroidery, print or embellishment, sometimes all at once if you think it works—but if the jacket is a lot, then team it with a lot less. A military jacket with brass detailing can work too, but keep the rest of the outfit slightly softer, with fluid fabrics, to stop it looking costume. Honestly, an evening jacket, paired with T-shirt or shirt, jeans or trousers and a pair of heels or evening flats is a tremendous combination.

Play with proportions too. If your jacket is fitted, wear it with wide trousers or a big skirt. If your jacket is looser, or a cape shape, then a narrow bottom silhouette balances it out.

Unlike the long dress or a cocktail dress, you should get a lot of wear out of the evening jacket. Even if you are just going for dinner with friends, throwing this on will show that you cared enough to make an effort. And that is always appreciated.

HAVE A CARE

I cannot hammer this home enough: you do not need to buy something new for every single event, party or fancy dinner you are invited to. And when you do buy, make sure you aren't buying for one event in particular, but for those in future too. That dress, suit, jacket, earrings or anything else you invest in needs to earn its keep over many, many invitations.

Shopping for an event in a panic will never result in something that you love. It will result in a piece you like, for a price much higher than you would normally pay. It's the fashion equivalent of doing your weekly supermarket run when you are hungry. No good comes of it. Instead, when you do your bi-yearly wardrobe edit (and you better do your bi-yearly wardrobe edit), see what the gaps are and look for those special pieces when you have the time and not a deadline.

As for the pieces you already have, which you may feel you have worn on repeat, try mixing them with other items you own to give them a new lease on life. However, it really, really doesn't matter if you have worn a favorite dress to a hundred different parties—that is why it is a favorite after all. Just make sure you look after it and keep it looking pristine. Other people won't notice if you are wearing the same dress, but they will notice a stain, rip, hole, threads unravelling or a hem that is partially undone.

It is really tempting to wear an outfit once, air it a little and then pop it back on the closet rack. But think about it: how many items on that rack have you done that to repeatedly? I bet you have beloved dresses in there that you have worn several times, danced in, eaten in and pulled across pavements while getting in and out of cars that have never seen a dry-cleaner or a delicate handwash. Again, this is something you need to attend to before you need to attend an event. Go look at hemlines and zippers now and see what needs mending or cleaning. Finding a long-forgotten stain on a dress just before you are leaving the house is unnecessarily aggravating.

Once you (and I) are happy that your events pieces are clean and pristine, please have some respect when storing them. Anything that is delicate, or creases easily, and would suffer from being squeezed between everything else in your closet deserves a garment bag. Long for dresses, shorter for tops and jackets. A garment bag will protect your pieces, but it also makes things easy for you if packing them for weddings that require travel. Look for those that can fit more than one item in them and have a little window so you don't forget what you have.

EVENTS IN BRIEF

1   It might sound cliché, but confidence is the most important thing to wear to an event.

2   Dress codes are a guide, not a rule.

3   Nothing feels better than wearing something you love yourself in.

4   Business casual basically means no pajamas and brush your hair.

5   Don't wait to shop for an event dress when you really, really need one.

6   Tuxedos on women are still the sexiest evening option.

7   If Cate Blanchett can repeat a look, so can you.

8   Hats at weddings should make a comeback.

9   Don't let Google dictate what you wear.

10   Airing dresses doesn't clean dresses.

UNDERWEAR
+
LINGERIE

REMI BADER

Content creator and a key voice in size inclusivity, Remi explains the difference between underwear and lingerie, and how to make each work for your body.

THE DIFFERENCE BETWEEN UNDERWEAR AND LINGERIE

Underwear and lingerie are two very different things. Underwear is for everyday; lingerie is for special occasions.

Underwear is about comfort, and it certainly doesn't need to match. I pull out whatever is in my drawer, usually in a neutral palette, black or something that matches my skin tone, that fits, doesn't dig into me anywhere, and works with what I am planning to wear that day. I always put my outfit together first; being a curvier girl it can be difficult to find clothes in the first place, so I choose underwear after. I often don't even wear a bra—not because I don't want to, but because of what is available to me, and often it is more comfortable not to wear one at all.

Being measured for bras is not an exact science. I used to get measured regularly, but I started to find it incredibly frustrating as it would be different depending on a brand's size chart. It's annoying that if your weight fluctuates, even a little bit, your bra size can change quickly. The last time I was measured, I was told I was a 42E. I tried on the bra they brought me—it was double the size of anything I would wear. It confirmed that I am not an E! Just because my band size might have gotten bigger, it doesn't mean that the cup size is bigger too. Finding the right bra can easily become a game of trial and error, just like trying on jeans. Your boobs change in the same way that your waist and hip measurements do, and there is no quick solution. The only thing for it is to try bras on and see what size works. I find this frustrating, which is why I often don't wear one at all. If I do, I like a lace bralette over anything with underwire, as they feel so much better to wear all day.

Lingerie is different. Lingerie is less about comfort and more about looking good (though the sweet spot is finding both). I went to the Victoria's Secret virtual fashion event in 2023, which was basically a big party. They wanted everyone to show off their lingerie so that you could see it under your outfit. Some guests wore a lace bra under an open blazer, which I used to do. (I don't do it as often anymore, but I should as I like it!) Instead, I chose a red lace bra and red underwear, over which I wore a super see-through Jean Paul Gaultier dress. I felt confident and sexy, and the fact that they were matching helped. This made me feel put together, like they were a part of the outfit in themselves. And so, I am convinced that, for the right occasion, matching sets start you off on the right foot. Putting on something colorful, cute and pretty makes me feel composed and confident, even if it isn't something I do every day.

When you invest in lingerie, you do want to be able to show it off—not just on Valentine's Day or the three days that I decide to wear it for my partner. I like that it is acceptable to reveal it in public, that you can make it an integral part of your outfit. If you've spent money on it, if it makes you feel good, why wouldn't you?

LINGERIE

In theory, this is where *How to Wear Everything* begins. For lingerie can make or break an outfit, even if you can't always see it. It can dictate how comfortable we are in what we are wearing, and it can dictate our mood, and therefore what we want to wear, from the get-go. So, you need to get this chapter right before you can accomplish the rest.

First things first, would you go out in public wearing clothing that is faded, maybe has a couple of holes in it, perhaps some loose threads, the shape long gone, so just how the pieces are staying on your body is some kind of anti-gravity feat? I am assuming the answer would be no, or, at least, not if you can help it. Now think of your underwear drawer. Like Remi, I am going to separate your underwear drawer from your lingerie drawer, as many of us will have an everyday pile of bras and underwear that we reach for regularly, and then we will have a separate section or drawer that contains the more elaborate or special pieces. So, think of just your daily underwear. I bet there are loose threads galore in there, some faded crotches (never thought I would write that in my career), broken elastic popping out all over the place, and multiple teeny-tiny, and not so teeny-tiny, holes. Yet I will also bet that you still wear them. Every morning you will pull on a pair of underwear that you once loved but now have more of a convenience relationship with; that have seen better days—or years for that matter; that don't support you, or make you feel your best, and yet that is how you start your day.

The same goes for bras; in fact bras are even more important. There have been many, many times when I have gone digging in my underwear drawer and rediscovered a very pretty bra that I had long forgotten. Thrilled with myself I have popped it on, admired the shape it gives me under my chosen outfit, and left the house wondering why I never wear it. It's usually halfway through my commute that I remember that this is the itchy/uncomfortable/painful/unwearable bra that I keep meaning to throw away. Sitting through a day of work in a bra that makes you want to scratch your own nipples off is unbearable. Yet, that bra still sits in my drawer now. I can tell you that it is snuggled in next to one that gives me no support at all and has frayed on both straps, and yet I wore it just last week, as it was hidden under a large sweater. In fact, I have a beautiful bra that I wore very recently knowing that my boyfriend would love it. He did, until it came off and he recoiled in horror at the two deep welts it had left between my breasts that did not look beautiful in the slightest. He demanded I get rid of the bra (I haven't, yet). But it stops now. Because who cares what you put on over the top of your bras and pants if you have started with weak foundations—that is going to pull down the rest of your effort. There is never an excuse for greying, torn, shapeless underwear, so if you start with that, you have already lost your battle with the day. Have some self-respect; you deserve better than greying, torn and shapeless, even on a miserable Wednesday—*especially* on a miserable Wednesday.

I am not suggesting you wear your fancy lace favorites every day, but after you have read this, I want you to pull out every single pair of underwear and every bra you have, and sort them into Keep, Get Rid and Mend (if it is worth it) piles. Be as ruthless, or more so, as you are with your clothing. You might be the only one who sees your underwear or lingerie all day long, but how you feel about what is on your body is more important than who is looking at it.

Keep those that fit on your largest or smallest days, even if you don't wear them often, though the true non-negotiable essentials are fit, comfort, support and structure, followed by the aesthetic. But what you choose depends on when and why you are wearing it.

THE EVERYDAY

These are the briefs and bras that you wear probably more than anything else in your closet. They are the backbone of your look and can govern the mood of your day. They don't need to be fancy, but goddammit they do need to be comfy.

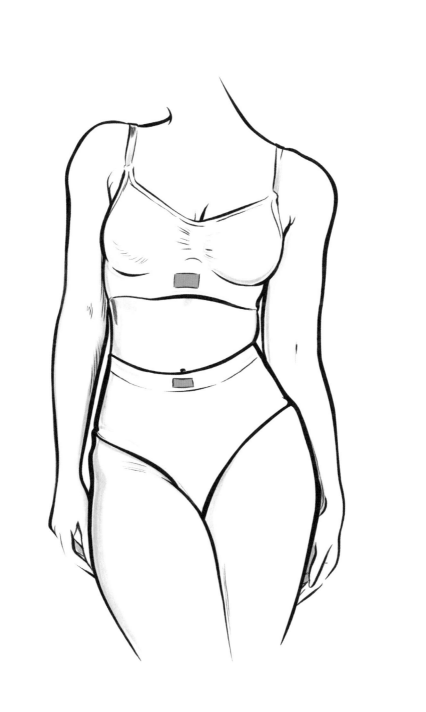

BRIEFS

I have three styles of underwear that I rely on. Low-waist black lace thongs as I tend to wear jeans or trousers that are fitted on the ass most days; low-waist black lace Brazilian briefs that claim not to have a VPL (they all kind of do, but we all wear underwear, so why try to hide that?), which I will wear with looser clothing; and seamless mid-waist black briefs that I wear for working out. I have another couple of pairs that I might sporadically sleep in, but that's it, those are the only styles that I wear. Yet my underwear drawer is full of all kinds of panties, collected in the days when I thought that just maybe I could be a girly girl who likes kooky printed underwear (I will never be that girl), or when I thought that men's briefs might be cool to wear (they are for a minute but look bulky under clothes), or those that fit when I was a size bigger or smaller. In other words, just as you know—or are hopefully going to get to know—who you are when it comes to clothing, you are that same person when it comes to underwear, and that won't drastically change.

Before I started this section of the chapter, I took my own advice and pulled everything out of that drawer. I now have a large pile for my local clothes bin, and for the first time in years I can see what I have, which is much more than I thought, though admittedly they all look identical to the untrained eye. You don't need lots of pairs of briefs, and the number that the internet seems to agree on is twenty-four pairs, but that includes the special pieces that don't get worn as often. Of your day-to-day I'd say you need no more than twenty, as that saves you washing the same pairs over and over and should extend their life.

Whether you prefer high-waist, mid-waist or low-waist, lace, cotton or silk (never buy synthetic), high-leg or low-leg, thong cut or more coverage, is completely personal, but your buy should be dictated by what you wear over them, and whether you want them to be a feature or not. I would recommend that if you are a creature of habit, like me, then repeat-buying the same styles from the same brand gives you peace of mind, knowing that you won't be desperate to pull them from your own rear in the middle of an important meeting. When it comes to size, I actually buy one size up from what I usually wear in clothing, as that gives a more flattering cut. But again you need to know and trust the brands, as I have done this in the past and ended up looking like I was wearing an adult nappy. Those underwear were long exiled from the drawer.

BRAS

Confession time: I have only been measured once, and that was many years ago. But I went in a 34A (sometimes an AA) and came out a 32B and was thrilled. When the woman told me the measurement, I thought she was deranged, but she reappeared with some bras for me to try, and lo and behold, not only did they fit, but for the first time ever I imagined myself in a period drama with a heaving bosom. Years later and I am still buying bras in a 32B, and while most of them fit, occasionally I will find myself wearing a cup with so much extra room that it could also comfortably store my wallet and keys in it. But after taking a small poll of close friends with breasts, it seems that even those who are fitted more regularly—once every couple of years is recommended, or more often if your weight has changed, or you have had a baby—say that a measurement is useful but isn't always accurate. Your breast size changes regularly based on hormones and the time of the month, so what works one week can be too tight or too loose the next. Then there is the added pleasure that different brands can come up larger or smaller. Honestly, finding the right bra is just as—if not more—difficult than finding the right jeans, and yet it is key to get it right. The correct bra can do more for us than any other piece of clothing, including preventing back pain, improving posture and helping to maintain the shape of our breasts. A bad bra, however, can cause back pain and shoulder issues, as well as deep indentations in the skin.

But what defines the correct fit? A friend of mine, who has also only been measured once, was told that she was actually a 32F after always wearing a 36D. Her initial reaction was, "Right, so now I have to move to LA and join the porn industry," until the woman explained that the correct cup fit of a bra is influenced by the band size. Are you ready for some boob math? For every band size you go down, you should go up one cup size. If you are wearing a 34B, and it feels a little too relaxed around the band, you can move down a band size to a 32 for a more secure fit, but go up a cup size to a C and the cup will be exactly the same. Basically, a 34B and 32C are considered the same cup size, as are a 30C and a 34A. That made my head explode initially. But if boob math isn't your thing, do leave it to the experts and get measured to see what they tell you. There are also many online services that offer a virtual fitting, but I think for first timers, in person is preferable.

Alternatively, you could take the advice my cousin gave me instead. She is "large of breast" (her own words!) and informed me that the only thing I need to say about bras is: "If you are large of breast and find a bra that you love, and that fits you comfortably, buy at least twenty-nine of them, in a range of colors. I regret my lack of multiple purchases almost every morning." And my cousin is usually right about everything. The bra that she has twenty-nine of is a balconette style that shapes and lifts rather than presenting her boobs like a shelf. I think balconette bras are very flattering on small boobs too, and give more shape than a soft triangle, though I don't think small or medium boobs can beat a wireless triangle bra for comfort every day.

THE SEX DRAWER

I say sex, but I don't necessarily mean crotchless underwear and pasties, though they absolutely can have their moment. By sex I mean lingerie that makes you feel at your sexiest, and if that leads to sex, then happy days.

The whole stockings and garters thing is undoubtedly a total nuisance, and when one garter hook has popped for the forty-third time when trying to pull it all together, it really can threaten to kill the mood. But at the right time, when you are in the right mood, with endless time and patience, it can feel empowering and, indeed, very sexy. I would encourage all those willing to try it. You don't need the full set to match exactly. You can add a garter belt to any lingerie set that you have, ideally in the same color, as your partner really isn't going to notice if it isn't the same brand or lace, or any other damn thing about it! Just that you are wearing it is enough. Wear the garter straps under your underwear, not over, while the 10 to 15 denier stockings should have a silicone coating to help them stay up, but not a silicone band that digs into your skin.

A lot of women wait for their partner to buy them the lingerie for this drawer, but that will often end in a selection of ill-fitting garish sets that are the subject of a 1980s sex fantasy and not yours. If you appreciate lingerie and like wearing it, don't wait for a partner to surprise you. If unsure where to start, go into a store, when you are in no rush, and bask in the glory of a sales assistant's expertise. Or if you are confident with your own sizing, browse online and explore your own boundaries when it comes to color, detail, shape, plunge, balcony, straps and buckles, and then try them on in the comfort of your own home with your favorite lighting. Do be sure of your size though, as understandably no company will accept a return on panties.

If you do task your partner with a lingerie purchase, make sure that they really, really know you and understand the brief. The best thing a man has ever bought me was not something obviously sexy. It's neither crotchless nor red, and it doesn't take me ages to put it on, but when I do, I feel sexy, feminine, desirable, and totally myself. It was a short, belted robe in white lace and silk. It is one of my favorite things and has a success rate that surpasses the bells-and-whistles garters get-up. Maybe because it is less obvious, or maybe because the man considered what I would like to wear, and not just what he would like to see me wear, which is the sexiest part of it.

You also do not need to save this lingerie for a partner. It feels spectacular to bring out your best lingerie just for you, to wear under your clothes, even if you have nothing special planned, as it makes the day feel instantly more special.

SHAPEWEAR

"My thoughts on shapewear is to wear as little of it as possible, and know that you will want to take it off after about three drinks," said my friend, who bought an all-in-one bodysuit to wear with a long loose sheath dress she bought that had no support. She loved how it made her feel when she put it on, as it felt instantly solid and toned and smoothed bumps. That bodysuit gave the sheath dress some structure to hang off, and she felt glorious in it. But then she ate and drank with it on and felt awful and boiling hot (they are completely synthetic, after all). Yet we all persevere with shapewear, due to the silhouette it can create. It can give us confidence when we need it, and it can encourage us to wear clothes that we often wouldn't dream of. Another friend relies on a bra minimizer to create a different line in some tops and dresses, so that they hang better. Yes, they are restrictive, and they won't massively reduce your breast size, but the right fit should never be uncomfortable.

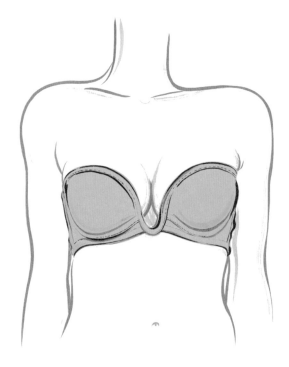

Shapewear is the opposite of the sex-drawer lingerie, for lingerie is a surprise underneath clothes, whereas shapewear gives you the confidence of sexy lingerie, and the perfect body, but when fully clothed. It serves a purpose, and being sexy isn't necessarily a priority.

But just like everything else, you need to try it to find the right fit for you, as it isn't always a miracle worker, and badly fitting shapewear can serve to create more lumps and bumps rather than fewer. I would recommend an all-in-one bodysuit to everyone, and shapewear bras can be revolutionary, but just know that you might hate it an hour into your evening.

UNDERWEAR AS OUTERWEAR

Years and years ago, I was meeting a friend that I hadn't seen for years for lunch. As I approached her, she said, "Oh my God, Kay, I can see your bra." Now, my friend is no prude, but wearing a colored bra under a thin white T-shirt was clearly more of a thing then. I was once commissioned by a fashion magazine to write about visible bras under clothes, as the editor said she had often seen me dress as such. This was in 2016, not 1940 FYI, but was still considered slightly risqué. She was also right though, as I love to wear a statement bra under something very simple, and I like to see it on others too, as it feels so personal and intimate. It means that they really thought about their outfit that day when getting dressed, as every single piece matters. The key is, and I wrote this in that 2016 piece too, to not be embarrassed or apologetic about it. If you are going to do it, own it. The bra is key: you want to make sure that you are showing it off for a reason, and not an error, so make it a really good bra. I like neons under grey, black or pastel shades under white, and just a bit of leopard under a gauzy knit. This isn't only for the small-breasted either, in their little triangle bits of nothing; this is about a confident reveal regardless of cup size.

Underwear as outerwear is not only about a hint of a bra through fabric; you can go all out if you like and treat your lingerie as a piece of clothing in itself. There is something hot about a bra or a bodysuit worn under a strict blazer. In fact, a bodysuit is an excellent evening addition, as they're designed to give you shape and support, and they are usually pretty enough to deserve a declaration. If corseted, look for those with boning on the inside rather than exposed on the outside. They are also great alternatives to matching lingerie sets if you are wearing a dress that is translucent; just look for one that has more cheek cover rather than a thong rear. If wearing a see-through dress or skirt, treat your lingerie very much as part of the complete look. A matching bra and brief set will make you look more put together, regardless of what color it is, and a fuller high-waist or mid-waist brief with a little more coverage and a high leg draws the eye without being distracting.

HAVE A CARE

Let's be honest here, how often do you wash your bras? After every wear? No, I doubt anyone does that. After the third, maybe the fourth? Or how often do you wear a bra once, then put it back in the drawer, only to bring it back out a week later and wear it twice, then put it back in the drawer again, until it finally ends up in the laundry basket after that routine has been repeated countless times because you have forgotten how long it has been in rotation? I feel we may have a winner.

Unlike underwear, which you must wash after every wear, bras are less clear. I mean, how dirty can they really get? But I think four times should be the maximum number of wears before it is added to the wash pile. As tempting as it is to throw all underwear in with the rest of our clothes, that is how we end up with a selection of very sad bras and briefs that make us feel depressed. Instead add them all to a delicate wash pile, and clean according to color. Do not tumble-dry—hang them up to dry naturally. That will extend the life of your underwear *and* lingerie and prevent you from having to replace them more regularly.

UNDERWEAR + LINGERIE
IN BRIEF

1   Underwear is for the everyday; lingerie is for the elevated everyday.

2   Bras should never be painful.

3   Matching lingerie sets really do make you feel put together from top to bottom.

4   Underwear is the most important step in getting dressed.

5   Have some self-respect and throw away your old underwear.

6   Get your boobs measured as a starting point, but know your boobs change all the time and a bra fit is not universal.

7   When you find a bra you love, buy as many as possible.

8   Don't wait for your partner to buy you sexy lingerie.

9   Wear underwear as outerwear with confidence, not with coyness.

10   Wash your bras.

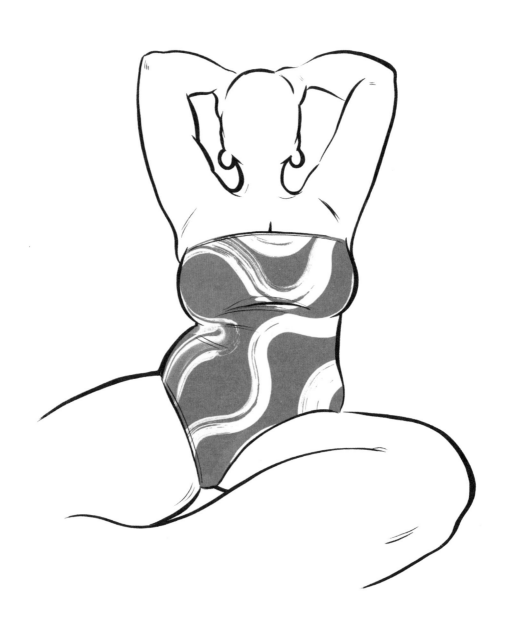

VACATIONS

NICKY ZIMMERMANN

Joint founder of the beloved Australian fashion and resort wear brand Zimmermann, and a woman who knows how to vacation really, really well.

THE IMPORTANCE OF EXCELLENT SWIMWEAR

Dressing for a vacation has almost become as enjoyable as the vacation itself. But this wasn't really a thing until the last few years; before that it was only for the elite, and now everyone gets a look-in. It used to be about flinging a couple of bathing suits in your bag, maybe a couple of dresses, and getting on a plane. Some may disagree, but I love how planning lunch, dinner and party outfits is now part of my vacation process. The most important thing to remember is that these are clothes to have fun in.

Of course, I say that, but on summer vacations it is also—probably—when you are at your most naked in front of people and there is a vulnerability to that. Stepping out in swimwear for the first time in the year is not *just* about having confidence in yourself. As a designer, I have all the resources at my fingertips, and I definitely don't have confidence. I always remind myself that everyone has their own personal body hang-ups, and everyone is in the same boat.

Like all your other clothes, you do need to feel good about your swimwear choices. I always suggest that pre-vacation, get yourself to your local department store, or shop online, and try on a *load* of different styles. Not just what you think is your go-to, as you'll be surprised at what might work. Don't take two options into the changing room, take twenty.

A good swimsuit is defined by the fit, cut and quality of fabric, and how that works with your body shape. I encourage women to be a bit adventurous in the styles they try on, because it's not necessarily the styles we think are right on our bodies that are most flattering.

For me, the most flattering swimwear is all about quality, while the cut is the difference between something being right or wrong for you. Stepping out in swimwear might not be about having confidence in yourself, but you need to have confidence in your swimwear doing what it needs to do. I don't really understand cheap swimwear because the fabric will be cheap, and the design will be cheap; it just won't do what you want it to do. It will quickly lose its shape, sag, the color will fade, it won't support you where it needs to, and it will cut in where it shouldn't. If you're sixteen, maybe, but otherwise I think you really need to look for a level of quality.

Don't think you are too old for a bikini. I am a big fan of the high pant, which sits on your waist with a slight high leg, offers coverage and works on all shapes and all ages. Pair with something as simple as a squared-off, elongated triangle bikini top with a panel under the bust, or an underwired soft cup if you need more support. Selling bikinis as separates remains a game-changer, as very few of us are the same size on top and bottom. I love a one-piece too, as I treat the swimsuit like a piece of clothing. I love to put on a big, beautiful skirt with it and go to lunch without the hassle of changing.

Personally, I like to keep accessories simple with swim, as if I am on a family vacation and covered in jewellery, they will tease me. But I'm really into it if it is situation appropriate. It's a whole thing—a way of personalizing your look and showing off your personal style, and I love that. Either way, if you look like you're just having fun, everything works.

Except for heels with swimwear. No, no, no . . . I can't say NO enough to that. That is absolutely wrong-town.

VACATIONS

When I was a kid, other than the time we drove from the north of Scotland to southern Spain for a fortnight summer vacation, the rest of our trips involved a car journey to visit cathedrals and castles in England. While I now look back with fondness at always being the middle passenger in the back between two of my siblings, at the time I was livid that we weren't at Disney World like my friends. I also wasn't allowed to go on group vacations with friends or school trips abroad. I'm not sure whether my parents didn't trust me, or the school and my friends, but based on subsequent behavior it was probably the former and they had a point. The one trip I was permitted was a week in Switzerland with the Girl Guides, during which I was told to change my outfit as the Guide Leader deemed it inappropriate. I was wearing high-waisted leggings and a minuscule crop top. On a boy-mad thirteen-year-old, she may have had a point. And while I still think that I looked cute (and basically still wear that combination), at the time I had no idea what to wear on vacation, as I'd never really been on one. I know, poor me.

I think my dad was trying to instill in us a love of the UK while, I now realize in hindsight, also hiding his fear of flying. However, rather than giving me an appreciation of British history, it instead served to make me vacation-obsessed. I didn't go on a proper vacation with friends or a boyfriend until I was in my late twenties and I have been making up for lost time ever since. It turns out that I am never happier than when I am in a bikini, on a beach, with a beer and a book. But it took me some time to figure out my vacation wardrobe. For it doesn't necessarily align with my usual style, as it can't really. In day-to-day reality I live in black, denim, shirts and great (if I do say so myself) jackets and coats. On vacation, everything is stripped back, there is very little to hide in, and it turns out that I love the freedom of it. Actually, the freedom *and* the fantasy of it.

On vacation I can experiment and exaggerate. In sweltering heat it turns out that I am not the world's oldest emo, as black clothing is not the answer. So, while the ever-goth in me is reserved for some swimwear and perhaps an evening slip dress, my vacation wardrobe is where I play with color. Tangerine-orange asymmetric dresses, Pepto Bismol—pink shorts and bikinis in bright pops of neon yellow, emerald, scarlet and cobalt, all blended. Sometimes successfully, sometimes not so much. But who cares? As Nicky Zimmermann says, your vacation wardrobe, regardless of where you are or what you are doing, should show that you are having a really good time (and on vacation I really do). You just need to know the basics of what to bring where, and how to pack them.

BEACH VACATIONS

If I haven't made this abundantly clear yet, beach vacations are my favorite. The distant promise of a beach vacation will get me through the longest of workdays and the worst of weather. But they are often the hardest to dress for, as they are so removed from our average day-to-days, so much of this chapter is dedicated to them.

A few years ago, my friend moved to Mexico for eight months, and I went to visit him in Zipolite, a destination renowned for being Mexico's first and only legal public nudist beach. I was excited at the prospect of not having to think about clothes for ten days, other than bikini bottoms and a couple of shirts I could fling on. And it was liberating for about two days, until I realized that I missed the consideration and playfulness of putting an outfit together. It did, however, confirm that you never need a lot of clothing on a beach vacation (albeit more than I brought to Mexico), for you will ultimately favor just a couple of the swimsuits or bikinis you packed, have bare feet 75 percent of the time, grab the cover-up that you left on the chair the day before, and alternate between two or three dresses at night. As I said, vacations offer delightful escapism from your day-to-day wardrobe: you can be whatever version of yourself you like, but be realistic about what you are actually going to wear, when you will wear it and what will make you feel comfortable.

SWIMWEAR

Let's start with the integral pieces, for if you are anything like me, then I assume these are what you will spend most of your vacation wearing. Shopping for swimwear can be as traumatic as shopping for denim, but it doesn't need to be. Firstly, Zimmermann is one of the most successful swim and resort brands in the world because Nicky knows her stuff and has done lots of the hard work for you. So please *listen* to her. Sure, it will take time to try on loads of different fits of bikinis and swimsuits ahead of your trip, but it will be time well spent in the long run. If you are not a bikini person, then rule it out immediately. I am adamant that there is a bikini out there for everyone, regardless of age or shape, but you know yourself better than I do, so if you are positive that you are really not comfortable in a bikini, then head straight for the one-pieces. However, let me stick with bikinis for a moment. I prefer them over one-pieces purely for tanning purposes—I am from the Highlands of Scotland, please forgive my (safe) tanning desires. For tops, I mainly wear bandeaus, with and without side boning, triangle string-tie options and a couple of seersucker styles that I can pull over my head and are great for sea swimming, as they are all good for small boobs. Bigger boobs benefit from the support of underwire, and adjustable straps rather than string. In terms of bottoms, I prefer a high leg but lower waist (though many prefer a higher waist for more hold), and with more ass coverage than many bikinis seem to offer. When trying on swimwear, always turn around and look at the rear view, as I have mistakenly bought pieces that look great from the front and then reveal a thong from the back. That's great for some, but personally I like a little more surface area. When it comes to the one-piece I prefer mine simpler, with high legs, a low back and narrow straps, and no bells, whistles or unusual cutouts (again, the tan).

With swimwear, no style is wrong if you feel right in it. It is about finding the bits that you are happy to get out and the bobs that you want to keep covered. Bought correctly, great swimwear has the power to elongate your legs, flatten your tummy, give you bigger boobs, reduce your boobs, lift your ass *and* make you feel confident to walk from lounger to the ocean. Which is why it is worth spending the time searching for the swimwear that does what you want it to do. Which styles are actually supportive, and which just dig in? Only you can decide if you prefer underwire and boning, a soft cup or padding. Though when trying them on, it is worth remembering that swimsuits get slightly bigger in the water, not tighter, so if you're between sizes, buy the smaller one if it's not uncomfortable.

"For me, your bikini or swimsuit is like every other outfit you have in your closet—what you want to wear is driven by mood and where you're going, so have a selection of different swimsuits or bikinis that fit in with your style," says Nicky. "Some days you might feel like a really clean, sleek and sophisticated style of swimsuit—one that's easy to have a swim in. On other days, you'll wake up in a girly mood and fancy a ruffled piece that's more romantic. Cater for your own moods."

When buying your swimwear, or digging out old favorites, listen to Nicky and know that everyone has their own personal body hang-ups, and wearing swimwear can be intimidating, of course it can, but only for the smallest of windows. This is *your* vacation; everyone is concentrating on *their* own vacation and really not looking at you. I promise. It can't be stressed enough: no one else cares about you in your swimsuit, and you shouldn't either. So, relax, bury those bare feet in the sand, enjoy feeling the sun on your body and have the glorious time you deserve. Nothing is more beautiful than the sight of someone having a lovely time.

COVER-UPS

Cover-ups can be anything: an oversized shirt or T-shirt, an official kaftan, a pareo (which is essentially a sarong but longer), a pull-on skirt or wide-leg trousers. It depends on what you feel the need to cover up and whether you're casually covering up poolside or covering up for a more chichi beachside restaurant.

For both occasions I am of the oversized-shirt school—in white cotton or linen, as then it complements all swimwear—as you can button it up, knot it or just pull it over your shoulders depending on desired exposure. It works on its own for poolside and knotted with shorts or wide trousers for the restaurant. Kaftans should take you everywhere and will be as appropriate at breakfast as they are at dinner. Make sure there is ample opening around the neck, ideally with a button-drop split to the base of the sternum, as there is nothing worse than struggling to get a kaftan on when wet or hot. I love pareos and sarongs as they are an easy way to add print and color without having to overly commit. Choose one in a lightweight fabric like silk or cotton, which

will drape easily without overwhelming and bunching around your waist. Perhaps opt against those with fringing, beading or embroidery, as they will show signs of wear and tear much faster. The ultimate cover-up does need to deal with being thrown in bags, pulled off and on repeatedly, and being abandoned on a lounger, so it should be relatively robust, even in the lightest of materials.

Similar to the pareo, I always think a long skirt looks chic when paired with a simple swimsuit or bikini as a top, and again silk or cotton is preferable over a denser linen. Wide-leg trousers do the same job, just make sure the fabric is loose around the top of the thighs and waist—you don't want to feel restricted. Or keep it simple and just wear a sundress that you are happy to pull back on over swimwear and are not precious about.

But you do not need all of the above—one pareo and a couple of oversized shirts have taken me through many, many vacations. Crucially, it is essential that your cover-up does one thing and one thing only: confidently takes you for lunch or for a sundown drink.

DAY

So, apparently some people don't just want to stay on the beach all day and like to get out and about on holiday. It takes all kinds after all. This is where the day dress comes into its own, closely followed by separates. For dresses I suggest three things: loose, colorful and light. Midi or mini is gorgeous, and still allows for a welcome breeze around bare legs. Play with prints, as you will feel far better stepping out of your comfort zone print-wise in a location that practically demands it than you would in your local park on the weekend.

For separates, it is about the shorts and the tanks and T-shirts. Shorts that sit on the waist and have a kick-out wider leg to mid-thigh are flattering on all body types, but if you prefer comfort in the heat then move the waistband down. Denim shorts are never a bad idea, but traditional gym shorts in velour or silk, though longer in length, are a great alternative. Just knot a half-unbuttoned white linen shirt over the waistband or slip on a linen T-shirt, and you're good to adventure.

EVENING

Unless you have a gala planned every evening of your vacation, after dark is often much more casual than you pack for. You want to make an effort, of course, but also feel relaxed about it. Again, I turn to the dress. Now I rarely wear dresses any other time of the year, but for a vacation in the sunshine I can't get enough of them. After a day in the sunshine, you don't want to make any decisions, so a dress is the easiest—and often most effective—option. I like long silk slip dresses as my go-to, as they are breathable and it's finally cool enough to wear black. But it is at night when I will break out the bold colors, favoring red, pink and orange, and I encourage you to as well. For those who like to cover up a little more, I would suggest an off-the-shoulder dress. That may sound contradictory, but a long-sleeved, long-hemmed dress that exposes the shoulders is universally flattering. A good friend who favors the off-the-shoulder told me that everyone has great shoulders, and do you know what, she's right.

Alternative to the dress is a pair of printed or block-color wide silk trousers with a matching shirt. Again, very easy and elegant, with a jet-set feel to it—and that is always a nice role to play, if only for a couple of nights on vacation.

SHOES

I have done all the research on shoes so you don't have to. I have been on a week's vacation with seven pairs of shoes and worn two, and I have been on vacation with one pair of shoes and desperately needed two. So believe me, all you need are two: one pair of casual beach slides and a slightly more elevated pair for evening. I like black rubber slides for day, and a flat chocolate-brown suede strappy pair for after dark, as they enhance all skin tones and seem to dress up day dresses and dress down somewhat extra evening looks. If you want to bring heels, please go ahead, and a heeled sandal in suede is more comfortable in the heat than leather, but I bet they never step out of that hotel room for the duration.

Now, I can't bear a wedge. My dad worked in shoes and once told me he hated wedges as they look so heavy as a woman walks away. Read into that what you will, but it stuck. However, they are a good alternative for that extra bit of height if you feel you need it.

On others I think that an espadrille version with straps that wrap up the leg can look elegant, so please be my guest and I will try not to watch you as you walk away.

BAGS

Ideally your travel bag should double up as your beach/day bag, choosing either a canvas tote or a basket weave with top handles that you don't mind getting covered in sand and suntan lotion. Then you only need one smaller bag for evening, ideally a cross-body so you can end the night dancing freely with not a care in the world.

ACCESSORIES

I do love to see accessorizing done perfectly on other people. Layers of super-fine gold jewellery all stacked up and knotted against glowing skin is the woman I dream of being on vacation, but alas I am not her . . . yet. I love to add some earrings at night, but that's about my limit. I am more minimal, but if you prefer statement jewellery, then please layer it up. Vacations are about being your absolute true self and exaggerating it. People-watching is one of my favorite things to do when away—and anywhere, actually—and seeing what women have chosen to wear and how they accessorize gives a little spark of insight into who they are. Especially on vacation, as the likelihood is they have taken their most personal trinkets with them.

Other than that, all you need are a leather or canvas belt for denim shorts, one or two hats—I have a trusty baseball cap with a malleable peak that has been around the world with me, but it may be time to upgrade to a larger straw hat for more facial protection—and as many pairs of sunglasses as you can fit in your case. Sunglasses are such a playful, and often affordable, way of expressing yourself, and I can't and won't put a limit on that.

CITY BREAKS

This is about seeing some culture, right? And making sure that people know you are seeing some culture. Content with a cathedral ceiling, or a gallery that you spun around on the way to lunch. Even if that is the case, you are already a better person than me on vacation. The short city break is about discovery, be that art, shopping, restaurants, bars, history or politics, which in most cases means walking. Lots and lots of walking. Dress accordingly.

As with all vacations, don't overpack, but that truly applies here. If it's just a weekend, be honest with yourself about how much you really need and where you are going to go. You need to consider the sightseeing outfit and the dinner outfit, which I can guarantee will be the same outfit on at least one day of your trip.

LAYERS
Layers are your friend. Assume that the weather will change quickly and temperatures will drop, and that's even before you have stepped into the cool shade of a magnificent piece of history. Shirts and light jackets that tie around your waist are fundamental, and work as well with day dresses as they do with light trousers.

BAGS
Now I am adamant that on a city break you just need one day handbag and one evening option if the day bag is rather big. Assuming that you aren't travelling with a laptop, you will have travelled with a shoulder bag and a small suitcase. Excellent work. In which case the shoulder bag becomes your day bag, and you can swap it out for something smaller in the evening. Oh, and I would leave a little bit of extra room in your case for that ceramic vase you can't resist.

My wonderful book editor also wants a special shout-out for the fanny pack, which I must agree with. They are ideal for moving in crowds in popular tourist locations where opportunistic pickpockets work, and flat leather ones (not big nylon ones from your youth) are super chic too. My editor has worn hers to Euro Disney and to festivals "without an ounce of shame!"

SHOES

All that walking needs a shoe that you trust. This means absolutely not a new pair of shoes. You want old, comfy and friendly. Shoes that will take you around an airport, up towering flights of stairs, along cobbled streets, through dusty souks and home again, without ever being thought of. I find if you are thinking about your shoes, then they are up to no good. These could be sneakers for some people, Birkenstocks for others, or even canvas slip-ons. But for evening, I encourage heels (though perhaps block heels if dealing with European cobbles), for there is something much more exciting and exotic about getting dressed up to go out in a city that isn't your own. Make the most of it.

EVENING

Making the most of it applies to clothing too. Whether you are on a romantic weekend, or away with friends, there is something sexy about evenings out in a different city, so wear something that makes you feel sexy. Go all out, at least one night, in the dress that you love but never get to wear, even if you are going to the hotel restaurant. Even if you are the most dressed-up person for miles, own it—this is your vacation, your choice. Feel and dress like you are in a movie. My "dressing like I am in a movie" outfits include a backless dress that makes me feel like I am Mireille Darc in the French movie *The Tall Blond Man with One Black Shoe*, while a black tuxedo in a European city makes me feel like I am in a Helmut Newton picture. No one else might think that, but this is my vacation, so I can feel like a Helmut Newton girl if I want to!

SWIMWEAR

Come on, you never know when there might be an opportunity for a quick sunbathe on a balcony or a rooftop. You've seen the city, you now deserve to bask in its shine. You will not regret packing just one.

ACTIVITY VACATIONS

I am going to assume that if you have booked an activity break, you will be more of an expert in that activity than I am, and therefore will know the technical clothing that you need to pack. I will not be responsible for recommending the wrong kind of boot sole, only for you to slip down a hill. So best for me, you and the legal department that I stick to bikinis and not hiking boots.

The same rule applies to skiing, as I've skied only twice in all my days. The first time I hated it so much I cried and wet myself, not necessarily in that order. The second time I hated it less, but I was older and excelled at the après-ski bit. All in all, I am no ski bunny. But I appreciate a good ski look and have spent many a year overseeing ski campaigns and working with the product. Which means that I can say with confidence that most of it is awful. Yes, I know that it's about substance over style, but I'm not sure that is an excuse for some of the salopettes I have seen. So, from a purely aesthetic angle, I would always recommend a ski suit over separates. They aren't as bulky, take up less room in your suitcase and, most importantly, they have Bond Girl vibes. See, that is why I shouldn't be advising on your activity packing.

PACKING

Speaking of packing, a very wise fashion designer, renowned for her resort wear, once told me that we all need to learn to love the art of packing. Bear with me. She packs one outfit per day, and her packing ritual takes an entire day. And this applies to every type of vacation. I used to think this was extreme, but I now see the benefit in it. She packs what she needs—not more, not less—and is committed to wearing all of it. When she gets home, everything is put in one place, including unfinished vacation beauty products, so she knows where everything is should a last-minute trip come up.

In the past, I would overpack and still find that I had nothing I wanted to wear. Then in the summer of 2022 when airports managed to lose everyone's luggage, I too learned the art of packing with only a carry-on case. I'm afraid there is no way around it: the key is to take time and plan. Nicky Zimmermann admits to being a terrible packer, but she too has realized over time and countless "Why the hell have I taken this with me?!" moments that trying on everything before you pack is a game-changer. "You need to think about all the different situations you're going to be in, and what you need for them," she explains. "I pull out everything at home and throw it on the bed—hats, shoes, bags, everything—and I stand in front of a full-length mirror and try them all on. If you have the time and can be bothered, it really does work."

TIPS AND TRICKS

Repetition is celebrated . . .

You don't need to pack something new for every night of the vacation. Pack for half that and repeat outfits, but plan what you are going to wear at the start.

Go light on shoes and bags . . .

If you can't close your suitcase, chances are it is because of an extra bag. Take it out. Same goes for those shoes that you sneak in because you love them but they wreck your feet. Leave them at home. They will still wreck your feet in another country.

Pack a bit of magic . . .

Another tip from a wise traveller I know, who advises that you be optimistic about where you might go and what might happen. Put a dress in your case that might be considered extravagant, or some amazing earrings you never wear but love. Be ready for anything, and if anything doesn't necessarily happen, wear it on your last night and go out with a bang.

Master the roll . . .

Right off the bat, I'm going to give full credit to my colleague, friend and packing guru Alice Casely-Hayford for the Packing Roll trick. She once went to Rome for a long weekend carrying nothing more than a cloth tote shoulder bag containing four outfits and a change of shoes. Before a trip to Tuscany for a wedding, she sent me an image of her tiny suitcase (photographed next to her foot so I would believe the size), which is smaller than an average carry-on, and which I always thought was pointlessly small. I was wrong. In that case she had eight looks (four of them gowns, the rest daytime dresses), three pairs of shoes, one bikini, PJs, toiletries, a makeup bag and hair straighteners. The shoes went in first, toe-to-toe to maximize space, then everything else was rolled and stacked side by side, bar the PJs which were folded and placed on top. Soon after, on a weekend away, I followed suit and had room for more than I had imagined. Alice is a hero of our time.

Learn a hat trick . . .

I love watching people at the airport wearing pieces that they couldn't fit in their case. Hats are the main culprits. Oversized straw hats worn with jogging bottoms and a tank at Gatwick at 8 a.m. is a personal favorite. But while Nicky might not be the most organized packer, she boasts that packing hats is, unusually, where she excels. "The technique is that firstly you pack a layer of soft clothing, probably about 8cm, then I stack my hats on top of each other—I pack a lot of hats, because being Australian I am terrified of getting sunburnt, so I wear one from the moment I wake up until it is pitch black outside. I then stuff the bottom hat with socks, T-shirts or my lingerie to hold its shape, and I pack soft clothing around the brims so I'm not changing the shape of the brim or anything like that. Then I layer the rest of the clothing around it. You can literally unpack and lift the hats out and they're perfect. But if you need to, another top tip is that if it's a straw hat and your brim goes wobbly, just get an ironing board and an iron and use steam to flatten it back into shape. They turn out perfectly every time."

The return to reality . . .

I am the kind of person who immediately unpacks and washes everything when I get home. I find looking forlornly at a well-rummaged suitcase, spilling out with dresses and sandals that will now be retired until the next vacation, makes my vacation blues ten times worse. Out of sight, out of mind works for me, but do what works for you to minimize the shock of a return to reality. Just don't let salty swimwear languish.

WHAT TO WEAR TO THE AIRPORT

One of the most googled pieces of advice sought is "what to wear to the airport," with search results accompanied by 90s pictures of Kate Moss and Whitney Houston. This blows my mind every time I remember it, until it comes time for me to dress for the airport. Of course, really, it's not about the airport, it is about what to wear on a long-haul flight.

Now if you were going to take advice from Kate or Whitney, you would be wearing jeans, crisp white shirts or tank tops, and boots. I am going to take the liberty of assuming that isn't what any of us will actually be wearing. I doubt anyone has been upgraded at the airport based on their outfit since 1985, so choose comfort over dreams of first class.

The aeroplane is the only place I allow loungewear, as the drawstring waistband was made for watching romantic comedies at 40,000 feet. Relaxed jogging trousers, leggings, cashmere sweaters or hoodies are the unofficial travel uniform, worn with sneakers or slides that easily slip on and off, but *always*, and I can't stress this enough, *always* with socks. You do not want to be caught barefoot anywhere on a plane.

HAVE A CARE

Even though swimwear isn't one of our most regularly worn items of clothing, it does break down quickly due to exposure to salt water and chlorine. So even though experts claim that you don't have to wash your swimwear every time you wear it, you really should if you've been in the sea or a public pool.

On vacation I wash my bikinis and swimsuits in the shower with me at the end of the day using a gentle soap, then hang them outside to dry, though not in direct sunlight as colors fade fast. When home, I put them on a cold cycle with a mild eco detergent and let them dry naturally, then store them in a cool, dry place with no humidity.

Once the pieces are past their best, it is worth doing your research on who accepts them for recycling, as due to the Lycra content, they are often tricky to dispose of considerately. There are a number of sustainable brands who take worn-down swimwear and upcycle it into new items. All you have to do is remove any attachments or fastenings, and pop the swimwear in the mail.

VACATIONS IN BRIEF

1   Cheap swimwear is cheap for a reason.

2   You are not too old for a bikini.

3   Never wear heels with swimwear.

4   Pack a bit of magic, even if you just wear it for a short time on the last night.

5   Experiment and exaggerate.

6   Treat swimwear like lingerie: wash after every wear.

7   Stepping out in swimwear is only scary for mere moments.

8   Learn to love the art of packing.

9   You do not need to pack all those shoes.

10   Dressing up for the airport will not get you upgraded.

COLOR

+

PRINT

JODIE TURNER-SMITH

Actor, model, and a woman who shines as brightly on the outside as she does on the inside. She also knows how to use color to bring joy to herself and others.

WHY EVERYONE SHOULD EXPERIMENT WITH COLOR

When I was young, my mum loved to dress me in bright colors. I hated it, especially yellow. I just didn't want to stand out. But as I got older—and my self-confidence grew—I found myself leaning into color without even realizing it.

Now, every time I wear yellow, I think about how my mum used to love me in it, how much I used to hate it and how wrong I was! To this date, one of the best fashion moments that I've ever had is the yellow Gucci gown I wore to the 2020 BAFTAs. That particular dress was meaningful on a number of levels. I was heavily pregnant, and I felt like I was sharing that space with my unborn daughter—it was just so magical. The experience was as positive as the dress color, standing as a beautiful affirmation of the fact that mother truly does know best.

By my nature, I am a joyful and enthusiastic person, and I try to bring that joy and enthusiasm into everything I do—especially dressing. My complexion complements nearly every shade, so I enjoy reaching for color when getting dressed. The right color will enrich your skin tone and brighten your eyes.

Something else I learned from my mum: whenever I am feeling down or low, I should try even harder to dig deep and allow myself to look my best. Perhaps how I feel on the outside will migrate to how I feel on the inside. Perhaps it won't. But sometimes the satisfaction of looking good is a way to reverse engineer a bad mood into a good one! Colors have been used since ancient times to treat mental (and even physical!) health conditions. If you can manage it, reach for a color that makes you feel your best and give it a try!

I'm often asked my favorite color, and the truthful answer is: rainbow. It's why I like to dye my hair different shades all the time. I am in a color-exploration phase of my life and no color is off the list. What is the harm in experimenting? The only thing in life I am resistant to is playing it safe.

I think there's this false idea that once you are an adult, that's it, you are who you are. You've finished becoming. Maybe that's why we are asked to make tremendous life decisions like who do we want to be in thirty years when we are only eighteen! In reality, we are all constantly evolving. We change our minds, our tastes, what suits us and what we want to wear. I would encourage everyone to stay open and experiment, to not be afraid of getting it wrong. If you are scared of color, there are ways to figure out how it can work for you. For all skin tones, it's important to have an understanding of undertones to see what complements you. Once you know if you have cool, warm or neutral tones, it will help you understand which colors suit you.

Start with what you gravitate towards and think about how a color makes you feel when you wear it. If it isn't resonating, then try another one. My daughter taught me this. There's something amazing about becoming a parent, because as you're watching your child grow, watching them try and sometimes fail, it reminds you that having such an open mind doesn't have to be reserved for children. We all actually benefit from living life this way, including experimenting with color.

By now you have probably guessed that my closet is pretty colorful! And the color black is a main character too! Black is creative. Have you ever noticed that even if you opt for black just because you can't figure out how to put an outfit together, it still comes across as effortlessly cool? Wearing all black is the shortcut to looking chic without trying too hard. Except, never wear all black to a wedding. Unless it is the dress code, if you wear black to a wedding, the message you are subconsciously sending is that you are going to a funeral, and no one wants to think of their blessed nuptials as a death.

COLOR AND PRINT

Before I jump into the rainbow, I absolutely respect Jodie's stance on black and weddings, but I admit that I have worn black to weddings, and I have been to many weddings when other guests have worn black. I talk to it directly in the Black chapter, but I just wanted to clear that up before we start.

Anyway, when I worked in a clothes shop, during quiet periods the staff would try on the worst items in the shop to entertain each other. While some were drawn to pieces that were universally awful—be that the shapeless, the overly directional or the I'm-not-even-sure-what-this-is—I would try on a seemingly innocent floral dress, and it would draw the biggest laugh. It wasn't necessarily the dress's fault; it was more what my body, demeanour, attitude and aesthetic did to those poor dresses. I looked deranged. The ditsier the print, the more unhinged I appeared. It is a skill I still possess. On me, I hate prints—stripes and polka dots aside—and quite a lot of colors too. But fear not, I love them on other people so still feel qualified to write this chapter.

I love to surround myself with color—contrary to popular belief, my home does not look like the Batcave and is in fact very bold and bright, even down to the pink wardrobes in my bedroom and the bright yellow window frame in the bathroom. Color makes me happy, and I like to absorb its positive energy. But when it comes to wearing it, I feel a little differently.

Black is my safe space, as it is many people's safe space, which is why I have dedicated an entire chapter to it. And for years it was all I wore. Perhaps it has taken me slightly longer to find my color confidence than it took Jodie, but it is never too late to start experimenting and get out of your gothic comfort zone. And it really doesn't matter if you don't get it right every time. For example, I have an orange miniskirt that I fell in love with, and after much financial deliberation I decided it *must* be mine and I bought it. I have worn it only once in three years as I can't quite figure out how to wear it without looking like I work for an orange-themed budget airline. Or like I am a member of a subpar 1960s girl group. Yet I persevere to find its perfect color complement. I have high hopes for slate grey. I also love pink, but when I bravely once bought a hot-pink top, I looked like Tonya Harding on ice, which was not my goal. I returned the top posthaste.

When I do wear color, or print, I always get more compliments than I do when I wear black, for everyone has an emotional connection to colors. When I feel the urge to compliment a stranger on their outfit, it is almost always because they are wearing something that has made me smile, and much of the time that is influenced by the color or print. There is nothing better than seeing someone unafraid to stand out and have fun with clothing. I knew that Jodie Turner-Smith was the right person to introduce this chapter because when I saw pictures of her in the incredible yellow dress at the BAFTAs, I was entranced. In that canary sequinned gown, she radiated positivity and cheer in a way that a black dress never could muster. Elegance sure, coolness of course, sexiness almost always, but rarely positivity or cheer.

Clothes are a form of communication: they reflect how you are feeling but also affect those you encounter. With color and print, both bold and subtle, the wearer conveys confidence and to me also imagination and hopefulness. Although that might be the optimist in me. The feelings generated by seeing Jodie in the yellow inspired me to branch out and have fun with color, as why wouldn't you want to make others feel that same way?

Every color isn't for everybody. Pastels are a complexion drain on me, for instance. But finding the colors that suit you will sartorially lift your spirits. Likewise with print: whether you love maximal decoration or minimal graphics, there is fun to be had. You just need a little direction.

COLOR

FIND YOUR SHADE

Back in that same clothes shop where I dressed up for laughs, there was a customer who visited the store every Saturday, at the same time, without fail, to have a look around. I can only assume that at some point, for some birthday, an aunt gifted her with a Color Me Beautiful appointment, as over a period of at least two years, that woman exclusively wore brown. The exact same shade of chocolate brown to be specific, from top to toe. Boots, cords, sweaters, T-shirts, shirts, bags—even her eyeshadow and lip liner were brown. Clearly, she believed she was an "Autumn," which Color Me Beautiful compares to "autumn foliage or exotic spice colors." Now to be fair to CMB, I don't think they intended for Autumn to be taken so literally, but autumn landscape she heard, and so brown she wore. I'm not deriding CMB, or any other color consultants, as I do think there are huge gains to be made from knowing what suits your personal coloring if you have no idea where to start. But I don't think it should be considered gospel, instead merely thought of as an initial point of exploration.

Much like everything else style-wise, finding the shades that suit you involves trial and error. Though there are no true errors, you simply try and either love it or hate it. I find that there isn't any middle ground with the colors people choose to wear. I have a friend with brunette hair and olive skin who looks tremendous in pastels, and she loves them. I know a blonde with rosy cheeks who looks incredible in every shade of pink, and while it shouldn't necessarily work with her complexion, it really does. I have dark hair and pale skin that is energized by rich, darker shades. I love red, love it, yet I must be in the right mood for red, rather than let red direct my mood. Sure, red is supposed to be empowering and courageous, and is associated with passion, but I need to feel powerful as a reason to reach for red, rather than using it to envelop me in those emotions. A good friend of mine told me that she also suits red, but she feels too self-conscious when wearing it. It's fascinating that colors have such individual influence.

When I was younger, my mum used to practically beg me to wear royal blue, and while it suited my coloring, it made me feel, well, a bit blue and not myself, I suppose. I still never wear blue. Unless it is denim. Suiting a color is not enough, regardless of the compliments you receive; you have to love yourself in that color and feel connected to it.

You will also be drawn to certain colors at different times of the year, if you change the color of your hair, and at different times in your life. Our skin tone changes seasonally, so perhaps orange is your friend during the height of summer, but maybe not in the depths of winter. It also changes as we age, so the colors that suit us change too. As we get older we all benefit from brighter, richer tones, though don't fear—that doesn't mean you have to throw out all your beloved pastels; you just need to layer a brighter shade underneath, and even a narrow edge will provide a youthful lift. Or, if bold is a step too far out of your particular palette, white can work wonders too. We have long been taught that black can be harsh on older skin, and while I believe this to be mainly false (which I write more about in the Black chapter), I do think that it can drain its surrounding colors, so it isn't always the best shade to use to support or frame pastels and brights.

I spoke with Joa Studholme, who is the Color Curator at Farrow & Ball, one of the most famous paint producers in the world, and the way we approach color in our homes can also reflect how we approach color in our clothing. "I always say to people that if you are wary of strong color, use small amounts initially," Joa says. "Try a bold shade in a downstairs bathroom, or the inside of a cupboard, in the same way you might wear a classic navy suit but it has a fuchsia lining or a flash inside a pocket. Because when you start small, it makes you a little braver every time."

HOW TO PLAY WITH COLOR

Black and bright colors tend to cancel each other out, or black makes the color stand out even more. If that is not what you are intending, and you are not wearing the color from top to toe, then pair it with a complementary shade or a less severe neutral like beige, khaki, navy or cream.

Trying color with accessories is a safe place to start. But not with a black canvas. Pair them with other neutrals of white, khaki, navy or grey to complement and not overwhelm. I love to see a surprise pair of brightly colored shoes with an otherwise staple outfit of jeans and a shirt. It is instantly chic and playful.

Wearing one column of color is as flattering as wearing all black. For example, a colored suit will work as hard as your favorite event dress, and the streamlined silhouette makes it as easy as a T-shirt and jeans. If you're running late and have no idea what to wear, reach for pieces that are all in the same (or shades of the same) color—that you love, obviously—and it will be easy to put them together. A monochromatic moment doesn't have to be a neutral.

Let the color lead you. Some days you might fancy dressing like Rainbow Brite, and others you will be reaching for a navy hoodie, and that will feel like enough.

PRINT

FIND YOUR PRINT

If you love, love, love print, then by all means fill your closet with every pattern that you can, and wear it heroically and clashingly at all times, but if you are timid, and yet still want to explore, then you only need one or two pieces.

A designer once told me that you should choose a print as you would a painting. "It has to speak to you. If you don't feel it, don't go there." Have a look at the paintings and pictures you have at home, as they are a good indicator of what you are drawn to both color and pattern wise. The art in my house is graphic and abstract, which is probably why I am attracted to stripes and polka dots over florals or anything overly feminine.

In early 2023, fashion designer John Lewis heralded the death of the floral midi dress; meanwhile, the *Guardian* newspaper claimed that the "floral midi and sneakers has become the de facto uniform across the country." They weren't wrong. Floral dresses see an uptick in sales in retail from late spring through summer, as they are considered

a summer staple for workwear and casual alike. Of course they aren't dead, they are a wardrobe perennial, and John Lewis was just suggesting that everyone who wants to wear them probably owns more than enough of them by now. A dress is the easiest way to wear print, so I get their draw. They offer a sense of ease to dressing, and the print—floral or otherwise—does all the work and draws all the attention. Ideal for day or evening, and you don't have to think about what works with the pattern. But print gets more exciting and enjoyable when you mix it up a little—I promise it is not at all intimidating, even for pattern newbies.

HOW TO PLAY WITH PRINT

Balance it out. Head to toe isn't for everyone. I like to see a print seemingly effortlessly blended into an easy outfit. Try a silk or light cotton shirt in the print of your choice—tropical, whimsical, ditsy, enormous, monochrome, rainbow, the print world is your oyster—and team it with your everyday wardrobe. You can't go wrong with denim, but a paler wash adds a good level of emphasis to the shirt. Add sneakers or ballet flats for more casual or pull out one of the colors of the shirt in a pair of strappy heeled sandals for evening. For work, take the same shirt and wear it with a suit. If your print is colorful, avoid black, and see if grey complements. If you are comfortable with color, then a single-colored suit in a corresponding shade serves to accentuate a print too, and if suitable for your workplace it will lift all Monday-morning spirits. There is also something sensual about the feminine romance of a printed shirt with the strictness of a pencil skirt or leather trousers. Especially if the shirt is slightly undone.

It works the other way too, of course. Printed trousers or a skirt worn with a simple T-shirt or knitted sweater is a great way to try it without figuring out if the print colors suit you, and it is far easier to experiment with something "out there" in bottoms, rather than right next to your face where we tend to dismiss color or print quicker. Oh, and top tip: striped trousers elongate your legs, as do any vertical geometric patterns. You're welcome.

For something more courageous—well, relatively speaking—try top to toe: coordinated prints can look elegant and stylish. One of the big, big bosses at work wears a deep-orange silk shirt and trousers with a white geometric print on them, and she looks effortlessly graceful in them. They really come into their own in the summer. Think of them like pajamas as they should be as easy to put on, yet they make you look like you are making an effort. Lighter fabrics are preferable to add a little movement, such as silk trousers, shorts or a skirt; team with a shirt, tank or top, and just add slide sandals. More interesting than a dress, just as simple, but much more impactful.

Embrace the clash to bring out the print big guns. If you are a maximalist or feel that somewhere in you there is one waiting to get out, then the print clash is for you. More is simply more here, and the best thing about it is that anything goes. Ditsy florals and stripes, why not? Add in some leopard, maybe some zebra? It's controversial, so hell yeah. Print clashing isn't about being sleek, it's about personality and standing out. If you don't feel comfortable going all the way, then dial it back a little. Or a lot. A pair of striped trousers, a plain T-shirt and a printed silk scarf tied around your head or neck still counts . . .

Treat some prints like a neutral. I don't know why it is true, but polka dots, stripes, checks and even classic leopard print are considered to be neutrals. Believe me, they really are; they suit everyone and always look chic. Yes, even leopard print. They are the print equivalents of black, white, navy and grey, they can be layered with almost anything and just, well, work. Day or evening, as the main attraction or the best supporting act, they will quickly become the hardest-working prints in your closet, and will be quite at home alongside your capsule wardrobe. If you feel that horizontal stripes make you look wide, then try vertical or diagonal. I have a black and white long dress with stripes flying in all directions, and it might be one of the most flattering dresses I own, as it makes me look about a foot taller than I am. Match the print to your figure. If you are curvier, you might think that larger prints will exaggerate your figure, but actually they serve to balance proportions, while smaller prints tend to overwhelm. If you have a small frame, the opposite is true, as large prints tend to drown you, while smaller prints look more refined.

HAVE A CARE

The one thing harder than finding clothes in the color that suits you is keeping them that color. I have a bright yellow bikini that was one of my favorite summer pieces. I say "was" because last summer I threw the top in the machine with other bikinis, and it came out a dull yellow. And no matter what I do, I can't get the color back to bright. I still wear it of course, but I can't wear it with the bottoms as they are still the original shade and make the top look dirty. Gutted. So don't do as I do, do as I say . . .

When washing your colored clothing, start by separating. That does not simply mean whites in one pile and dark and colored in another. You also need to separate according to color. Reds and pinks together, greens and blues, yellows and oranges—you get the idea—but only the richer shades; anything paler that falls into a pastel category is also separated into its own pile. Slightly laborious, perhaps, but worth it to make your clothes last.

Hot water can cause fading and bleeding, so 86°F (30°C) and below is the sweet spot. I now usually wash any color and print pieces I have on a handwash setting, as that sad bikini taught me a lesson. I asked my mum (no one washes clothes better than moms, and incidentally, after years and years of trying, I still can't make my clothes smell as fresh as she can) if there was a way to brighten faded colors, and she suggested adding baking soda or salt to the wash—FYI baking soda is the answer to 80 percent of all life's questions. Annoyingly it didn't bring the bikini top back to life, but I rated her advice highly enough to try it again with other items, and a pair of pink shorts came out looking brand new.

Another top tip is that when you buy new dark clothing, wash it on its own for the first and second washes to see how much of the color runs out. Then add it to the dark washing pile.

Personally, I have trust issues with any laundry product that promises it can "color catch," as I fear it will result in weirdly colored clothes and a broken heart.

Finally, and this should go without saying as it applies to all clothing, when storing richly colored items, keep them out of direct sunlight as nothing will fade color quicker than the sun. Think where you hang your coats, and if it is near a window, put your favorite items in your closet instead.

COLOR + PRINT IN BRIEF

1   Certain colors will improve your mood.

2   Never stop experimenting with color.

3   Monochrome doesn't just mean black.

4   Go big on color, or go small—it all makes a difference.

5   An emotional connection to color is integral.

6   A little print can go a long, long way, but don't be afraid to clash.

7   Choose a print as you would a painting for your home.

8   There is a world of print beyond a floral midi dress.

9   Consider some prints to be a neutral and invite them into your wardrobe staples.

10   Listen to your mother.

SUMMER

SOFIA RICHIE GRAINGE

The model and designer, whose sleekly simple personal style has been much admired and replicated by legions of dedicated followers, knows how to be chic in the heat without breaking a sweat.

HOW TO DRESS FOR A HEAT WAVE

Clothes, for me, are my way of self-expression. Depending on how I feel, kind of depends on how I dress. I can really represent myself and express myself through fashion. My personal style has evolved so much over the years—I would say now I try to be timeless. That's a word that I always try to incorporate when I'm thinking of putting together an outfit. And always comfortable. I definitely would say I'm not shy with expressing my style with what I'm going through at a certain time in my life, and it's kind of cool to look at it that way.

I was born and raised in Los Angeles. I've been experiencing heat waves my entire life. Surprisingly, actually, I much prefer dressing for colder seasons! That's probably just because I grew up somewhere so hot.

Dressing for heat waves starts with, let's be realistic, "am I going to sweat in this outfit?" I can't be in tight clothes in a heat wave, and I'm the first person to go for a slip dress with sandals, or a flowy dress; that's my go-to. I have girlfriends who wear tight jean shorts and sneakers and a little button-down top and they look adorable. So there are definitely different ways of doing it. It's honestly what you're the most comfortable in during a heat wave, which for me is loose and flowy.

I'm typically a neutral-tone girl. If I wear color, I'll just do a pop of color in the shoe or jacket. I love to over-accessorize. If anything, I'll do less with the outfit and more with jewellery. Lots of stacking, lots of bracelets, lots of necklaces and playful earrings. I think there is a way to be playful and fun and young while being sophisticated.

My ultimate style advice would be to dress with an item that you connect with, whatever the weather. I'm not a trend follower, but there are trends that I absolutely connect with that I'm gonna hop on. But I don't always dress because the girl next to me wore it. I dress because I feel comfortable and confident in myself.

SUMMER

Several years ago, I remember being on the Tube on the way to the office during the height of summer, wearing a T-shirt and a wool pencil skirt. Wool. I still now think of that sensation of sweat running down my legs, knowing that I couldn't sit down as I would instantly be sitting in a puddle of my own making. I foolishly thought that because I had bare legs, I would be cool. Nope. I have also worn skinny jeans in August heat, with high-heeled pumps, and the result was pretty much the same except with the addition of swollen and blistered feet. It has taken me many years and climbing temperatures to know how to dress for the two words that can bring even a seasoned traveller and sun worshipper to their knees: Heat Wave. Across the world, you would think that other countries more used to the heat—and with AC as standard in most homes and workplaces—would handle it in their stride, but on social media in August, most New Yorkers just seem pissed off. I don't blame them, for being on vacation in the heat is one thing (you can strip down to a bikini for a start and jump into the ocean or pool) but trying to tackle your normal day-to-day of public transport commutes, school runs, work meetings, appointments around town and any type of social engagement becomes an exhausting, rage-filled and sweat-drenched challenge. Sadly, due to climate change, the number of extreme heat waves will become more regular, so it is something that most of us will have to get used to and figure out how to dress for.

Not that you need a dedicated wardrobe for this—not yet anyway. Instead, it is mainly about repurposing what you wear on vacation to make it urban and profession-appropriate. Switching up what you wear, and when and how you wear it. When dressing for sweltering city (or town) heat, fabric and fit are everything—or, in this case, a lack of being fitted is everything. Oh, and before we go any further, spoiler alert: linen is not always the answer.

KEEPING YOUR COOL

While the choice of material is integral, the idea is actually to keep that material as far away from you as possible while still technically wearing it. Except for synthetics—synthetics need to remain locked away, far away, until the temperature drops and your body cools down. And even after that too, ideally.

What you need are lightweight, loose-fitting cottons and silks, which allow heat to escape rather than trapping it against the skin. A very, very light merino wool is also a good, if slightly unusual, option as the fibers draw moisture away from your skin and release it into the air. But don't assume that means your winter knits will keep you cool; I'm talking about delicate merino vests or slip dresses. They also don't wrinkle.

Which brings me to the subject of linen. Admittedly linen has many benefits in the heat: it is breathable, it also draws moisture—more so than both cotton and silk—and its weight means that it will fall away from the body and not stick to it. Which is ideal when off-duty. But assuming you have to look some level of presentable during your 9 to 5, linen's ability to look like a wrinkled heap in a matter of seconds will do you no favors. I have a pair of high-waisted, wide-leg linen trousers in beige that I love. When I put them on, I feel like I too could have starred in *The Talented Mr. Ripley*. But after sitting in those trousers for mere moments, my Ripley dreams are as crumpled as I look. I also love a white linen shirt, especially with a colored bra slightly visible beneath, but it never translates well from vacation to office.

If linen is your summer cooling crutch, then darker colors, especially a deep navy or black, hide the creases better than lighter shades, as do prints, and try to iron or steam linen when damp to get rid of the worst wrinkle offenders. Otherwise, I would recommend leaving linen to vacations, weekends and the bedroom. Linen bedding will keep you cooler, so I'd suggest you sleep in linen at night, and not just look like you slept in your linen clothes during the day.

THE HOT ESSENTIALS

Simplicity is your coolest friend. Think loose and easy (like my coolest friends). In a heat wave, clothing sticking to you is almost as bad as one of your bare limbs accidentally grazing one of your other bare limbs, causing a sweat fountain. Sorry to be gross, but we all know the hell of that. This is not the time to worry about accentuating your curves; it is about leaving a lot to the imagination.

DRESSES

I have a sleeveless A-line minidress in white cotton that I bring out when I can't bear to wear anything else. Which is why I love it. It has a generous neckline and a single button fastening to the back, and it easily slips over my head and falls to my mid-thigh. It allows for ventilation and sits away from my body like a doll dress. If I lived in a consistently hot country, I believe it would be all I would wear. A-line dresses in mini, midi or maxi are summer saviors. I prefer shorter to get my legs out to hint at some kind of shape beneath, and even lower calves and ankles in a midi are more flattering, but if maxi is your preference then please go all the way. The clean silhouette of an A-line does what it needs to do and nothing else, which means it is a perfect canvas for a bold color or print.

If you would rather cover your arms, shirt dresses are a good alternative, but ensure that the sleeves aren't too fitted and allow a little billow, or can be turned up easily without becoming uncomfortable. Many shirt dresses can become sack-like frumpsville quickly, so they benefit from a belt. If yours doesn't come with one, tie a complementary cloth belt around your waist to see how it looks, and if it works then take the dress to a tailor to add belt loops. But on the hottest days, tie it slackly behind your waist to offer some shape without the clammy restriction of being belted in.

Bare your legs under the skirt, and choose a longer length if you aren't comfortable getting your pins out. I know that bare legs and hot temperatures can lead to thigh chafing, so pop on some cycling shorts or longer SKIMS underwear to offer some protection.

COORDINATING SETS

This makes getting dressed as easy as putting on a dress, but with a little more interest and often much chicer—it is something those LA girls like Sofia Richie Grainge excel at. I like a printed silk shirt and matching trousers (or tailored shorts if appropriate), but they tread into pajama territory very quickly, so for work a tank or lightweight vest worn with nothing underneath paired with wider trousers is less bedtime, or a matching top and skirt. Look for silk and cotton styles in a single shade you love or a print you won't get bored of.

SHOES

When it comes to sandals, as much as you love the delicate ones with barely-there lacing, step away from them and into something a little more, well, substantial. City sandals take some pounding, and your feet also need the support as they tend to swell if you are on them all day in the heat. A pair with a sturdier sole and more significant straps will last many, many summers to come. If there are ankle straps and buckles, fasten them as loosely as possible without them feeling unstable. Save your pretty and elegant ones for evenings, holidays and taxis. If sandals aren't workwear appropriate, try a backless or slingback slide shoe with a closed toe in a soft suede or canvas.

ACCESSORIES

Do not use a cross-body or shoulder bag in a heat wave. Even as I write that I can feel the moist discomfort of past mistakes, for nothing will make you more hot and more bothered than a tight leather strap. Instead, opt for a handbag and don't overfill it if possible so it isn't too heavy.

Finally, as a finishing touch if you have long hair, tie a printed silk scarf around your ponytail. It serves to elevate, it's effective, it's easy to do and it looks cute. You can always untie it at the end of the day to blot your face and neck on the train home. After all, you have spent the day holding it together—now you can melt.

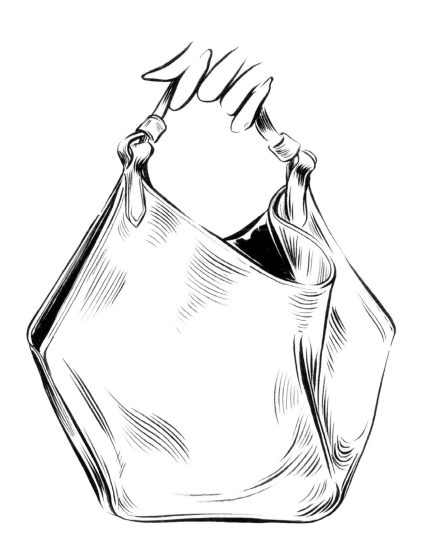

HAVE A CARE

This might be the least sexy chapter I have written, as it is basically all about sweat. Or trying not to sweat. Mind you, maybe that is sexy for some, who am I to judge? But like it or loathe it, sweat can damage clothing, so best to know how to deal with it. If sweat has impregnated and stained a piece of clothing, you need to act quickly, ideally before it dries. A little bit of lemon juice diluted in water will prevent it drying and start to work on the mark, and then soak the stain in white vinegar and warm water for an hour and patch-clean it before putting it in the washing machine. Obviously do a small patch test before committing to a larger area, but if you are strictly restrained with the dash of lemon juice, there is very little damage it can do to fabric. Wash items inside out so whichever parts have been in contact with the skin can be easily reached.

In the summer, I treat most items like delicates, so I change my detergent to something more gentle and wash on a cooler setting. Some cottons can withstand much higher temperatures, but I use that rarely. Additionally, to avoid excessive creasing, do not overfill the washing machine drum, and if you are lucky enough to have an outside line for drying, try to spread out the items, which will also help. But as mentioned earlier, ironing cottons and linens when they are still a bit damp will make it far easier than when they are dry. You might not want to do it at the time, but it is always better than revisiting a crumpled ball of fabric that your iron can't smooth over.

SUMMER IN BRIEF

1   Check the temperature before getting dressed.

2   Keep it simple.

3   Plan for a heat wave; don't let it take you by surprise.

4   Linen is not always the answer.

5   Keep your clothes as loose and easy as your naughtiest friend.

6   A cross-body bag in the heat is an instrument of torture.

7   A little sweat is inevitable, but damage to fabric doesn't
     need to be.

8   Make friends with your iron or embrace the crease.

9   Avoid synthetics till cooler temperatures return (and beyond
     if you can).

10   The reality of summer dressing isn't sexy: you will sweat,
     and your hands and feet will swell, so stay hydrated and try
     to keep your cool.

BAGS

TINA LEUNG

Stylist, beloved TV personality and one of the original fashion influencers, who calls her collection of bags her "babies."

LOOKING AFTER YOUR BAGS

The Chinese say that if you put your bag on the floor, all your fortune comes out: "A purse on the floor is money out the door." So, I am the kind of person who asks for a stool for my bag. I asked for one the other day in a restaurant and the waiter laughed at me. But, I mean, the floor is so dirty—it's just good sense. Then again, my big airport bag is often on the floor as I travel so much for work, and I constantly worry about my fortune spilling out all over the place.

My personal style is quite eclectic, and it changes all the time depending on my mood, the dress code and what is lying around (I am quite messy). So do my bags. I have fun little bags, shaped like bows and hearts, and ones covered in crystals (which probably reflect my eclectic style). But my go-to day-to-day bags are classics. I have a black Hermès Mini Kelly, and buying it was a momentous moment for me. I invested money in it and I know that I will have it forever. I'm carrying it today and currently it contains my passport (I always have it with me so I can go anywhere at any time), two lip glosses (I'm never without at least two), my wallet, loads of old receipts and my keys. It's classic on the outside, but all about me on the inside. As a bag should be.

When looking to buy a classic bag, look for the ones that have stood the test of time. The ones you have seen everywhere and in the history books (well, my version of history books: fashion magazines). Focus on the craftsmanship, and the sort of leather, like full-grain or uncoated, that gets better with time. Crucially, they should work with everything you wear, day to night. If you are going to spend a lot of money on a bag, it should be one that you can imagine passing on to your daughter, friend or niece as a future heirloom. I think of bags as watches—if you look after them, their value increases.

But there also needs to be a balance, as I think bags that are worn and loved look better—they've absorbed stories that give them character. I don't keep my bags in their original dust bags; once you wear them, they are dusted, right?! It always delights me when I use a bag that I haven't in ages and there is a ticket from a party (or that cloakroom ticket that eluded you at the time). I love finding bits of my personal history in a bag, little things that take me straight back to a particular moment. There is definitely something to be said for not keeping things pristine. Perhaps just keep them off the floor!

BAGS

Be prepared, for this is one of the chapters where you should put your money. Though not necessarily Hermès levels of money. A handbag has all the power, so if you are going to invest in anything for your wardrobe, let it be a bag. The first bag I ever saved up for to buy was by Chloé. It was deep green suede and had a chain strap, which I can still hear as it loudly clattered against furniture and rails on the Tube. It was insanely expensive to justify with my Saturday salesgirl salary, but I found a way to make it work. I wore it till it fell apart, as I didn't know then what I know now about looking after things, and it made me appreciate the beauty of the right bag.

A bag can make or break your outfit as only accessories can. It can elevate a perfect look as quickly as it can destroy it. Yes, yes, I know that that sounds dramatic, but if you saw the "ludicrously capacious bag" episode of *Succession*—or the hundreds of subsequent memes—you will know what I mean. If you didn't, it was described at the time as the "biggest handbag burn in cinematic history." Let me explain . . . In the episode, the date of one of the extended billionaire Roy family attended an intimate party, also full of the super-wealthy, carrying a vast Burberry tote handbag. Now there was nothing wrong with the bag per se, but as it was the wrong bag for the occasion it took down the rest of her look, which incidentally was a pretty and inoffensive floral dress. The bag overwhelmed the outfit and became the "look-at-me" focus, which should rarely—if ever—be the role of a handbag. Even if that bag was ludicrously expensive and you want people to know it. The ideal bag is not about labels: it's about style, size and suitability.

Though, saying that, my very favorite bag wears its label proudly. So proudly in fact that it doesn't look real. When I was a (slightly) younger journalist, Louis Vuitton thanked me for a feature I had written by gifting me a bag—"My very own Louis Vuitton!" It is a top-handle black coated canvas bag, printed with red LV monograms, and finished with a luggage tag embossed with my initials. It is just big enough to squeeze in a laptop, so I take it with me to work every day, and I love it. There is something about the black and red combination that makes everyone assume it is a knock-off, which is rather rude, but oddly, there is something about that which makes it even more right for me. It's unusual, unique and just the right side of garish. For Louis Vuitton.

Played correctly, a bag is there to enhance what you are wearing, while offering practicality, support and protection. I don't mean protection in terms of it doubling as a weapon (though I suppose that depends on the kind of bag you carry); I mean it as a form of comfort or security. When I go out, I keep my bag close to me. It's on my knee when I commute, it's on my desk at the office, it's in my line of sight when out for dinner, and it's strapped to my body if I ever find myself out out. Sure, that maybe makes me sound totally paranoid, but I don't care, as to me, my bag offers my escape. A literal escape home thanks to the keys it contains, an escape from boredom on a long journey thanks to the phone or book it holds, or even an escape to the bathroom during a dinner that just got interesting in order to retouch my makeup.

Your bag holds your most personal possessions. Phone, laptop, tampons, medication, makeup, gum, mints, distractions for your children, notes from loved ones, random old receipts that serve to remind you why you never have any money, perhaps a lighter that reveals you're a secret smoker when stressed or after a glass of wine. Sometimes I think I would rather let someone look at my recent Google search history than delve deep into my handbag, as my handbag and your handbag often hold the key to who we really are. How bloody terrifying.

The relationship that you, I and every other woman has with her handbag is incredibly intimate, and it is the most personal accessory you will buy. This means it is tricky for me to tell you exactly which bag is right for you, but I can advise you on what to consider when trying to narrow down your bag search.

FUNCTION

This is the place to start. What do you need the bag for? Is it a practical work bag, a small and elegant evening bag, a day-to-day shoulder bag or something light and fun for summer?

What are you going to wear it with? If it is a shoulder bag that you are going to wear over a winter coat, ensure that the strap is long enough. A bag that sits too tight on your shoulder will be relegated to the back of the wardrobe pronto.

How are you going to wear it? Do you want to wear it tucked under your arm? If so, it is a day clutch you are looking for, which is bigger than an evening one, or a small shoulder bag (think 90s) with a shorter strap that will work better with bare arms or lighter summer jackets and fabrics. Do you want to wear it across your body for hands freedom? Cross-body bags are a favorite of mine, but mainly as I am relatively flat-chested, so it isn't uncomfortable. Those with more generously sized boobs find that the strap separates them and cuts their body in half. Which sounds neither comfortable nor tempting.

SIZE

When it comes to bags, size is everything. While there is always a place for the oversized, there is such a thing as too big—you are not Mary Poppins after all. My dad bought me a bag when I was in my very early twenties that was comically big. It was a red leather clutch, but one that was 50cm long and 30cm high. In order to open the bag I had to sit down, as the top flap was too awkward to lift when standing. Practical it was not, beautiful it also was not, but to hell, I loved that idiotic bag.

A work bag needs to have practical value: your laptop should fit easily, not be a squeeze, but equally not be swimming around. You want to keep it relatively secure. When looking for a larger bag, check that it has a small pocket in the lining. Knowing where to find your keys and cards will save you so much time and panic that you may have lost them (you haven't).

And of course, there is such a thing as too small. "They are cute, but useless," says Tina. "At one event I had a small clutch that was just big enough to hold my hotel key card and a lip gloss. But I also had a camera and chargers, and I got in a jumble, dropped the bag and it broke, and someone stole the camera. My sister's wedding pictures were on there, so that was a lesson learned. Choose practicality over indulging in fashion wants and desires." Squeezing too much into a small bag will make you feel as uncomfortable as wearing something too tight. It's restricting and distracting, and things will eventually spill out.

WEIGHT

When I worked on the shop floor in retail several years ago, there was a trend for bags being festooned with chains, charms, locks and keys, and trinkets galore. The more the, well, more. One browsing customer picked up one of the jingle-jangle bags, and as she strained to get it on her shoulder said, "This was clearly designed by a man." That always stuck with me, and I've never forgotten the importance of the weight of a bag since.

If the bag is already heavy when empty, think of the punishment when it is crammed full of your essentials. A laptop might feel deceptively unsubstantial on its own, but pair it with other devices, a book, makeup bag, keys, wallet, water bottle and panic snacks, and you might as well book in with the chiropractor now. No bag, no matter how much you love it, is worth a bad back.

Consider the straps too. If you are looking for a work tote, you know that it will need to be pretty robust under pressure, so if the straps are slender, they may look refined and graceful but are unlikely to last the working week.

A short-handled, oversized tote may entice you to fill it to the brim with items you *might* need, but that's a bag you are going to be carrying in one hand and you can't distribute the weight. So, before you stuff it to within an inch of its life, remember the regret that always accompanies carrying home a supermarket bag that is too full.

MATERIAL

Once you know what you need the bag for, what it's made of is the next consideration. Let's start with leather. It has been the go-to for durable, long-lasting handbags, and for the most part it still is. Invest in good-quality leather, which isn't cheap, but if you look after that leather, it should age beautifully, get better with each wear and be a true forever piece. Structured or unstructured, supple or rigid, smooth or quilted, again it comes down to personal preference and your desired function for the bag, but do your research in terms of where the leather is from and where the bag was made. Remember that softer leather won't be as enduring as a harder alternative, but hard leather won't be as malleable. Leather bags wear the best, but they aren't scratch resistant, and they will be marked by stray makeup and life in general, and that is OK! Glossier or patent leather will show marks more easily, and scratches are harder to buff out, so consider what you are using the bag for—whether it is everyday or special occasion—before you commit to the patent. I also have two coated canvas bags with leather trims that I have had for nearly a decade, and yet they haven't aged a day (lucky them). They are so easy to take care of, as they can be wiped clean, and the only thing I've had to have fixed is a loose thread in the shoulder strap.

Then there is suede. Now, there is something about a suede bag that I love: soft, slouchy, seductive and indulgent, it somehow feels more adventurous than leather. However, it is also an absolute witch to keep clean, and even if you have treated it before the first wear, if you and your cherished suede bag are caught in a downpour, you will be trying to brush those raindrop tear stains off that bag for months. Though suede brushes do work, you don't want to use them too much as they make the suede thinner and more vulnerable. With a suede bag you can't be too prissy, and you just have to accept that the marks add character and be at peace with that. A bag is there to make your life easier; if you aren't relaxed with it getting a little bit roughed up now and again, it might not be the bag for you.

In recent years there have been great advancements in good leather alternatives. But to be clear, I am not talking about plastic-based leather alternatives; they are landfill fodder and should always be avoided. No, I am talking about plant-based alternatives which can be as durable, or more so, as animal, though they are currently quite an expensive option. Mycelium leather, developed from fungi, is far more environmentally friendly, but is so far still being developed in the luxury market. When buying new, it is worth researching what advancements have been made in new materials.

Basket and raffia have come a long way from picnics and tend to dominate the hands, shoulders and nooks of arms from May to September. Perhaps more synonymous with vacations and sundowners, but they are a great daytime alternative to a heavier leather bag when not near a beach too. A fresh uplift when paired with shirting and denim, and they are also light, which means you can pile them full and they won't cause injury. That might make me sound a hundred years old, but seriously, you've got to look out for your back!

THE BAG CLOSET

One bag is not enough. A bag can do a lot, but it can't do everything. I do believe, like the capsule wardrobe, there is a bag capsule too. You don't need them all, but you can pick and choose depending on your lifestyle and requirements.

TOTE

Occasion: Work, overnight, travel

What to look for: This should be your hardest-working bag. It will be your constant companion for work, travel and play, so you need to ensure that it works with everything you wear. If you want it to play a low-key supporting role, look for neutral shades in black, khaki, beige, grey, chocolate and navy, but you can also add a sense of positivity to more serious workwear with a singular pop of color in reds, blues and greens. Personally, I am rather partial to a leopard print too—after all, there needs to be some playfulness in our 9 to 5. If you are someone who tends to overpack, you run the risk of overfilling a larger tote, so measure up your laptop and only go ever so slightly bigger than that. Ensure the handles fit comfortably over your shoulder, even when wearing a large coat, and that they aren't flimsy. An inner pocket is always useful to keep the essentials. And finally, as this will probably be your most used bag, please take time to regularly clean it out—I'd suggest once a week. That dusty old Polo mint (at least I think that's what it is) doesn't need to be accompanying you everywhere. Get rid.

EVENING BAG

Occasion: Dinner, parties, events, date

What to look for: Ideally this is a bag that has a detachable cross-body strap that also acts as a clutch, or it could be a small bag with a strap on it that delicately swings from your wrist—basically what I am talking about is a small evening bag. But when I say small, as mentioned above, it should never be too small. You need to be able to comfortably pack whatever you need. Start with how your phone fits, then consider the space for keys, cards, makeup, mirror, mints and anything else to get you through the evening. It should never be too tight a squeeze, as that is how you lose stuff, and also how you distort the shape of the bag. Then think about how you would carry it. Again, I advocate across the body, which is great for being hands-free when dancing or trying to hold a drink while snacking, gesticulating or distracting yourself on social media. The wrist strap is also handy if the bag isn't too heavy and has a secure fastening, ideally a zipper. Furiously scrambling around on the floor picking up your possessions from a bag that unexpectedly popped its popper fastening should only happen to you once. But if in doubt, a clutch works with everything, and can be tucked under an arm for those hands-free moments. Just remember to edit the contents.

This is also a place to have fun with fashion, as when it comes to evening bags, anything goes. You want it to be encrusted in crystals? Do it! You want to play with color, print, fabric and charms? Step this way! Gone are the days of your bag matching your shoes, or the hardware matching your jewellery. There are no rules. They might be small, but they can pack one hell of a punch.

SHOULDER

Occasion: Weekend, casual, dinner, date

What to look for: This is the bag that maybe says the most about you, and perhaps the one you cherish the most. You don't buy it for purely practical purposes, and it is not there to look fancy after dark either. It is the bag you choose to complement and elevate you at your most relaxed. It might be the one that you have properly invested in too, and truly look after. This is not a bag that holds kids' toys, nor does it go on the floor. Maybe it is designer, maybe it has a logo or maybe it was just the bag that stood out to you in a sea of thousands and thousands of competitors. With Goldilocks' approval, it won't be too big or too small, it will be just right. For you. This bag should be considered a forever piece, regardless of price, so you want it to have longevity. For that reason I would campaign for black or brown styles, with gold or brass hardware—a subtle statement, but one that can make a white-T-shirt look like an evening dress. That is the power of this bag and it's what your family will be fighting over in the will.

BACKPACK

Occasion: Sports, travel, overnight

What to look for: OK, so the backpack is very much a case-by-case taste thing. Admittedly I haven't carried one since my last day of secondary school, but I think that is just because I haven't found the right one for me yet. I appreciate what they offer, and they are a damn sight cooler than the cloth tote bag I currently take to Pilates. They are also, and I will bang on about this repeatedly, very good for your back as the weight is evenly shared. For a backpack I'd say go all in and embrace the sport. Little leather backpacks are cute but do the same job as a shoulder bag, just not as well. You want pockets galore, clasp fastenings, comfortable padded adjustable shoulder straps, and room for everything. There are some great recycled shell fabrics on the market now, and they are better for the environment than nylon and polyester. Plus, as soon as you slip one on, you feel about sixteen, and there is no greater feeling than that.

BEACH TOTE

Occasion: Vacation

What to look for: Size, again, is important. And this tote should be big. Big enough for a couple of towels, endless sun cream, hats, water, books, food, drinks, crockery and cutlery. It's there to be packed, pulled, thrown in a car, and to end the day filled with sand and a little more sun-bleached than it was in the morning. This is not a bag to spend a lot of money on; this is a bag that should make you feel happy and organized. It can be canvas or raffia, which dries quickly and won't be damaged by a little bit of water. Again, ensure that the straps can hold a vacation load and then some, for there is nothing more depressing than returning from the beach with a broken bag and arms full of your damp possessions.

HAVE A CARE

Talking of broken bags . . . I know that some things can't be helped, and accidents do happen, but if you follow this advice it's unlikely to reach that point. You need to treat your bags like you treat your shoes or, in fact, a vintage car. Don't let it wear down or fall apart. Look after the leather with protectors and conditioners before using the bag and on a regular basis—at least once a year. Treat stains or water damage immediately with a damp cloth using a combination of water and soap, or a specific leather cleaner. If it's not your everyday bag, keep it in a dust bag between wears and not in direct sunlight.

Fix things as soon as they start to fray or there is a loose thread. It's much cheaper in the long run. Local tailors, cobblers and dry-cleaners are worth speaking to about repairs, but don't hand them your favorite accessory unless they've been recommended, or you've seen their work. You need to trust them. Don't go for the cheapest either; you often get what you pay for and that certainly applies to leather repairs.

Before you buy a bag, do your research in terms of what's offered as a follow-up service. Does the shop or brand you buy from offer free-of-charge repairs, or a bag

MOT service after a few years for some TLC? If not, they might be in partnership with a specialist repairs business such as The Seam or Leather Spa, or they can recommend the best service from alternatives.

When looking to buy a bag, pre-loved is a great place to start, which I explore more in the Pre-Loved chapter. Some bags are better when they have relaxed and been worn in a little. So if it is a specific style or brand of bag you'd love to own, a secondhand one will not only save you some money, it is also great for the circularity of fashion.

Finally, and this should go without saying, but as tempting as it might be . . . never buy a fake handbag. Even if no one else can tell, you will know. And even if that doesn't bother you, have a think about where it was made, how it was made and who made it.

BAGS

BAGS IN BRIEF

1   The ideal bag is not about labels, but about style, size and suitability.

2   No bag is worth a bad back.

3   Fake is never OK.

4   Don't put your bag on the floor.

5   Size always matters.

6   A too-small bag is the same as a too-small dress: things will spill out.

7   Clean out your bags on a regular basis before someone discovers the real you.

8   The right bag always makes the outfit better.

9   Look after them and they could look after you in retirement.

10   Sometimes old is better than new.

DATING

TINX

Social media phenomenon, presenter, bestselling author, digital creator and hilarious relationship expert, Tinx is the girlfriend we all need before hitting the dating scene.

HOW TO GET DRESSED FOR A DATE

Getting ready for a date is almost my favorite part of the whole dating process. I pour myself a drink, I put on an amazing soundtrack—almost always Beyoncé—and I do my makeup. Extra points if you can grab your friend and they can sit on your bed while you're doing it. It's fun and it's hopeful. I want to feel confident, but this doesn't mean that I put in masses of effort. I wouldn't plan an outfit beforehand because I *always* feel different on the day. I would never buy something brand-new to wear on a first date. To begin with, you're probably going to jinx it and set yourself up for failure. Second of all, you're putting the person on a pedestal and, look, they might be great but at the end of the day, you don't need to add any more stakes to the moment. A date is really just a vibe check. The human equivalent of dogs sniffing each other's butts. That's all it is. You don't need to elevate the other person; instead, all you want to do is say, "I know myself, I like myself, and I'm interested in getting to know you." The ideal first impression on a date is that you know who you are and that you are comfortable being you. Clothes can illustrate this on every level.

For me, feeling confident and sexy is all about a dress. I've always felt myself in dresses, and happily they suit my body type. I love a midi dress, loose and lacy, that makes me feel feminine. Then, depending on the season, I'll do a flat or a boot, and maybe put a little jacket over it.

I think about all the terrible outfits that I wore in my twenties because I wanted to appear a certain way or be attractive to guys. It was such a fruitless exercise—dating is like aiming for a moving target. When I turned thirty, I just thought, "This is so pointless," and I stopped dressing for anyone else. I have the most success when I feel great and when I dress for myself. Now, I have one dress that I've worn a thousand times and which has an excellent success rate. It is black, short but not a mini, has a square neck, and no matter what mood I am in before I put it on, even if I have had a terrible day, I feel good in it. It's undeniably elegant—women think it is chic and men think it's sexy. I think this is because of the cut, which doesn't show too much yet at the same time shows kind of a lot. The perfect dinner-date dress. It's actually more of a second-date look for me. On a first date I go pretty low-key, and then—if I like them and they get a second date—the wow dress comes out.

The more dates a guy gets, the more "fashiony" I dress, because a man has to love that side of me. He has to be ready for me to come down and be wearing something pretty out there, and while he doesn't have to conceptually understand what is going on, I want him to think, "I don't get it, she's wearing like a toucan or something, but she feels good, so I feel it too."

Even if you and your partner have settled down, live with each other and see each other at your worst, it's important to make time for dates. Get dressed up, flirt and have fun, remember the passion from the beginning, keep it alive and make it interesting for each other. But even then, dress for yourself and never for them.

If you are nervous ahead of a date and have no idea what to wear, close your eyes and think of yourself in an outfit. Something that you can sit in, eat in, are comfortable in temperature-wise (I'm a sweaty person, so silk is not my friend when I am hot) and, most importantly, choose something that doesn't need constant adjusting. Most of all, don't forget that at the end of the day it doesn't matter what you are wearing—it's only ever about whether you and your date are getting along. If your outfit is truly the reason why you don't have a second date, then they don't deserve you!

DATING

Now, I don't want to blow my own trumpet here, but I have been on many, many, many dates. First dates, second dates, twenty-third dates. Some successful, some not so much, and one or two that I personally believe might be considered the worst dates of all time. While some of the failures might have been to do with my personality (I know, it is hard to believe), their personality (easier to believe) or our collective lack of chemistry, I am confident that it was never the fault of my clothing—though some long-forgotten men might disagree. Over my dating years I have perfected my date outfits, and most have been far more successful than the relationships and have remained with me far longer.

To clarify, I am a cis/het woman who dates cis/het men, so my dating experience is confined to that space. However, when writing this chapter, I sought advice and experience from friends and colleagues, each with a differing understanding of the dating arena. But the unmistakable similarity for all is that dating has become more disposable. Thanks to the apps, going on dates has become more regular and normalized. For those who want to and have the time, it isn't unusual to cram in two or three dates a week—which means that, for many, dating is less of an event, so they make less of an effort. It is a numbers game after all. Dating has become casual, as has what we wear for it. Which is depressing. When I dated on a regular basis, I would occasionally notch up two dates a week, three if it was with the same person I couldn't get enough of, but I always made an effort, even for those dates I hoped would cancel right up to the moment I sat down in front of them. From first dates in a pub, to second dates for drinks and dinner, to those spontaneous ones that were organized with little notice and the dates in longer relationships, I would slip on a heel, an earring or two, and something that I thought I looked good (and felt good) wearing. While it is a bonus if your date appreciates the look, like Tinx advises, I don't dress up for the date's endorsement—I dress up for my own.

For Tinx to feel good it is all about dresses; for me it is about high-waisted trousers, jeans or skirts, and a cropped top that shows an inch or two of skin. The high waist makes me look taller, and I'm proud of my midriff so I get it out when I can, and dates offer up the perfect opportunity. My date looks are actually the same looks I wear when I go out for dinner with friends, and occasionally to the office, give or take a heel, and I suspect that my friends and colleagues will spend more time appreciating them than any man I've dated will have. From experience, a date will remember if they fancy you, and rarely any of the specifics of what you were wearing. On the other hand, I remember the man in the incredibly pointy shoes which established there would be no date two (there were other reasons too, I promise, I'm not that shallow), the guy in the obscene slogan T-shirt (he slipped through my pre-date vetting process) and the very nervous date who was in a box-fresh shirt, complete with pressed folds, who had panic-bought something moments before our date because he knew I worked in fashion. But then I find women are far more into the details than men are.

Date dressing, like every other form of dressing, is first and foremost for yourself and your own happiness, not anyone else's. So even if your partner, or potential partner-to-be, won't have any memory of the dress you spent hours deliberating over, and which was the subject of many WhatsApps between friends, dates are moments—no matter how many you go on—where you want to feel bloody fantastic about yourself so you can emanate that to the other person. Confidence is very seductive.

FIRST DATE

Regardless of how many dates you go on, or how much of a player you are or claim to be, I still believe that everyone has a little bit of hope and optimism for where a first date could go, be it a very, very short fling that night, or down the aisle in the future. There is potential in meeting someone new, and while we can dream of big love, one great night also holds much value. Not to mention great stories. So, clothes-wise, it is worth putting the work in.

Often there is pressure enough on the first date, so in line with Tinx's advice, go low-key rather than OTT for date one. I mean, unless you are going out for dinner somewhere amazing, in which case pull out the wow dress from the start, the reality is date one will be more informal. Pub drinks, cocktails in a bar or, God forbid, a walk . . . But regardless of the situation, first impressions are always everything. When you walk in or approach your date, you want to allow them to drink you in from top to toe, as that might be the only time during the date that they have the opportunity to see you from afar. Obviously it works vice versa too; the power is equal. This is your space to emphasize the part of your body that makes you feel the most beautiful: dazzle them with your ability to walk in heels, or simply show off the coat that you painstakingly chose for this moment. Make the most of it. For when you sit down—or again, God forbid, are walking—next to each other, the only focus is really from the waist up, or how you frame your face. If I was going to get all *Annie* the musical on you, I would say that it is what you wear from ear to ear that matters, and while I would love us to all be that profound, the primitive reality is that a plunging neckline on a great top can serve to beautifully support that smile.

THE PULL OF DENIM

When we try on jeans and turn around to judge how our ass looks in a mirror, dates are one of the reasons why. Wanting to look good as you feel eyes on you when you walk to the bar or bathroom is partly why we spend hours searching for the perfect jeans. A first date demands those jeans—your old faithfuls that you feel confident, sexy and totally yourself when wearing. They hold all the power and only need minimal assistance up top or below. A perfect white T-shirt, sheer enough to hint at the bra beneath, is always a winner, accessorized with some earrings or a pendant necklace. Then below, depending on your personal style and comfort zone, great sneakers can look cool and effortless even if you tried and rejected four other pairs in advance, ballet flats work well if you aren't in total mad denial about your height like I am, and *only* wear heels if you can walk in them. There is nothing unsexier than someone badly tottering around in shoes, and it will immediately make you feel self-conscious and uncomfortable, and you won't act like your best self.

TEMPTING NECKLINES

You have drawn them in with your strut across the bar floor—now that you have their attention, let's maintain it. Forgive me if I am being uncouth or heavy-handed, but a flash of skin, even just a trace, can be very seductive ammunition. I am not talking about extremely low-cut necklines, though if that is your weapon of choice, then please take your best shot. It could be off-the-shoulder to reveal the clavicle—sexier than the anatomy sounds; square-cut for an elegant reveal; sweetheart, which manages to suggest sweetness and naughtiness in each dip; or as round as you dare to bare. I am a huge fan of the turtleneck, and live in them through the cooler months; however, my male board of representatives unanimously agree that turtlenecks are not date attire. Apparently, they convey that you might be too strict and serious. Many men are basic creatures, you see, and turtlenecks are not.

LUCKY LINGERIE

Whether or not you are going to reveal your lingerie on the first date—that is your call—it still plays a vital part in the event. "I always consider underwear when getting dressed for a date," says Tinx. "But again, it is more for me than for them. I want to feel sexy, I want to feel hot, and lingerie definitely helps in the process." Even in your sexiest jeans, if you have on a threadbare old thong underneath (I don't care about its success rate in the past), you are not going to feel on your A-game. Do yourself a favor and pull out the lesser-worn foundations from your provocative pile—if you are the only one who sees them that evening, then you should still consider yourself lucky.

SECOND AND THIRD DATES

Dressing for the second and third dates is sometimes harder than the first. You have to maintain the elevation from date one, and actually raise the bar, especially if the destinations and nature of the dates become less casual.

The early part of dating is also when you start to reveal the true you. Again, like Tinx (my dating muse), for me that means I bring out the fashion guns. From my experience, fashion

tends to scare people, or they can have certain preconceptions about it, depending on the amount of *Devil Wears Prada*, *Sex and the City* or *Absolutely Fabulous* they have been exposed to. I love clothes, obviously, but some of them can seem slightly intimidating, or confusing, to a date who doesn't have the same aesthetic appreciation. So, I add bits in date by date. A crazy shoe, a T-shirt that is business from the front (plain) and party from the back (umm . . . lace wings for want of a better description), or a knitted tank that turns out to be considered very unsexy and a total buzzkill by some men but very stylish by colleagues and the lauded Italian designer who made it. That date's loss, I say.

I really don't believe in buying new items of clothing for dates, as you need to be you right off the bat, and if you are buying into the perception of being someone else for the first couple of dates, it becomes very expensive and difficult to keep up that pretence. I am me from date one, I just dial it down slightly. Then once the guy has held my interest, I dial it up until I am wearing something totally ridiculous, bewildering and brilliant by date seven and he's happy to just go with it.

LONG-TERM RELATIONSHIP DATING

In case there is any ambiguity, I mean going on dates with your partner, not dating outside of your long-term relationship.

It is very easy to settle into a relationship and stop making much of an effort. I get it—life, kids, work, resentment and lethargy get in the way. It doesn't have to be a weekly thing, or even fortnightly, but at least once a month drag yourselves off the sofa and go the hell out.

You have seen each other at your worst, so it is good to be reminded of why you were attracted to them, and them to you, in the first place. It doesn't have to be an extreme or expensive date—it could be a dinner at your local, a picnic for two, or a drink and movie, but please, for the love of God, make an effort clothes-wise. Pull out the lesser-seen "just for best" section of your closet and remember what impression you wanted to make when you initially got together. There is no shame in wanting to be found attractive, and even less in looking in the mirror before you leave the house and thinking, "Damn, my partner is lucky to have me."

SEXUAL POLITICS

It would be remiss of me to not discuss sexual politics in a chapter on date dressing. In the ideal world, there is no such thing as too much boob, there is no such thing as too much leg, too much skin, too much anything. To me, if it makes you feel happy, show it off.

Sadly, we have to have our body wits about us when we dress for an audience with one person, regardless of how many people are around. Different body parts mean different things to different people, as some lone figures see them as invitations to events that they are definitely not invited to. On this subject I can't speak to those who associate a low-cut dress or a miniskirt with solicitation for sex (though I would have much to say), but all I know is that you should never be afraid to dress in a way that you later think might have led someone on. It didn't. If you ever feel that or think that has ever happened, know that it had nothing to do with your clothing, or what your desire for the date was, and all to do with the other person.

HAVE A CARE

I have one little dating warning story. When asking the men in my life if they have ever recalled what their date has worn, or if they have dumped someone based on fashion choices alone, they all said no. Except one. On a first date, the aforementioned man drove to pick the lady up to take her for dinner. As they stopped at traffic lights, the woman crossed her legs in the front seat, in a flirtatious move I can only salute. Unfortunately, her actions did not have the desired effect and instead flagged to my friend that she had a hole in the sole of her shoe all the way through to her bare foot. This total disregard for her possessions horrified my friend, who managed to proceed with the date but never called her again. Get to the cobbler before getting coquettish.

DATING IN BRIEF

1   Dress for yourself first and your date second.

2   Don't let the casualization of dating casualize your outfits.

3   Always make an effort. It is for yourself, after all.

4   Don't buy new for a date. They (the potential partner and the outfit) are never worth it.

5   Be confident in how you look from the back.

6   Lingerie is important, but not for the reason you think it is.

7   A little bit of skin goes a long, long way.

8   Show off whatever makes you feel sexy and confident, and don't allow anyone else's judgement to cloud that.

9   Get your shoes resoled.

10   Your date will probably never, ever remember what you wore.

BLACK

MONICA BELLUCCI

The award-winning Italian actress and model brings a bombshell allure to dressing in black and knows why no other shade will ever be as powerful.

WHY THERE WILL NEVER BE A "NEW BLACK"

Nothing can replace black! For me, black is not a color; it is an essence that makes me feel protected from the world, and secure in a crowd. It is instinctive, feels authentic and is fitting for every single occasion. From Chanel's little black jacket to Saint Laurent's black Le Smoking suit, or even an iconic black dress à la Sophia Loren, black highlights the wearer's identity in a fundamental way. It tells the world—subtly and elegantly— that the wearer is perhaps confident or private, and it can even signify where they are from. So yes, wearing black is protective, but it also makes me feel utterly Italian.

I am quite a shy person, so I feel safe and secure entering a room or having to make an entrance for an event wearing black. I think that black can envelop you without hiding who you are, and that is what makes black irresistible and totally irreplaceable. Through clothing, one has the freedom to express who they are, however they want, and black is reassuring because it brings allure and elegance to every figure. I have a curvy body, and black honors shape rather than trying to disguise it. I want black to speak for itself, and not try to be something it isn't, which is why I like to wear timeless cuts and simple lines. While I love an LBD by Dolce & Gabbana, as their cuts feel practically made for me, most days you will actually find me wearing a black shirt and black jeans. I am very consistent in my style—even my cat is black!

Black might have an association with the gothic, and it is true that it can emanate a certain impression. Black can create a certain distance, it can suggest the wearer is aloof or solitary, but I don't think it does so with any aggression or imposition. Black brings light elsewhere, to the core of the wearer. No other color has the power to enhance and to veil in quite the same way. Yes, black is a little mysterious, and that is wonderful. Sometimes women need mystery.

BLACK

No one makes black look sexier or more desirable than Monica Bellucci. I would bet that when she pours her enviable curves into a black dress, she is responsible for more sales of LBDs than anyone else in the world—including the designers long famed for their little black creations. While I would love to claim that my long-standing allegiance to black clothing was inspired by Monica, I was sadly not that sophisticated as a preteen. Instead, it was another woman who was and remains responsible for my black obsession: Winona Ryder. As soon as she appeared on-screen as Lydia Deetz in *Beetlejuice* in 1988, I knew that never again would pastels or florals have any place in my life. Lydia was all teenage angst in black lace, layers and hats, and I couldn't wait to replicate it. Out of character too, Winona was a pinup for all preteens with angsty aspirations, in simple black dresses on the red carpet and excellent black leather jackets or masculine black suits for off-duty paparazzi shots, which I pored over, analyzing every detail. Winona wore black and was cool and mysterious, so I wore black to be cool and mysterious . . . with significantly less success.

Despite not transforming into Ms. Ryder when I slipped on a long black dress (maybe any day now), black has remained my style constant ever since Lydia Deetz spotted the ghosts in the attic.

I've used black to disguise my body and to celebrate it. I have worn it to seduce, or at least to try to seduce anyway. I have worn it to express my mood, both happy and sad, and I have worn it as a shield when I was deep in grief and didn't want anyone to talk to me—black became my armor. During that time I was picking up lunch in a sandwich shop in central London, dressed in a variation of my then go-to look: a dramatic black wool and leather A-line coat, with a funnel neck that grazed the tip of my nose; outrageously high black platform boots with a towering heel; and black spindly jeans, finished off with a ghostlike pallor and a short black bob. Approachable I was not. In the queue I bumped into a colleague, and as I took out my headphones to talk to her, she started to say how intimidating I looked but stopped mid-sentence and said, "Wait, are you listening to the Backstreet Boys?" I was. On the outside I looked, as my friend once described me, like "gothic Wizbit" (please google), but the impenetrable black exterior allowed me the space to start to heal on the inside, and part of that healing involved "I Want It That Way." Now I look back, I did appear terrifying, which wasn't the intention, or not fully at any rate. The intention was to build a wall, and black forever serves to be the most bulletproof front. Color studies have found that black has emotionally protective qualities.

As Monica said, black is fitting for every single occasion, and I completely agree. It is appropriate for everything, including weddings I believe, though Jodie Turner-Smith disagrees in the Color + Print chapter. It remains my go-to for everything, whether I am dressing up or dressing down. While I might not dress like a gothic Wizbit anymore, I still occasionally dress in a way that people might find "intimidating"—but honestly, who cares? Black has certain connotations—depressing, intimidating, bleak, somber, oppressive, funereal and ominous—and people tend to have an opinion about people who regularly wear black, more so than any other shade. "For God's sake, cheer up," I get a lot from not-so-perfect strangers. But black can also be sexy, sophisticated, dangerous, powerful, intellectual and authoritarian.

That is the beauty of black. It works effortlessly for you, and it can be anything you want it to be. Wear it because it makes you feel taller, slimmer, protected, sexy, smarter, pulled together and forceful. I am always drawn to people when they are wearing all black, as it makes them appear clever, even if the look is simply a black sweater and jeans. Wear it because it (mainly) all matches, and you can get dressed in a flash. As the inimitable writer and filmmaker Nora Ephron once said, "Black makes your life so much simpler. Everything matches black, especially black." Now I am not one to argue with Nora, but that is only *almost* always true.

If you love black, you will be drawn to black pieces like a bat, regardless of what you are looking for. But the following list is as useful for those who are devoted to black, and have many of the items already, as it is for those who aren't as obsessed, but like to lean on the black essentials in their closet from time to time. These are the pieces that I think excel in black more than in any other color, and while many are mentioned in more detail in other chapters, consider this your black inventory.

THE LBD

The little black dress—or LBD—is the hero in a capsule wardrobe and the essential in your black inventory, especially for after dark. It is the item you reach for to feel magnificent in when wearing it for an event. I have two. One has long sleeves, a high neckline, a maxi hemline and a slit down the back from the nape of my neck to the base of my spine. When I first got it, a friend told me that the only accessory it needed was a broomstick. I ignored him, and six years later I love it just as much as I did when I first tried it on. It's my winter LBD as it looks better with boots than heels and is more covered up. The other one is black silk with thin shoulder straps, midi length and completely backless. It is a special-occasion dress and one of my favorite pieces. If a dress has started many conversations in a restaurant bathroom, you know it was worth every penny.

The key to the LBD is wanting to wear it and wanting to wear it for a very long time to come. It should be timeless in terms of subtle details, without big statements, and never "on trend" for a specific season. It should also highlight the part of your body that you are most comfortable with. If you are comfortable with every body part, that is great news, but when it comes to the LBD, narrow it down to one. If it is your legs, make it short but with long sleeves. If it is your arms, opt for strappy but long. If it is your back, as I have just realized must be mine, then keep the front more modest for a posterior surprise.

When it comes to fabric, you know that I love silk, but the LBD is where I also encourage velvet. Velvet is not just for Christmas, and in black it looks chic and sexy all year round. A strapless black velvet column dress will always be a favorite, as the trick with velvet is to keep it simple. I don't know why designers see velvet and think "add ruffles, ruching and bows," because velvet is doing the heavy lifting already, and less is more. The sexiness of black velvet is in the desire to touch it, so if your partner can't keep their hands off it, you are on to a winner.

BLACK TURTLENECK

OK, OK, so I might be obsessing over turtlenecks as I manage to mention them in almost every chapter, but I love, love, love them. To be clear, I am not talking about a mock turtleneck, as I don't think they look flattering on anyone. I encourage you to commit to the high-neck turtleneck and not a poor imitation. Plus, I swear I haven't met anyone who doesn't look good—or taller—in a black turtleneck, whether it is fitted or loose. Personally, I like a fitted ribbed cotton or merino wool one as a go-to when I can't think of anything else to wear, but recently I have found the benefit of a men's lightweight knitted turtleneck—the neck is larger, so immediately appears more dramatic, and the fit is on the good side of oversized as the soft line of the shoulders drops flatteringly so it doesn't look too big. I wore it recently with narrow black leather trousers and large gold hoop earrings, and that turtleneck got a whole lot of love. A narrow black turtleneck looks perfect with wide-leg black trousers, while a more generously shaped turtleneck looks better when paired with a narrower trouser or skirt, especially if you tuck it in at the front or side to give it more shape. If you are tucking it in, length is everything, and the perfect turtleneck should sit just below your hip bone—that way it won't bunch too much if you tuck it in, nor will it ride up if you wear it with a lower waistband. If you want to wear it over your waistband, then a longer length to mid- or lower buttock is ideal. When it comes to the neck, I prefer mine to sit high under my chin so I don't often fold it at all, but if you prefer it neater, then try folding it in rather than out, as it creates a neater line.

A black turtleneck is simple and timeless, and it cleverly accentuates the face while elongating the body. I mean, come on, how could you possibly resist?

BLACK SUIT

When you buy a suit, you're really buying a 3-for-1—you could wear the full suit, or just the blazer or trousers. Your choice.

A black suit can be oh-so chic and incredibly versatile in terms of wearability and occasion. It's worth investing the time and effort in finding that special one that is the perfect fit, fabric and shape. No shine allowed so, as ever, avoid 100 percent synthetics as they start to shine up after just one wear. I have a virgin wool one that has only got better with age, and I have had it for nine years, but also look for those with a viscose and wool blend as they are very hard-wearing. Do check that the lining is silk though, as that is breathable next to skin. Traditionally for day or work, a more relaxed fit—a soft drop shoulder, a longer hem that skims the bottom of the bottom, and wider-leg trousers—works better and will be more comfortable, while an evening suit can be more sharply tailored. That doesn't mean fitted, but the shoulder should be stricter with a more defined edge, so the overall silhouette is straight and not narrow or pinched. However, the reality is that both fits work for both occasions, depending on how you style them up. A jacket worn with nothing but statement jewellery underneath for evening could easily be worn for day by replacing the jewellery with a dark shirt.

A wool suit or simply just the blazer is nicely complemented with a black silk shirt beneath for some texture play, but it is crucial to remember that just because two things are black, regardless of what Nora said, it doesn't mean that they automatically work together. This is particularly relevant to the suit, or trying to create a suit from existing items you have. If the jacket and trousers are different fabrics, textures or shades of black, or you have worn in one piece much more than the other, it can quickly look sad and shambolic.

Black trousers, whether worn as part of a suit or independently, are a great canvas to either set off other items or become the hero themselves. They have the ability to dress up a T-shirt or camisole but can appear more relaxed with a ballet flat or sneaker.

These should always be an essential part of your capsule wardrobe—if, and only if, the fit is right.

BLACK MAXI COAT

Ah, the drama of a long, sweeping black coat. Excellent for rushed entrances and exits as it sails behind you, and comforting when you wrap it around yourself and belt it on a chilly winter walk, teamed with a large scarf, sunglasses and melodramatic posing into the light. It should be considered a character in your closet, the one you bring out day or night when you are feeling a little operatic.

Ideally it should hit slightly below mid-calf, be straight-cut and single-breasted, with narrow lapels and a max of three buttons. If it has slanted pockets, do not be tempted to unstitch them and stuff them with gloves and other winter paraphernalia, for that will ruin the line of the coat. And that is literally what bags are for.

Perhaps the greatest thing about a black maxi coat is that you can wear whatever you like under it. Pretty much. Big boots, black turtleneck and jeans for day, and it serves to disguise barely there evening looks until you are ready to flamboyantly reveal.

BLACK SUNGLASSES

Black sunglasses are a functional accessory that suit everyone and lend a contemporary finish to every outfit. In layman's terms, they make everyone look cooler. Black frames and dark lenses (and I do mean dark, dark—the more mysterious the better) never go out of fashion; you just need to find the shape that is right for you. Cat eye, round, oval, Wayfarers, square, bug-eyed or *Matrix* tiny, there will be styles that suit you more than others, but there is no right or wrong pair and they will manage to elevate a look all on their own. They are also a more accessible way to buy into a designer brand, if you want; either way, just ensure they offer 100 percent UV protection. Always put them back in their case and don't throw them loose to the bottom of your bag—treat them with the same care as everything else you buy.

BLACK HOSIERY

Tights are an unsung hero of our closets, and yet they are one of the hardest-working additions to an outfit. They are what make us feel confident in a miniskirt and can be the difference between a black dress looking frumpy or sexy. It is all about the denier and the finish. If you'd like a little more coverage to get your legs out in short hems, then a 40 or 50 denier will give a semi-opaque finish, and always opt for a matte look. If you are looking for complete coverage, then 100 is for you, but they can feel very heavy under clothing, so save them for the coldest of days. But if you want to achieve a sexier finish with tights (or stockings) then a 15 denier is what you are looking for—very seductive when slipped into a high black stiletto court. I also recommend a 15 denier with very delicate dots or lace for special occasions. Tights with a shimmer are acceptable for the holiday season and the holiday season only.

I feel there needs to be a special mention for black socks here too, as it took me many years to find the perfect black socks: they are from Falke and they are 100 percent cotton. I have tried cashmere, which seemed like an unnecessary expense, and I was right, as life is too short to handwash socks. Cotton socks are harder-wearing, so won't thin in the heel as quickly, and my perfect socks are longer so they sit on the leg above ankle boots.

BLACK PUMPS

I talk about the charm of black pumps in both the Capsule Wardrobe and the Shoes chapters, so I won't bang on about how they transform the way you feel and the way you carry yourself in a single step. Nor will I repeat how even with a short heel they still manage to elongate your legs, especially with a more pointed toe. And of course, I won't say again and again that if, and only if, you are comfortable walking in a heel, then these are an integral addition to your wardrobe.

I have pairs in black matte leather and black patent leather: the matte ones work to dress up a more casual day-to-night look, while the patent ones have never failed to transform the simple combination of an LBD and a 15 denier tight into an outfit that always gets me what I want. On that note, I shall say no more . . .

BLACK ANKLE BOOTS

If you aren't a heeled-pump kind of a girl, or if you are but you funnily enough don't live in them, then boots are another black perennial. They will ideally rise to above your ankle bone, not too fitted around the leg, but not too wide either—you should easily be able to slide one finger between inner boot and skin. The heel height, or lack thereof, is entirely up to you. For a day-to-day ankle boot that will see much walking, opt for a flat Chelsea boot with a rounded toe in a slightly high-shine leather, as they offer a little style over stomp. Or for those who like a slight elevation all day long, just a two-inch Cuban-esque block heel and a slightly extended toe will remain comfortable but with added stature.

BLACK BAG

No matter how many bags you own, I bet it is the black one you rely on the most. A black shoulder bag works for *almost* everything (no one needs a black shoulder bag on the red carpet) and with nearly everything (evening gowns aside). Keep the shape simple, avoid too many bells and whistles such as buckles and hardware additions, and make sure the strap is comfortable enough to allow your arm to move freely, even with a jacket on.

BLACK AND SUMMER

Black is not just for the dark and cold months, as proven by the fact that "how to wear black in the summer" is one of the most searched-for fashion terms from April to September. There is no great secret to it: it just comes down to loose fit and the fabric. Easy, breezy black cotton and silk are your friends; black polyester or wool, not so much. I am very partial to a black silk slip dress worn with flat sandals and over-the-top earrings for a hot summer night out. It never disappoints.

BLACK AND WEDDINGS

Unless someone specifies that you *can't* wear black to their wedding, the general rule is that you *can* wear black to a wedding. So long as there is no veil involved.

However, consider the happy couple and the likely mood of the wedding before you commit to the dark side. If the wedding will err solidly on the side of traditional, then black is likely to be frowned upon, especially by older relatives, and it's never ideal to be the guest that others are judging. Or at least not for a fashion choice anyway. But ultimately, if you have a black dress or suit that you feel sensational in when wearing, then who wouldn't want a guest with that sensational mindset to be a part of their wedding day?

BLACK AND AGE

It has long been spread about that once we ladies reach a certain age, we must lay aside our black items of clothing as they will enhance our rapidly ageing faces in all their hideousness. Absurd. If you are someone who has used black as a style and emotional crutch, you do not have to stop because of some ancient wives' (men's) tale.

In 2015, at the age of eighty, the celebrated American writer and journalist Joan Didion became the iconic face of Céline dressed in a simple black sweater. Recently I saw a woman in her eighties wearing head-to-toe black, including a turban, and the only color was the gold of her drop earrings. She didn't look older than her years; she looked younger, and chic as fuck too, I might add. There are hundreds, thousands more examples, but it seems foolish to feel the need to mention them.

If you are still concerned about wearing black next to your face, then feel free, of course, to layer a shirt collar over the top in a paler shade that you are comfortable in. Just ensure it isn't a white round neck set against black, as it can get person-of-the-church quite quickly. But honestly, if black has always had a positive impact on you and the way you dress, never give it up. After all, if black made me feel cool and mysterious when I was a preteen, I can't see why it won't do the same when I am ninety.

BLACK AND COLOR

Right off the bat I am going to tell you that you absolutely can wear black and navy. In fact, I think it might be one of my favorite color combinations. It looks sophisticated and savvy, and also shows that you don't give two hoots about nonsense style rules. But, while it is easy to treat black as a canvas, if you are pairing an all-black outfit with a brightly colored piece or accessory, it can look a bit gimmicky, and can cheapen both the black and the color. Instead, break up the outfit with other textures and colors. For example, if you are wearing black trousers with an orange top, pull on a denim jacket to soften the impact of the shade. Even if you layer on a black coat, the additional denim balances it all out.

HAVE A CARE

Watching a favorite piece of black clothing fade is depressing and unnecessary. When washing clothes in the machine, turn the items inside out, keep the temperature low and ideally set to a handwash or delicate setting. When drying, keep them out of direct light for a long length of time.

But occasionally, even with the gentlest of care, the black still fades to grey. You can try to dye it, either yourself or ask your dry-cleaner if it is a service they offer. Often black dye doesn't take, and it depends on the fabric, but if you love the piece, it is worth trying. If dyeing doesn't work, or isn't an option, it is time to retire the greying item to the clothing bin. I'm sorry to say, there is no coming back for it.

Black clothing is also irresistible to lint, hair, crumbs and every other teeny-tiny piece of dust that suddenly becomes noteworthy when it makes contact with black fabric. I recently followed advice that suggested adding a cup of white wine vinegar to your wash to reduce static and therefore the lint attraction, and I can confirm that, once again, white wine vinegar is a working wonder. But mainly I rely on the joy of a lint roller, or, if caught in a lint trap without it, I use sticky tape. For larger items, if you have the time and the energy, another roll in the washing machine will dislodge most of the lint, but remember to clean the filter regularly too.

BLACK IN BRIEF

1   Black is a superpower; it hides and enhances.

2   There will never be a new black.

3   Wearing black doesn't mean that the wearer is melancholy.

4   Play with the opacity of hosiery to transform a look from sedate to sexy.

5   Black sunglasses make everyone cooler.

6   Whisper: *"You can wear black to weddings."*

7   Not all black items work together just because they are black.

8   Everyone needs an LBD.

9   Carry a lint roller.

10   You are never too old to wear black.

OFF-DUTY

ERIN WASSON

The Texas-born model and designer, and the ultimate pinup icon for the coolest off-duty style, knows how to make maximum impact with minimum effort.

FINDING FASHION TO RELAX IN

It's not about fashion, it's about style. Always.

Style doesn't mean that you have to have a lot of money; look at every single photo of James Dean—he's always wearing the hell out of a T-shirt and a pair of jeans. Don't let choice overwhelm you. Find your base, find your core, and work around that. We have handbags, jewellery, all the accessories—we can create so many versions of an outfit with a base as classic as a T-shirt and jeans. This is the secret of off-duty.

My mother can put four ingredients into a casserole dish, sprinkle something crunchy on top, bake it, and it comes out perfectly. This is how I try to get dressed. Accessories, no surprise, are my most important tool. White shirt, a perfectly cut pair of jeans, whatever shoes you want and a fabulous pair of earrings—just like that, you will be ready to go. I don't wear a ton of dresses and I don't often wear high heels. I dress low-key naturally, but I like to wear cute things depending on where I am. In New York everyone peacocks on the streets; it's a walkable city, it's a pedestrian city. The outfit that you're wearing in the morning is probably what you're wearing that night. You're flexing all day. In Venice Beach, the atmosphere is very much, "OK I'm walking the dog, I'll go get a coffee, maybe I'm gonna drive to the beach." The whole spirit around being in California is so relaxed, with all that nice weather . . .

I have always felt that the least dressed-up girls were the most confident, the ones that everybody wants to get to know. When I was working with my friend Alex [Wang], a fashion designer, we wanted to create a world of women who were the least dressed-up girl in the room—it's why we did sweatpants and high heels. And one of the greatest joys of my life was literally seeing every Chickaboom (that's what I call the girls in New York City who are free and having a great time) out wearing sweatpants and high heels. I was like, "hell yeah." Then it became all about the oversized blazer, denim cutoffs and high heels or great flats—the model off-duty look. It was confident, cool, totally at ease and it became, as they say, a moment.

Today, off-duty is just about wearing something so relaxed *to you* that it feels off-duty, whether you're wearing it for a Saturday morning coffee, to a meeting or a party.

"Relaxed" is the feeling I want to apply to everything I wear. When you're relaxed, you best believe your best self is going to come out. You're going to feel happier, your conversations are going to be easier, you might even find yourself being funnier. And, more importantly, you're not thinking about your outfit.

OFF-DUTY

I feel it is important to start this chapter with the admission that I am obsessed with Erin Wasson, which I admitted when I interviewed her, and while I'm not sure it made it any less creepy, she was incredibly gracious in the wake of my fandom. Sure, she was always one of my favorite runway girls, but for me it was more about what she wore off-duty than what any designer dressed her in.

Though she writes above that it was a look that coined the phrase "model off-duty," I would go so far as to claim that Erin herself was the inspiration. Street style in the 2000s became insanely popular due to her example: a great, just-slouchy-enough jersey T-shirt, front-tucked into the waistband of narrow jeans, worn with a low-key belt and teamed with a sandal or Cuban-heeled boot. A denim shirt with the sleeves rolled up to just below the elbow, worn over a black singlet, with leather trousers. Baggy blue jeans, a sports top and a long duster coat thrown over it all. A vest with nothing underneath, long before everyone was wearing vests with nothing underneath. And of course, the cutoff denim shorts with heels and a blazer. She made the casual cool in a way no one had really achieved before.

Because I have no shame left, I will also confess that after I saw a picture of her on Instagram in early 2022 wearing a pair of straight-leg white jeans, a white T-shirt with the sleeves pushed up to her shoulders, an overly long black belt and black loafers, well . . . I might have recreated the entire look myself the next weekend. Complete with the black duster coat she unknowingly inspired me to buy sometime in 2019. I sense Erin might unfollow me after this . . .

Anyway, forgive my gushing declaration of love, but my point is that off-duty style should be as aspirational as every other kind of dressing. More so even, as we wear it while enjoying *our own* time. We aren't dressing for anyone or anything else, just for ourselves. These are the clothes that we spend our personal time in, and we owe it to ourselves to make even the smallest of efforts—so why do so many find it so hard?

It is understandable to think casual and immediately think comfort, which quickly leads to frumpy. Which is the first mistake. The second is to think that we don't need to look good in our downtime. Now, while I am all for making no effort some of the time— we all have those days when we simply can't be bothered—you need to acknowledge how you feel when you are making no effort and are in your comfiest, and therefore I imagine frumpiest, of clothes. For me, and for many people I know, if I think I look good, I feel good—or at the very least feel better—and if I look terrible, I feel worse. It is that simple. If everything else is out of my control, I will control what I put on my body, and I find it makes even the smallest of differences.

Please understand that I am not talking about the clothes that you do your chores in—cleaning the bathroom is never a reason to dress up—and I am not talking about the clothes you revert to if you feel unwell or premenstrual. Those clothes are sacred and individual to each of us, and I shall not touch them. Instead, I am talking about weekends, uneventful days off, evenings if you change after work, and that weird time between Christmas and New Year. Basically, the times that you have a schedule that is your own (kids and real life aside), where it is very easy to slip into something comfortable but not exactly exciting.

So how do you dress down without it looking like you've given up? Well, it's really about your comfort levels.

LOUNGEWEAR

This is my least favorite word in the English language. The other is athleisure, which basically means the same thing. However, I understand that for many people loungewear forms an integral part of their downtime wardrobe. So fine, for all of you I will write about it, and start with it, as loungewear seems to be the "dress down" go-to.

Now, I am not sure why I don't like it. I wasn't forced into tracksuits as a kid, and in fact I had a yellow Benetton tracksuit that I adored. I didn't spend my weekends in sports

uniforms, running around cold Astroturf. Actually, as I write this, I think it is more of a personal aversion to hiding my body in loose-fitting stuff. I spent my teenage years hiding my body, for one reason or another, and now I like to reveal the shape of a waist, or the curve of a butt cheek. It's not that I want to show off my figure, it's more that I like clothes to give me a figure.

I own one pair of Adidas trackpants and four hoodies. And I have only worn them together when I have been unwell. I bought the three-stripe black-and-white trackpants after seeing some women I admire look very cool and comfortable, and you know what, they were comfy, and I understood the fuss. However, were they a little *too* comfy? Did I quickly have visions of myself on the sofa months in the future, still wearing the pants, but also with the matching zip-up top, surrounded by kitchen-cupboard debris and crumbs? Perhaps. I knew that I couldn't trust myself with that level of comfort to see a way back from it. And so back into my looser jeans I went. The kind of jeans that sit lower on the waist, are straight-leg, can be rolled up slightly at the ankle to give them a better shape, and look great with sneakers, loafers or ballet flats. I still have the trackpants of course, and now and again if I am changing after a long day, or a slightly fancy early dinner, I will slip them on with a white T-shirt or an oversized black turtleneck and thick socks, remote control in hand, and curl up on the sofa.

However, I have found myself in the fashion cupboard at work, speaking to the team and realizing that I have been stroking a pair of Loro Piana cashmere lounge pants for the duration, and I feel relaxed and comforted. My great editor likes nothing more than taking off her bra as soon as she gets home, and allowing her boobs to swing free in loungewear. My smaller boobs have been swinging free all day in a small triangle bra. So I really do get the draw of loungewear, especially if you work in a uniform all day and can't wait to rip it from your body as soon as you step over the threshold.

By all means hold on to your loungewear aesthetic—all I ask is that you keep it elevated. And clean. Trackpants are fine if they aren't threadbare and with remnants of last week's dinner on them, and if they aren't all you wear when you have time to yourself. If you love wearing loungewear, treat each piece with love. I recently saw a woman in green trackpants (the kind with ankle zippers that mean the hem falls over the shoes and aren't tapered) and burgundy sneakers, worn with a long navy coat and a cross-body black leather bag, and I've got to say, she looked great. Side note: it is remarkable how a handbag can serve to lift a loungewear outfit. A cross-body or shoulder bag works best.

Hoodies, however, I completely support. I once kept them strictly to sportswear, but I then saw their value over shirts and under oversized denim jackets, blazers or coats. A hoodie is a perfect layering piece that also adds a youthful element to a look, regardless of your actual age. It is the clothing equivalent of retinol or a really good facial. I have two cropped ones—a black sports brand, the other a red fashion one—both of which I wear off-duty with high-waisted jeans, shorts or trousers, and under a duster coat in the winter. I also have two cashmere ones, which aren't as fancy or pricey as they sound, as there are stores that offer excellent cashmere, or cashmere blends, for a fraction of the cost but with all the desired strokeability. Silk cashmere is more expensive than other blends, but it helps to prevent the cashmere from losing shape; cotton cashmere allows the yarn to dye more easily, so you are likely to find this blend in bright colors, though it isn't as warm; or you have wool cashmere, which is really warm, but look for a blend that is very soft to the touch as too much wool can make it itchy. I have one sweater in black cashmere and the other in grey, both slightly oversized. I wear these to work, and they look cool but suitably professional (for my workplace) French-tucked into the waistband of wide trousers. Some earrings or a stack of bracelets further serve to take the hoodie off the sofa, out of the gym and into the office. I also wear them, or an oversized sweatshirt, which works equally well, to travel anywhere—planes, trains, automobiles—as they are easy to pull on, or take off and throw over the shoulders. And, of course, they are a firm weekend staple.

SPORTSWEAR

You don't have to be doing a sport, or on your way to or from a sport, to wear sportswear. It could be worn with unfulfilled sporting intention, or no intention at all. It can be worn in transit, where you aren't really moving. And it can be worn for sport. By sport I don't mean sports with specific gear—fencing, cycling, tennis, football, swimming and the like—I'm more here for the yoga, Pilates and gym activities. Anything that involves Lycra.

For Pilates I dress like a ninja, all black at all times. High-waisted leggings (can you see I have an unhealthy addiction to the high waist? At 5'4" I do anything to create the illusion of longer legs, even when working out), or running "tights" if you prefer, matched with a sports bra or a fitted black breathable tank. Post-class, I do like to hang out in my sports gear for as long as I can, as subconsciously it makes me feel like I am still exercising. And while I know that is nonsense, you will find me in that outfit until lunchtime, when I force myself to shower and change into something more Sunday-wandering appropriate.

Personally, I think sports bras and breathable tops are for working out exclusively, unless you find sports bras more supportive. Leggings, however, have transitioned from sports to pleasure. And comfortable, flattering pleasure at that. Leggings work on all shapes and sizes, but please ensure the weight of the fabric is thick enough that you can't see your underwear through it. Bend over in front of a mirror and check, or bend over in front of a loved, trusted and now lucky person in your life for their view. Also, the more washes and wears a pair has, the more likely the seat will thin. During one Pilates move in a class, the mirror informed me that my favorite leggings had become transparent. I was delighted that was the day I was wearing a thong after forgetting to bring bigger underwear to change into. Those leggings were recycled later that same evening. So maybe do the mirror/ass check once a pair of leggings hits their first birthday. Once you have the weight right, there is very little else that can go wrong. High-waisted or mid-waist leggings are comfier, and again more supportive, especially those with a deep waistband, and length-wise they should sit on, or just above, the ankle bone. Leggings that are too long will bunch at the knee and at the ankle, but many brands offer them in varying lengths, so try them for size. Black is a wardrobe essential, but experiment with block color, like the girl in my Pilates class who dresses in all green on a Tuesday and all purple on a Thursday, though I would avoid print for leggings that cross the gym floor and into the everyday.

So, how to wear them in the everyday? Well, much in the same way you would wear skinny jeans. Except, unlike skinny jeans, leggings work on long-haul flights. They are great with flat knee-length riding-like boots in winter, paired with an oversized roll-neck sweater and a blazer that hits below the bottom. They also work with a white T-shirt and a denim shirt pulled over the top, either done up or left open. If wearing sneakers, or a shorter boot, thick longer socks are your friend. A chunky sock worn pulled up but then bunched back down a little above the top of the ankle boot, or beyond the ankle bone and over the hem of the leggings with sneakers, narrows your ankles and extends your legs. I swear. It's an optical illusion that works.

On the subject of sneakers, they are perennials and imperative to off-duty, and any style works (almost) any time, (almost) any place.

WEEKEND FITS

When it comes to the weekend, I get excited about what I am going to wear. It is a time to experiment, try different looks, change a couple of times in the day if I feel like it, and really enjoy my clothes. Not that I don't enjoy my Monday to Friday outfits, but weekends allow for a little trial and error, or a dress rehearsal if you like.

Once I have spent time languishing in gym gear, I then plan what to wear. I hate wasting a really good look on a day that doesn't deserve it, but Saturday is my day that deserves the looks. Not OTT looks, but maybe new combinations of pieces,

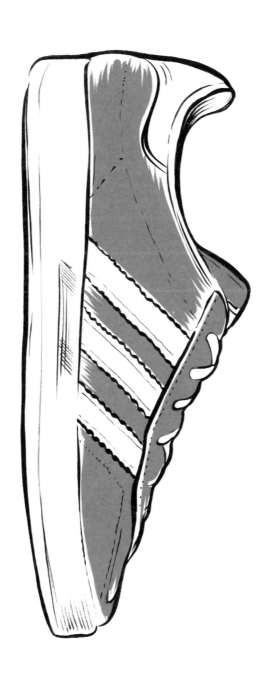

or the introduction and folding in of something new. As I type right now, on a Sunday, I am wearing a new oversized denim shirt that earlier this week I wasn't sure if I was going to keep. Turned out I just needed some time with it—it's been on my back since Saturday morning and now I can't imagine ever taking it off. It has accompanied me on errands, to the gym and to a casual lunch, and is big enough to layer over sweaters but also under coats. It's perfect, and I needed these two days off to figure that out.

There should be enjoyment in getting dressed when you might have the luxury to spend a little more time on it than you do Monday to Friday. I know, I know, kids and responsibilities don't stop just because it is the weekend, but you deserve some attention too, so give it to yourself. A little more time can still just mean mere moments—I'm not suggesting you dedicate hours to getting dressed. Though I wouldn't discourage that either.

If you aren't a loungewear person, then I will bet you either fall into the denim or dresses camp. Both are effortless ways to get dressed. With denim, start with the jeans and build around that, weather and agenda dependent. This is where you dip into that capsule wardrobe and layer or strip back as necessary. I like to select the jeans, then the ideal T-shirt in summer, or the tank top, shirt, then sweater in winter. After that it is about the coat or the jacket. I have been known to go home and change my coat or jacket if I don't feel quite right in it. For dresses, once you've selected the main piece, it's about the additions, the accessories and layers to ensure the dress works for all seasons. Again, for me, this is easy slide sandals in summer, or tights, chunky socks and boots in winter. Play with the contents of your closet and don't save everything for something special—sometimes nothing feels more special than a weekend doing very little.

Oh, and finally: weekends are the perfect time to break in new shoes. Start with short walks and then build up. Though be realistic about how long you will last in them. Weekends are precious; don't waste one looking for blister plasters through tears.

HAVE A CARE

Casual clothes should be maintained as much as anything else you own. And they should always fit properly . . . even your favorite trackpants.

When it comes to washing sportswear, it largely comes down to how much you sweat. If it is loads, that gear needs to hit the washing machine after every workout; if you are more of a glower, after every second wear is fine. But bacteria do love sweaty gym clothes, so make sure your sweatometer is properly tuned. Don't leave them lying in the wash pile for long either, as smells tend to bed in and it will be harder to get rid of them.

For synthetics, wash at 86°F (30°C) to preserve the fabric, but cottons can cope with a higher temperature. Once a top has started to smell, and I mean after washing, try soaking it in vinegar, then wash with a sports-specific detergent. If that doesn't work, recycle it. There is nothing worse for you, or those around you, than when you are mid-workout and your nose reminds you why you haven't worn that sports bra/leggings/tank in ages.

OFF-DUTY

OFF-DUTY IN BRIEF

1   The least dressed-up girls often look like the most confident girls.

2   Accessories can transform a basic off-duty uniform.

3   Feeling relaxed in what you are wearing is imperative.

4   Casual doesn't mean frumpy.

5   If you love loungewear, treat it with love.

6   Hoodies are a youth elixir.

7   Leggings are not just for the gym, or for pregnancy.

8   Off-duty dressing is when you are truly dressing for yourself. Enjoy it.

9   Break in new shoes on a day off.

10   Don't save your favorite clothes for special occasions, as weekends are special too.

PARTIES

MIMI XU

Acclaimed DJ, music producer, composer and performance artist, who creates the soundtrack to the best parties in the world—and knows how to dress for them.

GOING OUT OUT

For me, the ultimate party outfit *must* be dazzling.

Dazzling, but comfortable.

I like to stand out from everyone but I also need to be able to move easily, dance easily, go to the toilet easily . . . Years ago, I was all about the dazzle and less about comfort; now, I think it's 60 percent dazzle and 40 percent comfort. You live and learn, and I learned a lot about shoes.

Shoes are key to comfort. If your feet hurt, you're gonna want to cry and you're gonna want to go home. I spent years suffering in high heels, spending so many hours teetering in heels that I couldn't walk in, looking like drunk Bambi. I've got flat feet! So it doesn't matter whether you are trying to sell me a comfortable platform or a cushioned sole—I won't fall for it; I will not have my night ruined by footwear. I am completely and utterly a combat boots person—they go with everything and will take you everywhere.

The outfit, however, is totally dictated by the type of party I am going to or DJing. I like dressing for the occasion. Say it's a queer party: I will show quite a lot of skin and wear something tight—no one is going to bother you. At a Berlin rave I always tend to be more covered, because I want to be able to sit and not really touch any surfaces. It's about leather, but loose leather that you can dance in. As for how long I stay, it all depends on the music . . .

For club parties it's always about layers and never about the cloakroom. Why waste your night in queues? Wear pieces you can strip off and tie around your waist or your bag when you are hot and sweaty and throw back on when you leave. This is also where fanny packs come into their own. Hands-free and secure.

If you are unsure about what to wear to a party, I think it's cooler to be underdressed than overdressed. People are much more likely to say, "Oh, she's so cool, she doesn't care." But I have huge admiration for the ones who go for the opposite: overstatement no matter what.

When the night is over, French exit, no question. It is the quickest way to leave any party. Unless you are with your girlfriends. In that case, you have to follow the protocol. With your girlfriends you look out for each other from the beginning of the night right through to the end. No. Matter. What.

PARTIES

So, parties and events are different. Let me explain. Events are a bit more official, some could say straight-laced, whereas parties are a bit more low-key, where anything could happen.

I have been to fashion *events* where everyone is on their best behavior, posing expertly for the cameras and politely sipping champagne and water in equal measure during speeches and award announcements. Then I have gone to the after *party* where the same crowd has changed from gowns into clothes they can relax and dance in, while also changing from best behavior to someone who generates next-day gossip like: "Oh my God, did you see who was grinding against the man who is definitely not her husband in the corner?" and, "Was he wearing *just* leather shorts and a dog collar?" Chic. But that is the sign of a good party.

I wanted this chapter to be introduced by Mimi Xu not only because she is one of the coolest people I know but because as I write this in my mid-forties, the idea of what to wear to a club eludes me. To be honest, I don't think I ever knew. I am more of a dinner party and bed by 10:30 p.m. kind of girl, and I was born that way. Though I used to make it to midnight. One year on vacation in Ibiza, I was dragged to the superclub DC10. Dressing for that was almost as stressful as being there. Almost. But I don't want to feel like my clubbing days are over, no one should, so we need to be prepared for when the time arises once more.

Of course, this isn't just about clubbing, this is about all parties, and whether it is an age thing for me or a lack of practice (I'm really good at saying no to things), the only time I really second-guess my outfit choices is when I am going out out. Is this too dressy? Not dressy enough? Does casual really mean casual? Is it better to be overdressed than underdressed? And is there more to parties than just a nice top with a pair of jeans? I bloody well hope so.

Pre-lockdown—and I won't dwell on those lost years, but I do think they are key in this chapter—I used to go out almost every night of the week. Work dinners, friend drinks, weekend birthdays in bars and restaurants, the occasional bit of dancing, and never once did I question what I was going to wear. I knew my "party" outfits as well as I knew my working out or vacation looks. Then we all spent two years very much not going to parties, and many of us, me included, didn't easily step back into our dancing shoes in quite the same way. I finally understood that I didn't have to go to everything, which was liberating, not to mention an instant youth elixir. But it meant that when I did agree to drag myself off the sofa, I often stood in front of my closet and thought, "What the hell do people wear out?" And I wasn't the only one. "What are you wearing tonight?" was, and largely still is, the most rampant line of questioning in all my WhatsApp chats. But the answer is always subjective, for party dressing is about dressing for the promise of fun, and therefore it practically demands that you should have fun with fashion too.

Not to get all Kondo on you, but . . . when deciding what to wear to a party, any kind of party, do think about what pieces of clothing bring you joy. Watching a kid dance around in their princess dress, which they won't be separated from, is the feeling you want to capture—the enjoyment of clothes that brings such excitement. That is how you need to feel when you step out to go out, in clothes that truly reflect your personality.

I love that Mimi approaches her outfit as dependent on the party and the crowd, and that is how we all should think about party dressing. What is the occasion? Who will be there? How long are you planning to stay? And, of course, how long will you actually stay? There is nothing worse than choosing to wear your best-looking but most uncomfortable pair of shoes because you are only "popping in," only to find yourself at 2 a.m. sitting alone and with aching bare feet as you enviously watch your friends on the dance floor. We've all been there.

Parties can be fancy and extravagant or low-key and intimate, but you should always dress for yourself first, the occasion second, and the camera never. The idea of a party is always to relax, have fun and let yourself go a little (or a lot), and not to worry about what you look like on social media. In fact, the best parties are often the ones where the fewest pictures are taken.

You just need to find your perfect balance of dazzle and comfort and know what to wear where.

CLUB

I asked Mimi what she would dress me in for a club night. Incidentally, I don't think I have ever felt older than I did asking that question. Anyway, she started with the shoes, and certainly not any favorite shoes. "People are going to step on your feet, so don't waste good shoes on a dirty floor." Again, she recommends the combat boot. "No one will be looking at your feet, and you don't want open toes, *ever*, at a club." Oddly, I had never considered that, but of course it is true. If you are worried about someone accidentally stomping on your toes, you really aren't going to relax into the night. She also recommended black leather shorts, a sexy black bra and a shirt that should be opened and knotted when I'm hot from dancing, and then buttoned up when leaving back into the night. Or the morning. I have to say, I'm into it, even though I don't think I have dressed like that since I was in my early twenties. Though I am aware that it is a very specific look, and not for everyone.

But worry not, as being in a club is a collective experience and has always been about the music rather than the fashion. In a club you will not be judged for what you are wearing, as it is so far down the list of anyone's priorities. Assuming that you are going to dance, and not to catwalk for attention, then comfort is key, with a little disco dust of course.

What you are looking for in an outfit here is the party upstairs and the casual below. As Mimi suggested, the shoes need to comfortably take you from dusk to dawn, and then you can turn up the dazzle as you move up the body. I wouldn't recommend jeans in a hot and sweaty club, but if you don't want to expose your legs, and denim is your go-to, then keep them on the loose side. Otherwise, it is shorts and skirts all the way, with bare legs. Don't fret, no one is looking at your legs, I swear.

For the top, have some fun. If you want to keep it simple in a tank, make it a brightly colored one—which also makes you easy to spot when you have seemingly lost everyone you know. Have fun and experiment with the tops you have and never wear, or always fancied but didn't think you would have the opportunity to wear. Play with halter-necks, scarf tops, corsets, backless, barely there, or even the white shirt from your capsule wardrobe knotted at the front, with as much of a bra reveal as you feel content with. Though if you are getting it out, ensure that the bra is a bit more dazzle and a little less comfort, no matter how at home you are on the dance floor.

For something even easier, dip into the dresses in your wardrobe. Ideally the shorter options, though almost every LBD can be appropriately dressed down with a pair of boots or sneakers. Go to town with jewellery and big chunky pieces that make the statement that you want them to, though obviously nothing that is too precious to you. Unless it is only me and everyone I've ever known who tends to leave a club with at least one fewer thing than they arrived with, be that a necklace or a friend. Being less precious applies to your bag too. In an ideal world of handy pockets you wouldn't bring one, but if your look is pocket-free, then opt for a cross-body or belt bag, and keep it small. You really don't need your makeup bag.

Several years ago, also back in Ibiza, I went to a more me-friendly club—you know, one with a crowd of a certain age and plenty of options to sit down, and where it was totally acceptable to leave pre-1 a.m.—and I wore a pair of beloved Adidas sneakers and a slip dress. I felt free and relaxed, and dancing that night I didn't once think about what I was wearing. That is when you know you nailed it, and that you are having a really good time.

DINNER

Much like at a club, at a dinner party your shoes are null and void. But for different reasons (aggressive footsie aside). After you arrive, remove your coat, do a turn of the room and sit down at the table, your shoes don't get seen. Dressing for dinner focuses on what you are wearing from the waist up, so dress from the ears down.

This is where great earrings come into their own, and almost every pair of earrings has the power to dress up almost anything. A simple white T-shirt is party-appropriate with a pair of drop earrings—even just one earring makes the difference if you prefer a little asymmetry, but put a small stud or hoop earring on the other side to prevent people from suggesting you have lost one. I have a couple of pairs of large gold earrings that always attract the right attention. One pair are elongated hoops that almost graze my shoulders, the others are big gold teardrops that envelop my lobes. In fact, I bought the latter pair after sitting next to a woman at a dinner, when I didn't listen to a word she said—I was focused on her earrings. She told me where they were from, and I bought them online then and there at the table.

With a captive dinner audience, consider your neckline. In this book I often harp on about every woman having great shoulders, and how perfect to get them out around the dinner table to serve as a frame to your face. Off-the-shoulder dresses and tops with long sleeves work well as a cheeky but modest cover-up, and even a clean boatneck can be super flattering, though if you feel confident, I love a halter-neck which exposes a bit more skin. This is also the ideal opportunity, if it is your thing, to celebrate your assets. Get them out. Or out as much as is appropriate for the company at your dinner party. A top that plunges to the edge of the table will always draw a gaze, or a silk shirt unbuttoned beyond the center gore of your bra is seductive and yet quietly cool and nonchalant at the same time. Ideally worn with a slowly swinging pendant necklace.

Bright colors and bold prints often work well under low lighting, so don't be afraid to bring them out after dark. While velvet benefits from low lighting as it reduces any potential shine and looks at its most luxurious, I would avoid anything overly embellished, as it tends to be distracting.

Whatever is happening below the table—*fashion-wise, I mean*—is anyone's guess. However, this is not a news anchor or Zoom situation where not a lot of thought goes on below the waist. No, you still need to make a little effort. Jeans and an excellent top

are made for an excellent dinner, but if denim feels too casual, opt for tailored trousers or a relaxed skirt, paired with a heel to stop them feeling too worky.

BIRTHDAY

For my fortieth I organized a dinner for thirty friends. On the invite I wrote "Dress Code: Do me proud." Apparently, this instilled panic in my guests instead of pride, which was not my intention, and resulted in thirty people mainly wearing white T-shirts (the men) and black dresses (the women). Personally, I was in a white fitted dress, which might sound relatively low-key to some, but it was out of my usual comfort zone and I felt bloody delighted with myself.

My dress code may have been too vague for my guests, but whether it is your special day or you are celebrating someone else, you can absolutely go OTT for a birthday, regardless of where it is. Whether it is in a pub, bar, restaurant, club, their living room or a picnic in the park, do yourself proud, do the person of honor proud, and if you think what you have on is too much, add on something else! Take the opportunity to wear that thing you love but never seem to have an occasion to wear. Go all out. Channel Kate Moss on her thirtieth, fortieth and fiftieth birthdays; actually, think of Kate Moss on every single one of her documented birthdays. She knows how to dress for a great time. Personal favorites are the vintage sequinned blue gown she wore for her thirtieth at Claridge's hotel, and the relatively demure feathered black knee-length dress she wore for her twenty-first in LA. Thanks to the sparkle color choice (navy-blue vintage sequins win over gold or silver every time), and the less-is-more approach to feathers, she managed to make both sequins and feathers look chic and not cheap.

If it is your special day, regardless of which milestone you have hit, for they are all milestones, treat yourself to something new and don't worry about needing to justify it. I'm not talking about a shopping marathon down Bond Street here, though if that is how you celebrate, then please may I come to your next party? Instead, it could be a small piece of jewellery, a pair of shoes or a whole new outfit—just a little somethin' somethin' that makes you feel proud of yourself. You made it through another year.

THE FESTIVE SEASON

According to any magazine I pick up, or TV show I turn on, it would appear that any party scheduled between November and New Year's Eve demands sequins, feathers, crystals, bells, whistles and all the velvet you can gather. Now, I am by no means a humbug, but I own not one thing on that list, yet I can turn my hand to holiday dressing rather well. I mean, I say holiday dressing—I obviously mean the one or possibly two parties I attend during that period, which again conflicts with the media suggesting that there is nothing else to do but party for two straight months. So firstly, don't be drawn in by the great parties that you think everyone else has been invited to—they haven't. Secondly, sequins are not mandatory, despite what a window-shopping walk might suggest.

Whether or not this time of year contains a festival that you celebrate, the parties that occur during this season are usually less about religion (though not for all) and more about togetherness and friendship. I think that is always something worth celebrating, just not necessarily, for me, in sparkle and shine. However, I do love a little shimmer on someone else—a little shimmer goes a long, long way—and one of my favorite things to see is someone interpreting that in their own way to bring something unexpected to an outfit. Like a classic black turtleneck covered in crystals and worn with some casual boyfriend-cut jeans; or a white shirt, layered under a grey cashmere sweater, looking preppy, but then paired with a silver metallic high-shine midi pencil skirt. For these are women who have introduced that unpredictable hit of dazzle (thanks, Mimi) into their everyday closet, and not felt the pressure to allow their well-honed personal style to be overwhelmed by a season.

It is at these types of parties that your accessories come out to play and take center stage. As I said above, a little goes a long way, and that also applies to your final touches. Jewellery, bags and shoes can take a casual outfit and transform it into a mini celebration. In fact, consider them your collective fairy godmothers. Once again, those drop earrings—though choose something opulent rather than too subtle—have the gravitas to change a shirt from desk duty to after dark, while a switch out of a work tote to a small clutch suggests something more playful. And heels, well . . . heels literally raise your spirits.

OFFICE

I'm afraid that I can't raise the subject of parties without mentioning the—dreaded by some, beloved by others—office party. However, as much as I have feared them in the past, I think that office parties are an awkward tradition that must be protected at all costs. Plus, they are always more fun than you think they are going to be.

Your work colleagues know who you are sometimes better than your friends. They know your morning routines, eating habits, mood swings, stress levels, tendency to gossip and, of course, your personal style. Well, the style that you care to reveal in the workplace. It is often difficult to surprise your colleagues, but an office party is the opportunity to reveal a little bit more of the off-duty you. Though it does depend on the location. A party in the office space does not tend to encourage a grand reveal of your best party look, but you can still dial it up a little, even by dialling it down. If you have a smart office uniform, then mix it up in denim. Once again, the jeans and a great top combination is probably your best bet here for being comfortable, elevated and not too overdressed.

If in doubt, I really do think it is better to be underdressed than overdressed. To any party. Underdressed does have its limits, of course—it is never acceptable to turn up to a party in your sofa-friendly loungewear. But if you are not sure how dressed up the rest of the guests will be, then best to avoid a gown. If you feel uncomfortable or out of place in what you are wearing, it will make you feel insecure and exposed, and you will want to go home.

If, however, your workplace is splashing out on a lavish space, then be lavish. I used to love nothing more than seeing how co-workers glow-up for a special night out, as seeing someone in their saved-for-good outfit is like having access to a whole new person who is 100 percent themselves.

THE "FUN"DAMENTALS

Based on the above party categories, you actually only need a small number of outfits, and the beauty is that the pieces can mix and match per occasion, *and* you will possibly already own most of them.

THE HIGH/LOW

This is most people's party go-to. It's a safe place, guaranteeing you'll be neither too "done" nor too casual. For most people, it starts with denim. But not your everyday, knocking-around-the-house denim—in the Denim chapter I call them "occasion jeans" and they come into their own here. I like very high-waisted with a wide leg that falls to the floor over heels. They are too long for me to wear day-to-day, thus them being my occasion denim as they need a heel, and the highest of heels require an occasion. Once the bottom half is sorted, it's about creating the party up top. The casual below can handle the dazzle above, so don't be afraid if it seems to conflict. Cropped, bustier, corset, barely there, oversized, modest, printed, bold, subtle, velvet, feathered, ruffled, lace, buttoned up, undone, matt, metallic and everything in between all complement denim.

It works the other way round too. Party below, aloof up top. A narrowly fitted crew-neck sweater, or T-shirt, is taken somewhere different when paired with wide-leg silk trousers or a patent leather pencil skirt.

Alternatively, you can go casual from top to toe and dress it all up with an evening jacket. Again, it is unexpected, and it makes a statement on arrival. Whenever I am in a vintage shop I always search for a jacket, as vintage ones offer up something different,

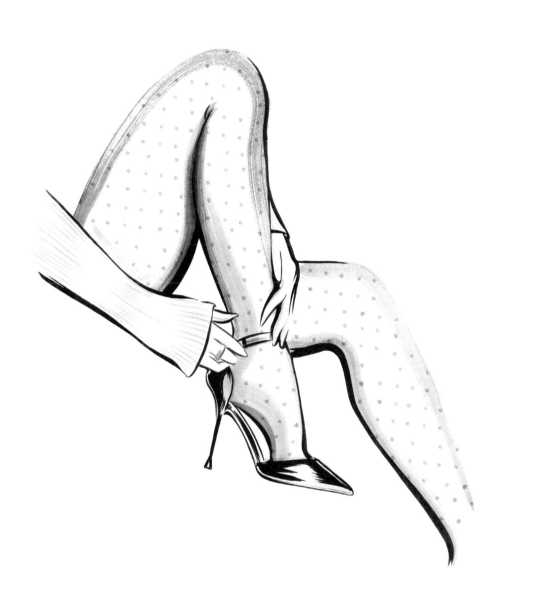

whether that be a cropped silhouette, a beautiful fabric or its own particular narrative. Look for something lighter, as you want to be able to keep it on for as long as possible and not relinquish it to the cloakroom.

THE GO-TO TO GO TO EVERYTHING DRESS

There just needs to be one, and yes, you can wear it as often as you like to parties with the same people and it doesn't matter one bit. This is the dress that isn't a gown but it also isn't something that you would wear to work. It could be your never-let-you-down LBD, or it could be a short A-line dress in your favorite color that makes you smile. It is still significant, and you love how it makes you feel and look. For those who aren't that comfortable dressing up, try something in black, as it won't feel too far out of your comfort zone, and you can push a style, fabric and silhouette in black, whether it be a mini, midi or maxi length. It should be a dress that works throughout the year, and is as at home in a bar as it is at your friend's dining table. But if it is long, make sure that it exposes your arms or décolletage, as it should be a dress that signifies fun and not a dress that suggests you want to hide.

Recently a friend asked me what the consensus on tights is, and I think that tights get a totally undeserved bad reputation. Many people are not comfortable getting bare legs out regardless of the time of year, and tights are a saving grace. They pull you in where you need it and support you elsewhere. My advice would be to embrace that you are wearing them, rather than trying to hide it with a nude version. In which case, if wearing a black dress, wear black tights, or wear colored or white if you really want to make a case for tights. In the winter months, opt for up to 40 denier, as anything above that and you might as well be in leggings. But try a 15 or 20 denier for something more sheer that looks super sexy with heels.

THE SUIT

If you aren't a dress person but want something more polished, a suit does the same thing as the go-to dress. It works for everything and everywhere, and you can wear it as much as you like. Also, it is practically a complete outfit—well, it can be if you opt for just a bra beneath (see below), and you don't even need to worry about a coat with a suit: you are good to go. For something more evening-appropriate, look for a velvet iteration, which gives a 1970s nod but is a true forever purchase. Black, maroon and midnight blue will never be out of style. The jacket should be slightly fitted and single-breasted with one or two buttons, while the trousers shouldn't be too narrow, so ideally straight or with a gentle kick flare. I understand that a flash of a bra can be a risk, so a silk shirt, camisole, tank or that hardworking white T-shirt are perfect alternatives.

THE ACCESSORIES

I have a grey marl T-shirt that I have had for fifteen years. It has been washed so many times that it is practically threadbare, and admittedly the neckline has seen better days, yet I refuse to part with it. For with the right bra underneath—black with lace edging—and great earrings, it is transformed into something perfectly undone, sexy and party permissible.

A good bra or bralette, even if you just see a flash of it, can revolutionize the most basic of outfits, and can even replace a top altogether with the right jacket buttoned over it. Not convinced? Try it—it's less revealing than it sounds.

When it comes to jewellery, necklaces and earrings are fundamental. If you are looking to elevate something for a night out, I would suggest one larger statement choker that sits on your clavicle rather than lots of smaller pieces. All you need is one pair of really good earrings that delight you. For partywear they tend to be the hardest-working piece with very little effort from you. I have a pair I return to again and again (even in the daytime when I need a boost) that are gold and wrap around my lobes. Regardless of what I am wearing, they are the items that receive the most compliments. I also advocate for a sprinkling of rings or a couple of stacks at a dinner party, especially if you are someone who talks with the aid of their hands, as they tend to draw focus in the best of ways.

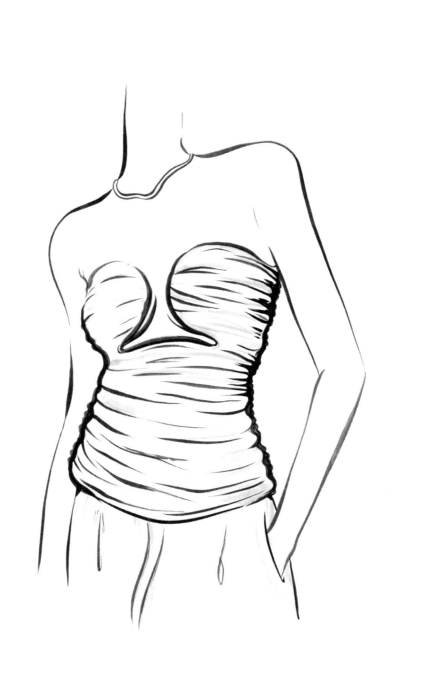

When it comes to bags, the key is to edit your belongings down to the bare minimum and take your smallest bag with you. Regardless of whether it is cross-body, shoulder, belt or clutch, keep it small, and ideally keep it on you. If it isn't going in the cloakroom, you need a hands-free way to avoid leaving it on the side only to never see it again. Call me paranoid or call me experienced.

Finally, the shoes. Other than for clubbing, a party will always bring out a heel for me, but ones that I know I can walk—and definitely dance—in. It might be tempting to buy new shoes for an exciting night out, but you will regret it. Party shoes need to earn their invitation. The same applies to flats, for they can equally hurt you, but the pain is somehow worse as the suffering is less expected. A ballet flat or pointed-toe flat brings just as much confidence—often more—to a look than a heel.

HAVE A CARE

Not to be an immediate party pooper, but party outfits are one of the biggest fashion polluters. There are people out there who will buy a brand-new outfit for every night out and then never wear it again, which is maddening, wasteful and financially insane. Don't do that. You absolutely do not have to buy something new for every invitation— you can always make something work with what you have, and play with different combinations in order to create something new for you. Remember that you are dressing to have a great time; you are not dressing for the other people in the room, so who cares if they have seen it before? Chances are they won't remember.

You may have gathered how I feel about sequins, but it's not just me—they are also terrible for the environment. As they are usually made of plastic and there are all types of synthetics involved, it is likely that they will long outlive all of us. So, if you are drawn to their sparkle and simply cannot resist them, please try to look for vintage pieces, or those made with biodegradable sequins. And make sure that you are buying a piece to wear again and again, forever and ever, as that piece will be your damn legacy. Sequins are literally for life—and well beyond—not just for Christmas.

PARTIES IN BRIEF

1   Find your dazzle-to-comfort ratio.

2   Dress for the occasion.

3   No one is too old for a party.

4   Dress from the top down, not the feet up.

5   Party shoes need to earn their invitation.

6   Festive dressing does not just mean sequins.

7   Embrace unexpected combinations.

8   Accessories are your magic disco dust.

9   Dress for yourself, not for a camera.

10   Being underdressed is always a safer bet than being overdressed.

PREGNANCY

VERONIKA HEILBRUNNER

Content curator, editor, style icon and mother of two on how to create your own maternity style, and how comfort trumps cool every single time.

THE LOWS—AND SOME HIGHS—OF MATERNITY DRESSING

If I was going to advise a newly pregnant woman on the one item of clothing that she needs to buy to get through the next nine months, it would be compression tights.

My eldest son was born in June, and from the beginning of April until that date it was 90 degrees in Berlin. Every. Single. Day. The compression tights were so hot in that heat, but I wore them anyway to stop my feet swelling to comedic sizes and to stop peeing eleven times in the night. I was told that the tights prevent water retention in your legs during the day, which meant I wouldn't have to pee so much, and it worked for me so I am going with it! Towards the end of my pregnancy, I had three go-to outfits. The first was tights teamed with an oversized black or white T-shirt and really big Birkenstocks, as my feet grew from a size 10 to 11½ and I couldn't get any other shoes to fit (it was Birkenstocks or men's sneakers). The next day I would wear a black ribbed tank-top fitted dress with knee-high compression socks—yup, had them too. Then, on the third day, I would be like, "Fuck, the compressions are in the wash," so I would wear some sports shorts and a tank top. I washed everything constantly and literally re-wore the same outfits for months. It was brutal, and I'm not sure how my partner survived it, but I didn't want to invest in any maternity wear—everything "maternity" that I tried on was horrible, and I just wanted to be comfortable.

But even before I reached the point of my three-outfit rotation, pregnancy changed my style completely. I am quite a tomboy and like everything to be a little oversized, which suited the early part of my pregnancy well, when my body started to change. But when everything oversized became a little on the tight side, I had to re-evaluate. I am tall and I have broad shoulders, so when I tried to cover up my big belly in big dresses,

I felt gigantic. Instead, I went the opposite way and decided to try really tight stuff and bought a lot of ribbed dresses, which I never did pre-pregnancy, as I never showed my body in that way.

By the time I was pregnant with my second child, Rihanna had done more for pregnancy dressing than any maternity jeans ever had and it was a new playing field. I was inspired by her and wanted to have fun, get my belly out and just go for it. I wanted to invest some money in a few pieces that were going to make me feel better than I did the first time. During months five to seven you feel kind of cute and cool—it might just be the hormones, but your skin glows and you feel pretty good about yourself. Embrace that time, because before and after you can feel horrible, as there is so much going on and changing. So, I bought clothes that were going to make me feel better when I was feeling dreadful.

From the start, I bought myself nice underwear (when I am not pregnant, I have small boobs, so I don't wear bras). First pregnancy I had no clue how to dress for boobs, but second time around I was prepared for them. Fashion-wise I went tight again, basically the dress equivalent of compression tights. I also wore a lot of crop tops, even though I swore to myself that beyond 2002 I was never going to wear them again. That's the Rihanna effect. My friends, colleagues and followers on Instagram were thrilled that I was finally showing my belly. There are always, sadly, the other people, the ones who asked, "Why would you show that, it's so private?" I mean, have you seen people in the street? But also, come on, it's 2023.

Post-pregnancies, I slowly reverted to my original style. I became fixated with getting my feet back into ballerinas, as I couldn't squeeze my gigantic pregnant feet into a single pair. I was in no rush, but they were my goal: ballerinas, loose-fitting jackets and big jeans. I mean, it's hardly ground-breaking in terms of a look, but it's the opposite of my maternity choices, and it is my style comfort zone. As for the compression tights, they did their job brilliantly, but they are back in the drawer for now.

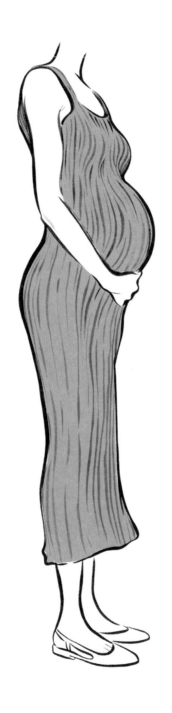

PREGNANCY

For much of my career, most of my colleagues have been women, many of whom have become very close friends. During that time, lots of these amazing women have had amazing children, and I have lived through countless pregnancies—and their changing styles—with them. When one of my friends was eight months pregnant and about to hit a horrific fast-fashion retailer for an outfit to wear to a wedding, I talked her off the ledge, led her away from the cheap and the flammable, and loaned her a very clever and generous dress of my own. I have never been pregnant, so have zero experience of my own to share, and while I feel like I was on the journey with many of my friends, for this chapter I have relied on their advice and wisdom, as well as that of my family and colleagues. My sister: "At least I had boobs to dress for a while— that was nice. Didn't last though." My mum: "As long as you are comfortable and healthy then anything goes." Friends: "It's like the world thinks because you are now pregnant you suddenly love Cath Kidston." The forever stylish, who found it a fun challenge: "Just because you are pregnant doesn't mean you need to lose your style identity, just enjoy evolving it." And those who did not: "This should be a chapter to forget and never talk about again."

One of my brilliant friends and colleagues filmed a style video for NET-A-PORTER when she was nearly five months pregnant with her second child. She advised women in the same condition as her to choose loose jeans with a button fastening so they could undo buttons as the bump grew, and then simply roll down the waistband to accommodate the extra girth. Cut to four weeks later, my brilliant friend and colleague was wearing her one and only pair of maternity jeans, complete with stretchy stomach band, that she had bought under duress the first time around, and when referring to her earlier style advice she said, "What a tit I am—as if that is going to work for nine months." In her defence, the jeans did serve her well earlier in her pregnancy, but as soon as that bump popped, it was a case of either retiring the jeans or swapping them for a really big size. She chose to retire them but pointed out that they will come in handy in the postpartum months, when you can't face your maternity clothes but you're also not ready for your old clothes, so her advice wasn't totally misguided.

I asked a large group of women for their styling tips and tricks: the clothes that kept them sane, the pieces to avoid, how to get through the different seasons when too hot or too cold, and any insight they could pass on. Whether they loved pregnancy or loathed it, the overwhelming consensus is that comfort is everything—but that doesn't mean you have to give up who you are for nine months and beyond. So, from them to you, here are the essentials to dress for work, rest and play, and how to deal with your madly changing body—the downs, but also the ups.

THE ESSENTIALS

First things first, you do not need to leap into maternity gear as soon as pregnancy is confirmed. The blanket advice from everyone I interviewed is to stay out of any official maternity clothing and in your own clothes for as long as possible, and then borrow or buy only what is absolutely necessary. Make concessions for comfort. At first that can be sizing up in pieces that you normally wear, like jeans and trousers, or pulling out the old denim trick: for a little extra give, loop one end of an elastic hair tie around the top waist button of your favorite jeans, then the other end through the button loop, and then back around the button. But that won't last for too long before it becomes uncomfortable.

Many refuse to wear or buy any official "maternity clothes" at all, finding them lacking any style or individuality and even panic-inducing. "Even looking at those ranges it felt so far removed from who I am, like I suddenly had to dress like a totally different person just because I was pregnant," said a friend of her first pregnancy. "Being pregnant doesn't mean you have to lose your identity. There is so much change that comes with impending motherhood that can feel totally overwhelming at the best of times, so it's important to keep true to yourself—your style and how you dress can be fundamental to that."

Much in the same way you can't control other aspects of your pregnancy, be prepared for your body to defy any style preconceptions you might have. "I had this idea of wearing a lot of cute tank tops with light layers over the top, or tight knitted dresses to show off my shape," a colleague told me. "But in reality, there was only a small window of time when I felt like revealing my belly, as before I just looked bloated, and after my boobs got huge, so the proportions didn't work for me. Instead, I opted for oversized sweaters or shirts, a little looser, that made me feel comfortable and cocooned."

In other words, everyone is different, and everyone will tackle their maternity style differently. However, I have compiled a list of saving-grace items of clothing that came up again and again, to help you through even the most uncomfortable of months, and tips on how to style them.

LEGGINGS

Without a doubt, you aren't getting through the nine months without leggings. They are versatile, as you can dress them up for work and evening, or down for the rest of the time. They are comfortable and allow you the freedom to move into all sorts of positions as required. They are supportive but not too restrictive. The advice is to buy two or three sizes upwards of your usual size, but if in doubt, go bigger, as there is nothing worse than being uncomfortable.

Don't be fooled into thinking that you need expensive "fashion" leggings, and instead opt for sport styles. Those intended for yoga or Pilates are preferred over running tights, as they are literally designed for stretching, while running tights can feel too snug. While I don't want to lead you with brands, the leggings that were mentioned on repeat were lululemon's Align, due to the weight, the stretch and the high waist— after all, you are wearing them over the bump and not under it.

For work, wear them with a fitted tank top under an oversized button-down shirt, and throw a longer-line blazer over the top. Pair them with chunky ankle boots or flat knee-highs in the winter, if that feels comfortable on your feet, and generous chunky sandals or ballet flats in the summer, whichever still fit. For play, switch out the shirt for a silk alternative, or just add cocktail earrings. Jewellery is your switch-up maternity saver. And for rest or off-duty time, add a sweatshirt or a knit, and sneakers.

WIDE-LEG TROUSERS OR SHORTS WITH ELASTIC OR DRAWSTRING WAIST

I never thought I would ever write this, but here we go . . . elastic waistbands and drawstrings are crucial. If you aren't relaxed in leggings, wide-leg palazzo trousers are a good alternative. Sitting towards the bottom of the bump, they also allow freedom of movement with less constriction. Look for those with a bit of stretch in the fabric, but nothing too heavy. My friend lived in a pleated pair that had just enough stretch to take her through the pregnancy and comfortably into postpartum.

Style them as you would leggings, but stay on the more fitted side on top rather than oversized, to ensure that the proportions don't overwhelm. If you are happy to get your bump out, sit the waistband of the trousers under the bump, and team with a fitted T-shirt or camisole that clings to the bump above the belly button. If you prefer to keep your bump covered, wear with a longer fitted T-shirt or tank and layer a shirt over. Button the shirt from the neck to the top of the bump and allow the shirt to fall on either side of the bump. Roll the sleeves up to mid forearm to show a little bit of skin.

MATERNITY JEANS

These are mainly discussed as a last resort, and only when nothing else works. Not everyone opts for them, preferring a legging or a trouser. But if denim is usually the foundation of your outfits, being without can be even more challenging when it comes to getting dressed. Maternity jeans don't have the best of reputations, and when friends have worn them they point to the elastic panel with disdain. But they have come a long way, or so I am told. Once upon a time you could only get skinny styles, and that is no longer the case. As with all jeans, you need to try a few before you commit. Look for jeans with straight or loose legs, which might suit you better in

pregnancy than they did before, as they help to balance out proportions. You only need one pair, in either an everyday classic blue wash or black. It doesn't matter if you wear them on repeat. No one will notice or indeed care.

Then style them as you would your jeans pre-pregnancy. Don't feel the need to hide the belly elastic; you don't need to fool people into thinking that you are wearing your regular jeans. Embrace and celebrate the stretch fabric; show it off under a white tank or T-shirt, and swap a cotton shirt for a denim one, as there is something about double denim on a beautiful pregnant woman that looks really youthful and fresh.

KNITTED DRESSES

Ah, the joy of one-piece dressing. Knitted and fitted dresses are a very easy choice to make in the morning, and literally pull you together. If you are happy to reveal your body shape, then a couple of these will see you through. Sleeve or no sleeve is weather- and body-temperature dependent, but longer-length dresses are better, as the bump will pull the hem up. They look great with tights or without, depending on how you feel in them, with boots or loafers in winter, and sneakers or ballet flats in summer. If you need a cover-up, try a shorter denim jacket if running hot or a long coat when colder. Don't worry about being able to close the jacket—if you need extra weather protection, pull on a large scarf, which is also a great way to add some color or print.

As an extra selling point, knitted dresses grow as you grow, so they work perfectly post-pregnancy too. One woman invested in a gorgeous knitted dress in her usual size when she was seven months pregnant, squeezed that bump in for her brother's wedding, and two years later it is still one of her favorite things and she wears it regularly.

WRAP DRESSES

Alternatively, if you aren't convinced by tight dresses, wrap dresses allow room to grow too. Wear the belt above the bump, and either move the belt loops higher or lower, or ask a tailor to remove them completely if you can't do it yourself.

JUMPSUITS AND OVERALLS

Like dresses, jumpsuits and overalls are a favored easy go-to, though look for those in a more relaxed cotton or silk fabric rather than a rigid denim or stiff cotton, and forgo a waistband. Feel free to add a tank or fine knit underneath, and unzip or unbutton from the top down to feel content (I am told that zippers are less time-consuming for the numerous toilet breaks that pregnancy brings with it).

BUTTON-DOWN SHIRTS

Some women can wear their pre-pregnancy shirts, leaving them open or only buttoned from top to sternum, and either layering fitted pieces underneath or having lovely taut skin peeking out. But if you need something more generous or want to button your shirt all the way down, look for styles with split side seams to give you the flexibility to move and grow in them. Alternatively, borrow from any men in your life if they offer a larger fit. You can return them after, if they are lucky.

BIG KNITS AND SWEATSHIRTS

When it comes to comfort, nothing beats a great big sweater. Cocooning, reassuring, reviving and protecting, it's no wonder we reach for them when we are feeling a little vulnerable. They really come into their own during pregnancy, so take advantage of them, and feel free to live in them. Some will feel better in oversized, but something a little more fitted over your belly might make you feel less boxy, especially when worn with leggings so you aren't overwhelmed by material. Keep to natural wool or cotton fabrics if you can, or layer a tank or T-shirt underneath, which will also help with constantly fluctuating temperatures. (Can I just take this opportunity to say that my friends have really sold pregnancy to me?)

T-SHIRTS AND TANK TOPS

The foundation layers remain fundamental in pregnancy. As with leggings, choose basics that are two sizes up, and wear them under shirts and sweaters or on their own as you feel comfortable. Again, you only need the bare minimum, so I would recommend a couple of white and black ones in breathable fabrics—either cotton, light wool or silk, or technical sports options.

SILK PAJAMAS

Turns out there is a reason that you gift every single mother-to-be a pair of pajamas before they set off to give birth, as that is what they want to live in for the last stage, and then long postpartum. Drawstring waistbands, buttons to be undone and ignored, and a fabric that is hard-wearing but feels luxurious.

COATS AND BLAZERS

If you have oversized blazers, coats or jackets in your closet already, wonderful. Coats, especially longer ones, become a great cover-up when pregnant, and serve to hide whatever you are wearing underneath (if you want to). Again, it's not about fastening them, but you might like to wrap them and, if an option, belt them over the bump, not under it. Men's coats and jackets also come in handy, and don't worry if the shoulders seem too big on you—they will help balance out the bump.

VACATION ESSENTIALS

If you are fitting in a relaxing beach vacation pre-birth—as you should—you shouldn't need to buy much that you either don't already own or that you won't wear again. The drawstring shorts or trousers I mentioned above are also a hot-weather savior and look chic teamed with a matching shirt. Basically, like pajamas, with the same level of well-being. Then one or two soft cotton summer dresses that are light and easy and have loads of room to grow into; if you don't already have them, I promise you will wear them well beyond that one vacation. Finally, the swimwear: to two-piece or not to two-piece? Well, you could say that if you don't normally wear a two-piece, now is the time to try it. You have a big, beautiful, tight belly—why not show it off in a bikini? But if you decide on a one-piece, I also hear that when it comes to Hunza G, one size really does fit all. So it might feel like an investment but, again, it will last long beyond the pre-birth trip.

LINGERIE

"I knew Rihanna was pregnant before she announced it," Jodie Turner-Smith told me. "When she accepted an award in Barbados, I saw her and knew that they were pregnant titties. I think the breast reaches its peak in pregnancy! The female body is a wonder to behold, and those hormones are incredible. There ain't no titty like a pregnant titty." Which is true, as for the women in my life there were those suddenly trying to manage big breasts for the first time ever, and those whose already large breasts became almost unruly. Reading between the lines, I think the former had a better experience. But neither is easy. Dressing a new bump, bigger hips and bottom is one thing, but also having to fit new boobs into the equation and get used to them can take a little longer.

Buy nice but comfortable bras (if you want to wear them) that make you feel good about your body. There are lots of T-shirt bras that offer support, have a huge range of sizes, look great and aren't going to break the bank. Get measured as you grow to ensure that you are wearing the right fit, as badly fitting bras are distraction enough even when not dealing with pregnancy body changes.

Although there are maternity underwear out there, the general consensus is that you don't need them. However, as one friend put it: "You just have to resign yourself to the fact that it's French underwear no more and granny panties galore." We all have those panties that we gravitate towards on certain days, the ones that sit low on the hips and are lovely soft cotton; well, by the sounds of it, those are the ones you are going to rely on, so maybe get a couple more pairs.

Do try to lean into all the changes, and marvel at your body rather than feel alienated by it. Once you feel at ease with it—even those unruly breasts—enjoy it, as it won't last forever, and you'll be back to your new normal before you know it.

"On a good day, seeing my body change to create new life was a beautiful thing, and I felt like a superhero," my superhero colleague told me. "I was less precious about how I looked, and while I still wanted to look polished, I was less worried about the details and that was rather liberating."

THE PICK-ME-UPS

I know you aren't always going to feel your best during pregnancy, especially towards the end when sleep eludes you, and you are feeling overwhelmed and exhausted. The times when pulling on a trusted outfit isn't quite enough to make you feel better, or together. That is when you need to have your little easy treasures that will lift your spirits. For me this is always a pair of earrings, which is a quick fix and doesn't involve sizing issues when pregnant. They immediately boost your look and, in hand, your mood. Alternatively scarves can do the same thing, especially in your favorite color, and they also offer a little security if you feel like hiding your bump on certain days when you are understandably feeling a bit vulnerable.

IN OR OUT?

When Jodie appeared as a guest on *The Graham Norton Show* in 2020, she wore a crop top. "There's a certain point in your pregnancy when your belly gets really fucking huge," she says. "I wanted my belly out, and it's a lot easier to have it out than to cover it up, because it doesn't fit in anything. Not in anything cute anyway! I think the pregnant body is so beautiful, so I wore my little crop top as it felt best on my body." Naturally the internet trolls rolled into action. "This may be an unpopular opinion," one wrote, "but I don't think pregnant women should wear outfits that expose their bellies." Nothing quite brings out other people's opinions like other people's pregnancies. Jodie responded with a picture of herself in the outfit, and the caption, "Gives zero fucks about your disdain for pregnant women's bodies on British television." Hear, hear.

Two years later, when Rihanna announced her first pregnancy, she wore an open vintage Chanel coat with ripped jeans, her beautiful belly exposed and adorned with jewels. Looking phenomenal. As Veronika celebrated earlier in the chapter, RiRi's looks continued to redefine maternity dressing until she gave birth, and did so again with her second pregnancy in 2023. "When I saw women dress during their pregnancy [in the past], I'd think that was the only way," Rihanna said at the time. "So I challenged myself to push it further and just have fun." Fun it was. Bralettes and low-slung relaxed trousers, baggy jeans that followed my colleague's advice of unbuttoning the fly (I mean, if it works for Rihanna . . .), naked dresses and lingerie, form-fitting bodysuits and dresses, miniskirts, big boots and big bare belly—every single time she looked sensational. You could almost smell the cinders as women around the world burnt their maternity dresses in response. "Thanks to Rihanna pregnancy is so much more visible," says Veronika. "Pregnant women are happy to show their bodies and feel more comfortable with the changes."

Of course, Rihanna is Rihanna, and hers isn't the everyday woman's pregnancy journey, but there are lessons to be learned and inspiration to be had. First and foremost, if you want to get your belly out, get it out. It is no one's business but your own. If you want to celebrate your body, as we should all feel comfortable to do, whether pregnant or not, then please celebrate it as much and as often as you can. "What it is really about is that we need to normalize wearing what makes you feel good in the moment and make that OK," says Jodie. "Once I saw a picture of Rihanna and she was out with her partner late at night, and she was wearing sweats and I thought, 'There we go, sometimes that's all you want to do. Just put on something big and cozy, to just hug that body and tell it it's safe.'"

POST-PREGNANCY

The fourth trimester (the twelve weeks following the birth) is really an extension of the third, but now more than ever comfort is key. Loungewear is integral, as are open tops or easy-access dresses if you decide to breastfeed. Stick with natural fabrics because the postpartum night and day sweats are no joke, and also choose to wear items that wash easily and dry quickly, as newborns are stain generators.

Loose waistbands are a must, and ones that you can easily adjust to a position of comfort. Those sweaters you relied on during pregnancy will remain key, but layer over camisoles or nursing tank tops if necessary.

"I didn't leave my house properly for two weeks after I had my son, so that first fortnight was a whirlwind of PJs and tracksuits," a colleague recalled. "But soon after that it was important to reclaim my identity and return to my old wardrobe, where I could."

Most moms will start losing some weight naturally, and the day will come when you are feeling comparatively you again, so you decide to try on your old jeans. Do not do this. It is too soon. Instead, revert to the staples you bought mid-pregnancy that were a couple of sizes bigger. It's not maternity wear, and it offers a good in-between capsule look that will make you feel better about yourself and your new body that just did a marvellous thing. No one needs a pair of jeans to make them feel bad about themselves. You'll get back into them when you do, or maybe you won't—there is no rush, it doesn't matter and you should feel no pressure.

HAVE A CARE

Like the advice that new moms ask for, maternity wear should be passed on. Borrow what you need and then pass it on to friends who need it next. Even if you are planning another child, there will be enough maternity jeans or social-life-saving jumpsuits in circulation for you to borrow then too. Ask friends for pieces before buying new, or search marketplaces for anyone else selling or giving away their maternity clothing. Yes, it is important to feel like you, and be true to your personal style, but that doesn't mean you need to buy a whole new pregnancy closet.

Additionally, rental services are a great source if you need a dress for a special event that you are only going to wear once.

Everyone I spoke to, from the ages of twenty to eighty and beyond, told me that you really don't need a lot of clothing to get you through the nine months. For the first three you can mainly wear your own pieces, just with a little give and room; the middle three take a bit more wiggle room and adjusting; and in the final three you just want to wear whatever you feel comfortable in. The one positive that most moms mentioned, regardless of how they felt about maternity dressing, was that in the end they appreciated the edit and not having to think hard about getting dressed. No matter how stylish you are, you only need a small handful of outfits. Enjoy the edit.

PREGNANCY IN BRIEF

1   Comfort is essential.

2   Don't plan your maternity style in advance—like everything else, that is also out of your control.

3   If you feel good, chances are you will look good.

4   If you want to get your belly out, get it out.

5   Your own jeans will only work for so long, regardless of what stylists on the internet say.

6   Try to stay true to your own personal style if you can. You are pregnant, but you are still you.

7   Learn to love leggings.

8   A knitted dress can take you through nine months of work, rest and play, and still be ready for more.

9   Borrow from the (bigger) boys.

10   If in doubt, ask: what would Rihanna do?

WINTER

OPRAH WINFREY

Global media leader, talk show host, producer, actor, philanthropist and author
on why she is never happier than she is in cashmere, with a stack of books to read,
in front of a roaring fire.

THE APPRECIATION OF CASHMERE

I prefer winter over summer, because of cashmere.

When I was a young girl growing up in Mississippi, reading *Seventeen* magazine, they used to run these features of clothing items that every girl should have. On that list was a cashmere sweater. Now, I didn't even know what cashmere was, but the idea of having a cashmere sweater was the most exciting thing for me. I remember thinking, "Whenever I grow up and get a job, I am going to get a cashmere sweater." Of course, when I got my first job, and held my first paycheck, a cashmere sweater was out of the question. Many years—and paychecks—later, I still love the comfort of a lovely cashmere sweater. But the joy is more symbolic than anything, as it stems from not being able to have one as a kid.

I have passed on my passion for cashmere to others, too. At one point, there were twenty students at college from the Oprah Winfrey Leadership Academy for Girls studying in the United States at the same time. I invested in a hundred cable-knit cashmere sweaters from Ralph Lauren, and every year when the girls got good grades, I would send them a cashmere sweater in celebration.

For me, the power of clothes is their ability to express who you are and how you are feeling on any given day or occasion. It's an outward expression that is always about being grounded in one's self. But I also want to express my joy, my delight, my calmness, my ease and always my comfort. And I tell you now: there is no such thing as *too* comfortable.

First of all, wearing a really lovely tracksuit, that has some shape and structure, is my favorite thing to wear around the house. Though that's if I am not staying in my PJs all day, as—of course—the best thing in the world is to stay in your PJs all day. HANRO cotton pajamas to be specific—tops and bottoms. I have stacks of them. When the weather is bad in California, I am the only person in town who wants it to continue, because the combination of HANRO cotton PJs, a lovely blanket, building a fire, and a stack of books to get through, well, Holy Moses . . .

I am most comfortable in clothes that remind me of pajamas. But I can be wearing sweats on the bottom, add a white shirt on top and I look presentable and show that I am taking things seriously. I treasure cashmere, but my favorite item of clothing is a white shirt. Nobody did them better than Gianfranco Ferré in the 80s and 90s, and I still have ten shirts that Ferré made. They are my favorite space to go to in my closet. I love a crisp white shirt—the crisper it is, and the stiffer the collar, the better. They lift you and make you look fantastic. When I need to feel cocooned, I have a long, buttoned shirt that belonged to [film director] Mike Nichols, a dear, lovely friend of mine. Diane Sawyer gave it to me at his passing, and if I am feeling blue or if I want to feel embraced, I put that on.

I won't say that I am a fashionista, but I will say this: during the twenty-five years of the *Oprah* show, I wore a *lot* of color. Everyone said that I needed to pop when I was on television. When I ended the show, I got rid of almost all of the color in my closet—I now own a single red sweater. I have a closet of neutrals, which makes getting dressed very easy. I have two cashmere onesies, one in taupe and one in rose beige, which Donna Karan made twenty-five years ago. I tried to get her to repeat them years later, as they are like wearing a sock over your whole body.

Oh my God, when it is cool enough, that is what I am wearing—a cashmere onesie with cashmere socks.

WINTER

I grew up in the Highlands of Scotland, so I know a thing or two about dressing for cold weather. Unlike some of my tougher friends who grew up in the North of England, Highlanders aren't the type to go to the local club (club is an exaggeration) dressed to the nines with no coat on ready to immediately fill the dance floor. Call us softies, or sensible, but we hit that club (community center) ready to fill that cloakroom. Growing up with the importance of layers, vests, sweaters, woolly tights, thick socks, sensible boots, coats for all weather possibilities, electric blankets and hot water bottles drilled into me for years is probably why I love dressing for beach vacations so much. However, while many of us might loathe the cold weather, boy does it result in some brilliant clothes.

Come on, let's face it, vacation wear is great and all, but it will never, ever give you that feeling of comfort and protection like a big sweater can. A knitted sweater can make us feel consoled if we are sad, it can soothe us when we are sick, and it can make us feel enveloped and safe after a crappy day. A bikini wishes it had so much power.

Similarly, I am sure that you will have often heard, or read on some social platform or another, someone declaring that coat-and-sunglasses weather is a favorite way to dress. I have to say I agree. There is something about a sunny but coldly crisp day, one that requires both wrapping up warm and adding a summer essential, that puts a spring in your step even in the midst of winter. In the UK we might get about four of these days a year, but the sheer joy of stepping outside only to run back for sunglasses is enough to warm your core for longer.

In cold months, we need to lean on our clothing for preservation but also for positivity, and there is an art to dressing "up" for winter that will stop you from feeling down. It's about ensuring that you have the essentials, and knowing when to—and how to—wear them that will make you feel ready for all weather eventualities, from the "Oh, it is surprisingly mild for the time of year," through to "Oh my God, it's deathly out there, let's hibernate till the great thaw."

WINTER

SWEATERS

I am going to start with sweaters, as over many, many years I have proudly built up a core collection suitable for all occasions and temperatures. I have also (mainly) saved them from moths, but more on those evil little devils later. This may sound like a humble, or not so humble, brag, but finding the right sweaters doesn't happen overnight. You really must put the work in to overcome itchiness, unflattering hem lengths, sleeves that are too long or too short, the endless pilling that some knits torture you with, too heavy a knit, or too light, the ones that make you sweat regardless of how cold it is, and those that were once perfect but now are ruined by overzealous washing. I have literally been there, done that, got (and rehomed/ruined/lost) the sweater.

You don't need lots of sweaters, as regardless of how many you have, you will return to the same ones repeatedly. But you do need enough in rotation that you don't ruin them through overwear. I have an oversized navy Aran cashmere-blend knit that I love. I got it about eight years ago, and for the first three or four winters I wore it over and over. It worked as well with silk trousers and earrings for business-casual winter dinners as it did with jeans, sneakers and a bomber jacket. It also worked well every single night I came home to a cold flat and put it on to keep warm while having dinner on the sofa. Thanks to careless eating and other general carelessness, that sweater is now resplendent with mystery soup stains, thread pulls, thinning elbows and repeat pilling, and would no longer be welcome at a business-casual winter dinner. However, I still love that sweater, and when I am feeling unwell that is the item I reach for, as it's no longer pretty but it sure is practical. When talking sweaters, practical is the magic word.

The sweaters that you need should fall into the following categories: light, medium or heavy, but also work, rest or play. For sweaters aren't just for casual; even the simplest style can be the perfect partner for a statement skirt or pair of trousers for evening. These sweaters usually fall into the light or medium sections, ideally with a fitted turtleneck or classic crew neckline. These sweaters are clever, for while they dress down the OTT, they can also dress up the plain and simple. A cream knit will do wonders for blue denim, whereas a black or grey turtleneck can make any outfit look sleek. Recently I wore a pair of oversized blue jeans with an ivory mohair sweater to the office, and I don't think I have had more compliments for an outfit, both on the day and even a week later when someone sidled up to me in the work kitchen to ask where each piece was from. The jeans I had worn multiple times before, but it was the sweater's debut outing, and it made the look. I obviously didn't tell any of the admirers that I have had to take a lint roller to my entire house due to that sweater, or that the tiny bits of flying fluff jeopardize my contact lenses, because it is one of the softest and most comfortable items I own, while also giving new life to well-loved and worn pieces. This is a sweater that falls into the heavy category but also the work and play boxes. Heavy sweaters are tricky, as you can't often fit a coat comfortably over the top, but if you can, you end up overheating very quickly. They should almost be treated as coats or jackets in themselves, as before the weather dips from cold to bitter and freezing, these are great items to put on as the final layer to head out.

Knitwear is also a great place to experiment with color and pattern; after all, when it is freezing outside you need a little something-something to bring some joy. I am not talking novelty sweaters here—they are reserved for a festive dare and nothing else—I am talking about knits that are bright colors, striped, checkerboard, patchwork, leopard, camouflage and anything else that warms your soul. I have a red sweater with a deep V-neck that I reach for when I am in a bad mood, but for it to have its full mood-enhancing power I must pair it with a white tank underneath, a certain pair of jeans in a pale blue wash, gold earrings and a pair of chunky Chelsea boots. That is the winning combination. I think it is easy to dress down sweaters, but the beauty is in dressing them up, and those that are patterned or bright look more elevated when you make more of an effort.

When it comes to all sweaters, try to avoid synthetics, even a low-percentage blend. They may wash well, but you want a sweater that will keep you warm, not make you sweaty. If you try on a sweater and it makes you itch, take it off immediately. Do not buy it, or if you have, return it. An itchy sweater will *always* be an itchy sweater and it is too high a price to pay, even if you love everything else about it. The speculative cost of cashmere may panic you, but you can get great-quality cashmere in some beloved high-street stores that is worth investigating, especially in the men's department if you are looking for a looser fit.

COATS

Ah, our trusty winter saviors. We don't always give coats the glory they deserve, but they are up there with some of the hardest-working clothes we own. For not only are they designed to keep us warm and dry (I am talking winter coats here, not evening coats), they also disguise what we are wearing beneath, and serve to make us look put together and practical in a flash. Do you think that elegant-looking woman on the school run, wearing that lovely buttoned-up long coat and scarf, isn't wearing an old hoodie beneath, one that she grabbed off her bedroom chair before leaving the house? You will never know, as that is the beauty of the coat.

A coat is always worth investing in, because if you buy it correctly and look after it properly, you will have it forever. But you should never buy a coat when you need one, as when the temperature plummets, it may already be too late to find the one you want. Most stores have their coats in stock from September, and I don't care if you aren't going to need to wear that coat till late October or November. Buy the coat before you need it, hang it away and then smugly pull it out when everyone else is desperately searching for their size up and down the country.

Like everything else we wear, one coat does not fit all; you must find the one that is right for you and your lifestyle. But the one thing that applies to all coats is this: if there is a vent on the back of the coat that is closed with cross-stitches, *please* cut them off before wearing. They are meant to be removed.

CITY COAT

Also known as the long-tailed coat, when bought in a neutral color this will be a forever classic. You will never regret buying this coat and can be confident that it will never fall out of style. I promise. Long, lean and just-fancy-enough, this coat is perfect for work, elegant enough for evening and also suits being dressed down with a hoodie for casual. It can do it all, but naturally fit is everything. Opt for a more restrained shoulder width; even if you buy it during a time when strong 80s shoulders are a thing, they won't be forever, but you want your coat to be. Try it on with a medium-weight sweater beneath, as it is unlikely that you will need anything heavier, to ensure you have enough room to move your arms freely and that the armholes don't feel restrictive. If you are unsure on a size, it is better to go up rather than down. Single-breasted with medium-width collar and lapels is more universally flattering on most body shapes, and if you don't want to go all the way in ankle length, mid-calf is a happy medium and more elongating than a coat that hits the knee. If this coat has pockets that are stitched together, best to leave them closed, as any temptation to stuff those pockets with gloves and phones will ruin the line.

PUFFER AND QUILTED

It is possible to be functional and fancy, but, when it comes to a puffer, practicality should be central. After all, why try to make it something it isn't and doesn't need to be? A puffer is one of the warmest coats you can wear, especially those with a natural down insulation rather than synthetic, and they are also lightweight and perfect for layering. Depending on the size of your puffer of choice, it can be worn as a layer under a coat, or as the outer itself. If compact, it should slip easily under a peacoat, parka or scarf coat, for extra lining. But if the puffer is more of a girthy statement, make it the showpiece—a walking duvet will keep you very toasty indeed.

PEACOAT

The peacoat is like the child of the city coat and a parka, for it is a little on the elegant side, but also sensible. The ideal peacoat should be double-breasted with wide lapels and come no lower than the under curve of your bottom; it should also fit narrow to your body, but not fitted. The peacoat's origins are in the navy, so military details are common, but those without epaulettes and brass buttons will have longevity. I think they look their best when paired with a chunky funnel-neck sweater poking out of the strict neckline.

LEATHER

I am including the leather coat in the list, as I know that for some people, they are an essential. However, I will tell you that no one is kept warm by a leather coat. They have that amazing quality where they are too hot for summer but too cold for winter. A leather coat has a window in October for about three days, if it doesn't rain, when the temperature will be ideal for it. Before and after that point it is rendered useless. Faux leather is the same, but worse in that it is non-breathable, so even during those three days in October you will be sweaty rather than satisfied.

PARKA

I'm not sure what it is that I have against parkas, but I hate them. Maybe I have a long-buried childhood trauma in which I was forced to wear one, as otherwise I have no idea where my loathing comes from. I understand that they have their purpose, but I am yet to meet one that I don't find completely depressing. Maybe it is the length? That mid-thigh hit will do you few favors if you are not 6 feet tall, and even then, I am unconvinced. Or maybe it's that they suggest that the wearer is active, busy and leads a lifestyle that has no time for anything other than the very down-to-earth, and that the pockets are guaranteed to be full of poo bags? Although there is an argument to be made for the hood.

Now, if you have a parka and that is your coat for life, then you do you. You're wrong, but you do you. I am sure it is perfect for all those dog walks, and your life is much more active than mine.

SCARF COAT

Born in Stockholm—where they know how to dress for a freeze—and designed by TOTEME, the scarf coat and the brand are getting a special mention here, for this is a coat that generated multiple newspaper and magazine columns, and a bonkers amount of Google searches, since it appeared on the market in the winter of 2021. Instantly recognizable for its oversized silhouette, inbuilt fringed collar scarf and blanket-stitch edging, it has become something of a fashion favorite, and has "inspired" many, many copycats. Now I am nothing if not a fashion cliché, and I very luckily have one of these and so understand why it became a phenomenon. With the built-in scarf it is practically a two-for-one purchase; it is warm and snug on its own, but the generous size allows you to layer up beneath too; and it is smart enough to elevate everything else you wear with it, but also doesn't look confused over casual sportswear. I live in this coat for three straight months at least.

SHEEPSKIN

An absolute forever piece, as sheepskin coats are built to last. Durable, practical and stylish, the sheer volume makes them a great coat statement. I have one that is a biker-jacket style, and when I wear it I don't need to wear anything heavy underneath, as it does all the work of keeping me warm. I do find, though, that the sleeves can be quite restrictive, and if I am on the phone for longer than five minutes when wearing it, my hand tends to go numb. Ah, the suffering for fashion. So do check you can easily move in it. There are very oversized styles, but I would recommend that you look for something slightly narrower, whether long or short, as you will get more wear out of it. Big is great, but you will only pull it out on the very, very cold days, and a sheepskin is an investment that you will want to wear as often as possible. They will dress up even the most casual loungewear, but they can also hold their own with an evening dress.

WINTER

LAYERS

Once you have all the pieces required, the trick to sensible winter dressing is layering. I am not sure why the idea of layering disheartens and intimidates people so much; it really is simply a case of trial and error. What is the worst that can happen? You get too hot, you take something off; you get too cold, you put something else on. Nothing to be scared of. But, to gently guide you in lessons in layering, I have put together some combinations that work for me and are easy to achieve.

TURTLENECK + HOODIE

A lightweight fitted turtleneck under a generously cut hoodie gives a sportswear piece a more polished finish.

TURTLENECK + SHIRT + SWEATER

Again, take the same fitted turtleneck sweater, button up a loose shirt on top (not fitted), leaving just the top button undone and a couple at the bottom, then pull a crewneck sweater over both. Pull the shirt collar to sit over the sweater's neckline, and allow the shirttails to hang out beneath the sweater's hem.

TURTLENECK + JACKET + JACKET

This is an autumn favorite of mine, when it is too cold for just a denim jacket, or just a bomber, but not quite coat weather yet, so I combine them. I have a cropped, fitted denim jacket that is perfect for layering over light knits, and under slightly larger jackets with breathable fabric.

JACKET + COAT

I will often substitute a jacket for a sweater instead, I think mainly to get as much wear out of my jackets as possible. Again, a denim jacket works for something more casual, and a bit of blue denim does add a freshness to winterwear, but a blazer or leather jacket also suits if it isn't too bulky.

Obviously a long city coat is ideal, as the hemlines won't compete with each other, but if trying this with a peacoat, puffer or scarf coat, make sure that the jacket beneath is shorter.

COAT + COAT

It's official: it's freezing. You don't want to leave the house as it is all looking a bit *The Day After Tomorrow* out there, but you have to, so there is only one thing for it. Well, two actually: the double coat. Now the proportions here are everything. I do this with a short belted puffer that is down-filled, so isn't too heavy, and pop my scarf coat over the top. It still allows freedom of movement, and I don't look like the Michelin man (not that that is a point of bother when there is a chilly wind). Wool can only do so much on its own, as elegant as it is; sometimes it needs that extra layer of practicality to help seal in the warmth and keep out the cold.

ACCESSORIES

For years, my mum, siblings and I haven't bought Christmas presents for each other. It was a unanimous decision, and presents are bought for nieces, nephews and grandkids instead. However, one year it was just going to be my mum and me on Christmas morning, and as the thought of no presents was too depressing, I suggested we buy something for each other. I went to three different stores for three different presents (I have either all the chill when it comes to buying presents and buy nothing, or no chill at all and go totally over the top; there is no middle ground), excited for Mum to open her gifts. On the morning in question, we exchanged gifts, and she was thrilled. I opened my beautifully wrapped present to discover a black cashmere snood, which matched the one Mum had bought herself at a local craft fair a year or two prior. I remembered as she had complained about the price for just as long. "I know how much you admired it," said Mum. "So, I wanted to give it to you." Mum hadn't bought me a matching snood, she had wrapped up and given me *her* snood. For Christmas. Now, admittedly, I was an ungrateful little sod for a moment or two (sorry, Mum), but it turns

out that that gift has become one of the most worn items in my wardrobe. It is toasty, versatile and chic, and I would be lost (and cold) without it.

Winter accessories are integral for practical, keeping-warm reasons, but aesthetically they are also a quick and easy way to update a look, or to play with color and print. My winter coats are, for the most part, black, but my scarves include a big hot-pink mohair one, which brings me joy every time I slip it around my neck, and a black, red and caramel striped one, which I think adds a cerebral air to my look, in a similar way to a pair of glasses. Admittedly I own one single black beanie, as I look certifiable in a colored or quirky hat, but I do appreciate a flash of color on others, and even think there is a time, place and person for a bobble hat, but that sure as hell ain't me either! Same with gloves: I am a black leather pair kinda girl, but I am drawn to those who have matched their gloves to their hats and scarves, or simply have chosen a colorful pair to brighten up a miserable winter's day. Color truly comes into its own in the cold and the grey, and it not only brings optimism to the person wearing it but is absorbed by those around too, so even a little goes a long way.

HOW TO TIE A SCARF

I have just fallen into a YouTube black hole of scarf-tying videos that would suggest you need to be a weaver or professional sailor to achieve the knots, which seems unnecessary. So instead, I am going to keep this simple and classic for you, and for myself. Firstly, come early autumn and the debut scarf outing of the season, I like the plain drape. Just a scarf hanging loosely around your neck offering a little bit of extra warmth in those days when it could go Baltic or balmy in a moment. I especially like this when worn with a lighter jacket, be that denim, leather or a bomber. Next, and this is my colder weather go-to tie, is to wrap the scarf around my neck to form a loop with the ends falling equally on either side at the front, which I tuck into my coat or knot together in the front. If it is really cold, and the scarf is long enough, I wrap it around twice. Alternatively, one that offers equal warmth but looks a little sleeker is to fold it in half, twisting it if you like, then wrap it around your neck and pull the ends through the loop. Pull it tight enough to secure it, but not too tight obviously. This is how the newsreaders on TV used to wear theirs, and as a kid I thought they looked like the chicest people I had ever seen. I still stand by this.

THERMALS

Whenever I return to the Highlands I never, ever bring the right clothes with me. It is always colder than I am prepared for, regardless of the time of year that I have returned, and I always end up borrowing something of my mum's. From December to March, that is usually her thermals. If you are visiting a cold climate, or know that cold weather is coming to you, get yourself down to Uniqlo and stock up on HEATTECH. Thermal vests or long-sleeved T-shirts in black and white are essential, as are leggings, gloves, hats and socks. You don't need many, but you will never regret what you buy.

HAVE A CARE

Winter clothes might be some of the best clothes, but they are also the most troublesome. They are some of the biggest, so they take up the most space; they are also the tastiest if a moth's taste levels are to be trusted; they are the most vulnerable to wash; and they pill and molt. But the care is worth it to preserve their lifespan.

STORAGE

I am not one of those people who swap out their summer clothes for winter clothes, and then perfectly store everything away. Everything is in its place all year round, apart from some T-shirts that get shoved to the back of a shelf as some sweaters move forward. I keep all sweaters folded, as hanging them can lead to them stretching and losing their shape.

All coats are hanging in the closet and not out in hallways where they can fade in direct sunlight or get attacked by moths when I am not paying attention. My more precious coats are in garment bags, while others are hanging not too squashed on wooden hangers when not in use.

All winter accessories are also kept with the heaviest of knits, with gloves inserted inside my winter hat (yes, I am adorable), as there is nothing worse than finding just one glove in October and waiting another month for the other to show up.

MOTHS

Nothing makes my heart sink faster than a moth erratically fluttering around my closet, but nothing makes me act faster either. I have tried everything over the years, from conkers to moth strips. I might have been using them incorrectly, but I never caught a moth on one of those strips. But now I think I have cracked it (she writes while touching all the wood she can find). I am using a ludicrous number of cedar wood rings, on hangers, in drawers and placed inside almost every sweater I have on the cupboard shelves. Now I really, really don't want to tempt fate, but in three winters I haven't discovered new holes. You do have to replace the rings every six months, but they are relatively inexpensive, especially in comparison to invisible mending. I also have wool coats in moth-proof hanging bags, and they are also doing OK. But excuse me while I quickly check on them . . .

PILLING

You can't prevent it, but when it happens tackle it quickly. A little pilling can become all-over pilling in a blink. You can avoid it by washing knits together and on a very gentle setting with a specific wool detergent, but pilling wear and tear is inevitable. Invest in a cashmere comb or electric fabric shaver, and very gently pull it across the knit. Please do not do it with an at-home razor; you might think that it's the same thing but it is not, and the knitwear will not survive. I sadly speak from idiotic experience. Removing pills always takes longer than you think, so don't do it when in a hurry or the fabric will pay for your impatience.

WASHING

I used to have all my sweaters dry-cleaned, for which I would like to apologize to my bank account, my sweaters and the environment—not necessarily in that order. Then my local dry-cleaners closed, and rather than test out others, I turned to handwashing everything instead. I gingerly tested out the handwash setting on my washing machine, and ever since that first load came out cleaner and not teeny-tiny, all sweaters are popped in the wash with a handwash gentle detergent, and I have never looked back. Never spin dry, and try to dry flat. Some creasing is inevitable, but I have found that steaming is better than ironing. However, if you don't have a steamer then put a damp dish towel between the iron and the knit, and make sure the iron isn't set too hot. You also don't need to wash your sweaters after every wear; if they just need a little freshening, there are plenty of environmentally sound clothes sprays on the market that are the clothing equivalent of dry shampoo.

Ensure that you are regularly adding your gloves, hats and scarves to the wash too—they don't wash themselves, you know. But if your gloves are leather, wipe them with a damp cloth while you are wearing them, to make sure the leather keeps the shape of your hands.

Finally, dry-clean your coats after each winter. Don't look at me like that; that is a perfectly reasonable request!

WINTER IN BRIEF

1   Being warm is more important than showing off any outfit and freezing.

2   Winter clothes are the best clothes.

3   The perfect sweater is the clothing equivalent of a cuddle.

4   Sometimes a men's sweater is the answer.

5   Coats can hide a multitude of style sins.

6   Don't wait till you need a coat to buy a coat.

7   Hats, scarves and gloves are not self-cleaning.

8   Layering is not difficult.

9   Tying a scarf shouldn't require a three-minute YouTube video.

10 You will never regret buying thermals.

PRE-LOVED

RUTH E. CARTER

Academy Award–winning Costume Designer, renowned for her revolutionary work on Marvel's Black Panther *blockbusters,* Malcolm X, Do the Right Thing *and many more, who understands that the influence of clothing goes far beyond the fabric.*

ON THE POWER OF CLOTHING AND WHAT IT CAN BECOME

People often think that costume designers only wear vintage clothing and accessories. I am the antithesis of this. I am a bit of a collector, though, and I have a Jean Paul Gaultier knitted hat from the 90s, and a coat by him too. They are pieces that felt ultra-special and I bought them in the hope that one day I would wear them, and lo and behold that day comes some ten or twenty years later.

I came up through the Madonna era: mismatched earrings, scrunch boots, 80s punk, but I have never felt beholden to any one era or any single style. And I am not, and have never been, someone who wears the traditional costume designer uniform: a hat from the 40s, jacket from the 50s and shoes from the 60s. I am more about a genre of dressing than an era. What a piece of clothing means—what it might reference—is important, but so too are the clothes that instill confidence, that give a sense of pride and a sense of self in the day-to-day.

My aesthetic has always been rooted in "Afro-future," which explores the imagined future through the black cultural lens. We have long had legendary images of the civil rights movements, like the Black Panthers in leather jackets that everyone wanted to wear, or the hip-hop of the 80s and the 90s. When you put on oversized jeans with a men's 60s jacket and a cropped T-shirt, suddenly you were emulating your favorite hip-hop artist. For me, it is about being part of a genre, or a movement, rather than paying homage to a particular era.

Clothes mean different things to different people, and an item of clothing can come to symbolize something far greater than itself. When we see Martin Luther King, John Lewis, Diane Nash and Amelia Boynton wearing trench coats during the civil rights marches, we might not notice that their hands were in their pockets as they marched. But this was to project an image of non-violent protests. When I think of Trayvon Martin, the seventeen-year-old who was fatally shot by a neighborhood watch volunteer on his way home from a convenience store, I think of the hoodie that he was wearing in the images the media used. That single piece of clothing was adopted immediately by a huge number of people who showed their support by also wearing a hoodie. For me, this was incredibly powerful; when we wore the hoodie we all became Trayvon Martin. His hoodie became a symbol of innocence, and I think it will forever be that. A form of activism that everyone recognizes and understands.

What we wear, I've learned, can become more powerful than we ever intended. In early 2020, I collaborated on a clothing line with a brand. We created a T-shirt that we gave away for free. On it was a line drawing of my face, while underneath was written "Trust your Voice," which is a mantra I have applied to my life and work. During Covid and the Black Lives Matter protests, there was a college student here in Atlanta who was dragged from her car with her boyfriend and tased. When she appeared at a press conference shortly afterwards to speak about what had happened to her, she was wearing my T-shirt. This impacted me deeply; when I said "Trust your Voice" I was referencing my own journey, but that young woman woke up that day and decided to trust *her* voice. The symbolism of clothing is incredible, and how people interpret it for what they need in that moment.

Clothing is meant to be shared, recycled, and reworked. A certain piece might mean something special to me, but I always hope that someone else will build on its story. This is the beauty of vintage. And I tell my family and friends the same thing—let some things go. It will go on to be a gem for someone else; they will appreciate it and do something wonderful with it, so that its journey continues.

PRE-LOVED

When I interviewed Ruth for this chapter, her passion for clothing and what it is capable of—in terms of how it can make you feel, and how it can become a symbol for something far, far greater—served to remind me of the importance of clothing as a communicator. What we wear says a lot about who we are and how we are feeling, which is why what we buy, and how we buy it, should be given appropriate consideration.

Remember that whole period when we were told that more is more, and fast fashion and mass greedy consumerism were celebrated? Yeah, well the thing about that is not only did it financially ruin people, it turns out that it also screwed the planet. Not single-handedly, of course, but it has played a significant part. It's been reported that at the beginning of this decade, the fashion industry accounted for around 10 percent of global carbon emissions and 20 percent of wastewater—to give that context, it takes an alarming 10,000 liters of water to produce one pair of jeans. The fashion and textile production model and supply chain have long been acknowledged to be environmentally damaging, and while integral work has been started to try to change that, it is a long and precarious process. There are global communities that have been built around factories and producers, and pulling at one string of that could unravel the already precarious economic situations of hundreds of thousands of people. The fashion supply chain is so complicated that until every single element of the production chain is transparent on every level, many brands won't know with certainty exactly where and how every element of a piece was created. For the majority of us, the production line isn't something that we can directly solve; however, there are smaller steps that still make a difference.

In early 2020, supermodel, icon and the then Contributing Sustainability Editor for *British Vogue*, Amber Valletta, presented her manifesto for "being green." Amongst her "10 Ways to Live an Eco-Friendly Life," she included: "Reduce, Revamp and Recycle: The fashion industry produces an average of 100 billion pieces of clothing annually, with only 7.7 billion people on earth. Buy for long-term style not short-term trends, repair damage, shop vintage. Lastly, don't bin clothes! Donate or use a designated textile recycling bin," and, "Take Ownership: You are responsible for the impact of your choices. Make mindful, conscious purchases, because there is a hidden environmental or human cost to almost everything we buy. Our power lies in the pause before we reach for our wallets."

A reported 85 percent of textiles needlessly end up in landfills or are incinerated, and each of us must take responsibility for the large or small part we may play in that. Buying less and buying better isn't going to immediately solve the environmental impact, but every little bit helps. We can make better use of what we already own, either by wearing them or putting them back into circulation for someone else to fall in love with. At every given opportunity, everyone should shop in their own wardrobes first, and the wardrobe of someone else second, before we consider buying anything new. Make considerate choices and always ask yourself: how much is enough, and do I have too much?

It will take time to change our shopping habits, but the huge increase in the popularity of resale sites and fashion rentals proves that the demand for these services is huge. But the bigger they become, the harder they are to navigate. Selling and buying pre-loved pieces takes trust, patience and focus—you need to know what you are looking for, and where you are likely to find it. It always starts in your own closet, with a thorough take-no-prisoners cleanse before you can know what you want to sell and what, if anything, you need to buy.

EDITING YOUR CLOSET

How often have you opened the doors to your closet and lamented having nothing to wear? We have all done it, and of course it usually has nothing to do with what is facing us on the rack and more to do with the mood we are in that day. Like going grocery shopping hungry, trying to decide on something to wear when in a foul mood will end with some terrible decision-making. Instead, reach for an old favorite, close the doors and revisit the closet in a better mood to fully appreciate what you have and to hopefully dig out some long-forgotten treats.

The wardrobe edit is hugely beneficial, but it is also time-consuming, so never approach it thinking you can do it quickly. Not dedicating the time to it will result in you feeling furious and resentful for ever starting it in the first place while staring at a bed covered in piles of clothes. Set aside at least two hours but be aware that it will likely take longer. Start first thing in the morning, and never in the evening—no one will have good judgement about a six-year-old, once-worn jumpsuit at eleven at night.

Once you have the time, you need to be methodical. Do not pull everything out and throw it on the bed or floor—that is just transferring the problem from one place to another. Instead, work piece by piece and start to build out four piles: keep, sell, charity, recycle. I start with the drawers and then build to the racks, as the drawers tend to take longer since that is where we are likely to have more items pushed to the back that need attention. Lingerie is first up. Any underwear with holes is unacceptable, I don't care how comfortable they are, and should immediately be thrown into the recycle pile. Everyone deserves better than threadbare underwear. Please also add any bras that are uncomfortable, tights with holes or runs, and socks that are worn in the toes and/or heel (unless you can darn, in which case darn the darn socks). Then move through T-shirts, tanks, gym gear and any other treats hiding in the drawers. Be ruthless. Anything that is discolored beyond saving, ill-fitting, unworn or unloved gets added to a pile. After the drawers, hit up the shelves and then finally the racks, and if you aren't sure if you still like something, try it on. It is also important to note that when doing the closet edit, you need to be feeling good about yourself, as you will look at yourself in the mirror a lot. If, for whatever reason, you aren't feeling on your personal A-game, do not edit your closet. Go do something to make yourself feel better instead.

If you aren't sure if you want to keep an item, ask yourself questions. *When was the last time I wore it? Do I love it? What does it mean to me? How do I feel in it?* Be honest in your response. If you haven't worn something in a long time, there is always a good reason for that, and it means you probably won't be wearing it again any time soon. If it is now the wrong size, be realistic as to whether it will be the correct size at any point in the near future. You don't want anything hanging in your closet that makes you feel bad about yourself in any way. Life is too short to feel judged by a pair of jeans.

Once you have worked through everything, revisit the piles. Do you definitely want to keep, sell, donate or recycle it all? Work back through it pile by pile and edit as need be. If there is anything you are unsure about, defer to a friend or loved one whose taste you trust. But ultimately it comes down to whether you will genuinely wear the piece and feel great in it. If you won't, then get rid of it.

Editing your closet is completely personal, so only bring in outside advice if you feel you need some help and direction. Friends can be distracting, as it almost always involves wine (I know, I have been that friend), and they can try to change your opinion on pieces that you might love. I helped a friend and colleague edit her closet, and while she wanted me to be ruthless, she managed to hold her own on a couple of pieces that I urged her to donate. One was a velvet harlequin jumpsuit that I told her should only be worn with juggling balls while riding a unicycle, but she told me her husband loved her in it, and who am I to argue with that (and I really tried).

Once you are set on your decisions, bag up the pile to be recycled and find your closest charity clothing collection bin, as you need to get it all out of your house quickly in case you go searching for holey pants. Decide which charity shop you'd like to donate to, and drop that pile off, and then it is just a matter of figuring out how to sell what is left, and what closet holes now need to be filled.

HOW TO SELL

When selling clothes, you must be reasonable and unsentimental. Acknowledge where the item came from (i.e. is it fast-fashion, mid-market, vintage or designer), what condition it is in (please, please, please ensure it is at least clean and ironed), if there is a market for it, and if so, where that market is. There are many platforms available on which to sell clothes; some that you do yourself, others that you hand over to professionals.

Do your research: search for similar items so you know what the market price is, and where they are popular. To avoid disappointment, it is very unlikely that you will get what you paid for the item, so be realistic with your financial expectations.

For non-brand vintage and good-quality items, eBay, Vinted, Depop and marketplaces are just a selection that have proven successful, and not too traumatic, when it comes to taking pictures, uploading and selling. Before you sell, check what they charge per sale, as some take more than others. Be honest about any marks, damage or wear and tear, as anything you fail to mention will come back and bite you in the form of seemingly a hundred messages back and forth with the buyer, and a terrible rating. Selling your own items does take time, so again, dedicate an afternoon to photographing it all and writing detailed descriptions, including sizing. Yes, people will want to know the length of the sleeve and the depth of the hem. Just get out your measuring tape and think of the pocket money.

For designer items, the luxury resale market has been growing steadily and is more popular than ever, and Vestiaire Collective, The RealReal, HEWI and even eBay are great for special finds. Renowned stylist Clare Richardson, who has worked for *Vogue*, *WSJ Magazine*, Calvin Klein, Hermès and COS, launched Reluxe in 2022, a luxury pre-loved shopping platform. The idea of "slow fashion" has always been important to her, and she wanted to be able to encourage women to shop in a more sustainable way, rather than buying new. "When it comes to designer, buying 'brand new' is not always as appealing as it once was," Clare says. "But when buying anything, it should still feel like a special experience. You are treating yourself, so it is important to feel treated in the pre-loved space. The curation of items is fundamental to me, as the resale market can feel as saturated as every other part of the fashion industry, so when it comes to what we sell, we apply the same approach that you should to your closets: less is more." Using her massive network of fashion icons and stylish women, Clare encouraged them to join the Reluxe community and sell pieces from their own closets. It's a pre-loved treasure trove. "So many women have items that they have never worn, some that still have the tags on. Or something they have worn once, and it's since been gathering dust. There is no excuse for them to languish when they could be loved and adored by someone else. When I visit the sellers' homes, it never fails to amaze me the amount that some people have unworn in cupboards, lofts, drawers and bags. I'm desperate to get it all out of hiding and encourage more people to buy pre-loved before they buy new."

Additionally, it is worth checking if the place that you purchased your piece from offers a resale service, as it is something that bigger retailers and single brands—both designer and fast-fashion—are starting to do to encourage the circularity of fashion and keep their items out of landfills.

HOW TO BUY

Obviously the most sustainable approach to shopping is not to buy anything at all. So, once you have edited your closet, think carefully about whether you truly need to replace what you have gotten rid of. A cleanse is a cleanse after all. You certainly don't need to replace it all—I am sure that many of those expelled items were unnecessary purchases or gifts in the first place. However, do look for legitimate gaps, and I would almost place money on your gaps being closet essentials. Refer to the Capsule Wardrobe chapter before buying anything.

Once you have decided what you need, research the brands that you like and discover where the majority are sold. I will just mention here that you shouldn't buy pre-loved underwear or swimwear, but anything else, in my opinion, goes. If you are looking for pre-loved items that are mid-market, then eBay and other marketplaces should be your first port of call. If you are looking to spend a little bit extra, take your time on luxury resale sites to explore the brand offering and the average prices expected. Look for items with longevity, that you know you will wear forever, are not trend led, and are durable, as you should be seeking quality over quantity always. You are buying something to have for the foreseeable, and not something that will end up in one of the piles during your next closet edit. Every time you edit your closet there should be less and less in those piles—that is the aim.

If buying designer, please buy from reputable sellers that have the items authenticated. Usually, if a well-maintained designer item looks like it is a bargain, it is likely to be a fake, so be wary. If in doubt, find another listing elsewhere of the same item, or same brand, and familiarize yourself with all the labels, tags and signatures. Always read the description, ensure the size is accurate for you (as returning pre-loved items because you didn't check the size is just as bad environmentally as returning something new), understand what the faults are and don't be afraid to ask questions. A pre-loved, vintage or secondhand purchase (they are all the same thing FYI) is still a purchase, so you need to make sure you are buying wisely and buying something that you will wear.

Designer pre-loved pieces are often considered to be collector's items, and the price will reflect that. Just because it is secondhand doesn't mean that it will be cheaper, especially when it comes to bags by Gucci, Chanel, Hermès, Louis Vuitton and the like. Bags, like watches, often go up in value rather than down, so if you know you want a particular style, and it's not about the thrill of the hunt for you, contact a resale platform and they might be able to source it for you.

It is worth setting alerts for certain designers or pieces on your favorite pre-loved sites. I know someone who has alerts set for 80s Saint Laurent jewellery, 90s Gaultier, vintage Gripoix glass jewellery when they were producing for Chanel, 80s and 90s Ralph Lauren, early 2000s Blumarine, and *anything* from the Alexander McQueen 2013 runway collection. Incidentally this woman leads an incredibly busy life, so I imagine that most of these alerts are set and maintained in the hours when she should be sleeping. It makes my alert for absolutely anything from the Nicolas Ghesquière Balenciaga FW2006 collection and a 90s slip dress from Narciso Rodriguez look small fry. A lot of it comes down to the time you are willing to spend searching for these items, and how much you really want them. But knowing what you want is more than half the battle.

WHAT TO SEEK OUT

BAGS

Bags do get better with age—if they have been looked after. If you are looking for a specific designer bag by a certain brand, hunt high and low and you may get one cheaper if it has more wear and tear. However, buy it only if you can repair it and bring it back to life, otherwise hold out for one that is a little more expensive but in better shape.

Brands to look for: Gucci Horsebit, Christian Dior Saddle, Louis Vuitton Speedy in traditional monogram, 1950s top-handle frame bags, Chloé Joyce

COSTUME JEWELLERY

What is junk to someone else can become treasure to you. Big, chunky jewellery goes in and out of fashion, which means that there is a lot of it on the resale market. Original pieces from the 80s are what you are hunting for as they are the ultimate in statement costume, but avoid anything that is discolored or the plating is peeling off, as it will never shine back up. A little tarnish, however, can be rubbed away with some baking soda and lemon juice.

Brands to look for: 80s Saint Laurent, 80s and 90s Chanel, all Schiaparelli, 80s Vivienne Westwood

PRINTED SILK SHIRTS AND DRESSES

I have a friend who can't walk past a vintage store without popping in to look for silk negligees and nightshirts. Now she has discovered some beautiful pieces, but she has definitely bought some haunted and cursed ones too. Personally, I would recommend that you stick to shirts and dresses—and maybe a robe or two—especially those in intricate and richly colored prints. Do check that they are 100 percent silk and not a polyblend, and wash them on the handwash setting when you get home.

Brands to look for: Versace, Hermès, Céline SS2011, Prada, Isabel Marant

DENIM

Remember that 10,000 liters of water it takes to make one pair of jeans? Well, that is one very good reason to look for denim in charity and vintage stores, and on resale sites (add Levi's to your search lists immediately). The bonus is that the more denim is worn, often the better it becomes. Jeans and jackets are usually a bit tougher and will have worn well, but don't always trust the measurements on the labels as people often tailor denim to suit them, so if possible try before you buy. Or be prepared to recycle once again.

Brands to look for: Levi's 501, 70s Lee, 70s Wrangler, current Agolde, current A.P.C.

LEATHER JACKETS

Brand-new leather can be very expensive, and it sometimes takes a bit of time to relax. When it comes to pre-loved leather, however, someone has kindly paid the price of both so that you can benefit. Do watch out for overly faded leather, as that can't be easily fixed, but I think that a little bit adds character. Do a zipper and snap test before buying if possible too, to ensure they are all in working order, as replacing zippers is an expensive fix.

Brands to look for: Acne Studios, Rick Owens, traditional men's motorcycle jackets

SHOES

I know lots of people are a bit weird about secondhand shoes, and I understand it. But there are many poor unloved once-worn shoes out there that were kicked off at the end of a wedding, or a night of dancing, with someone swearing to never ever wear them again, and they deserve a second chance on someone's more resilient feet. Look for evening sandals so you can see if there is any damage on the inside sole, and check that the heel is in one piece. Even one night of dancing can shatter the sturdiest of stilettos.

Brands to look for: any runway shoes, as they are more likely to become collector's items, including Prada, Nicolas Ghesquière Balenciaga, original Alexander McQueen, Alaïa ballerinas, Phoebe Philo Céline

BIG COATS

When some lucky so-and-sos move from the Northern Hemisphere to warmer climates, they often leave their biggest coats behind. The packing weight is just not worth it. Again, most of them are in fine fettle, but check for moth damage, rips and fabric thinning across the elbows, hems of the sleeves, where a crossbody bag may have rubbed and the seat. Vintage often conjures up images of women in huge fake-fur coats, but I feel that has had its time in the (winter) sun and should be retired forever.

Brands to look for: Toteme, Max Mara, Burberry, Moncler, Joseph

HAVE A CARE

From personal experience, the items in my wardrobe that I don't wear are often passed over because they need to be tailored or mended; same with shoes that desperately need a trip to the cobblers. There is nothing more satisfying than finally fixing a piece that you love and feeling like you are wearing something new. Shopping in our own closets is one of life's tiny pleasures, but it happens so rarely if you don't keep on top of things.

While I don't expect you all to learn the art of shoemaking, there is something to be said about learning to sew. Again, I'm not suggesting that we get all crafty, but when was the last time you sewed back on a button? Be honest. I have a small sewing kit that I am now building out. I can sew on a button, though I'm not confident how long it will remain on the item, nor will I let you see my handiwork on the reverse. But I do try. If threads become loose or have snagged, I know how to pull them through using a needle so they don't get worse. I know that doesn't technically make me Martha Stewart, but it sure makes me feel like an accomplished adult.

The art of make do and mend got lost as fast fashion got its claws in, so as fast fashion's popularity wanes, let's shine a light on those sewing boxes and fix what we can in our closets ourselves.

PRE-LOVED IN BRIEF

1   What we buy is as important as how we wear it.

2   Clothes are meant to be shared, recycled and reworked.

3   Always choose quality over quantity.

4   Buy less, buy better.

5   Edit your closet when you are feeling energetic, time-rich and positive.

6   Recycle holey underwear and uncomfortable bras.

7   Clean and iron everything before selling. That really should go without saying, but here I am saying it.

8   Do you really need to fill the closet gaps?

9   Selling and buying pre-loved takes time and research, but it is always worth it.

10   Own a sewing kit and learn how to sew on a button.

THE
FINISHING
TOUCH

KATE YOUNG

The most in-demand A-list stylist for A-list clients, including Selena Gomez, Dakota Johnson and Rachel Weisz, who knows that the style devil is in the final details.

THE TRANSFORMATIONAL POWER OF JEWELLERY

Great jewellery should do one of two things: make people talk or make them ask a lot of questions. It is the key to standing out in even the most generic outfits.

But jewellery is very personal. A piece that looks silly on me often looks great on someone else. So, finding what is the stand-out for you can take some trial-and-error practice.

The power of jewellery is its ability to transform an outfit. When I travel to the Cannes Film Festival with clients, often attending a few events, I take just a couple of dresses— usually one in color and one black or white. The bulk of my luggage is jewellery options. One night I might wear a dress with my favorite gold bracelets, the next I'll wear a huge necklace and do my hair differently and—like magic—the dress becomes something else. Jewellery offers flexibility, and given how expensive clothes can be, and the fact that so many of us are trying to buy less, I like to think how I can change up what I have with something unique.

My mom has *really* fantastic jewellery, collected from her mother, grandmother and aunt. She'd let me play with her jewellery boxes when I was little, and I was utterly obsessed with her charm bracelet. I think this is where my love for jewellery started. She had two charm bracelets, one of which I now have, which has charms from every place she visited before she was twenty-five. It is something I take great care of. (Her other bracelet is more special, and firmly in her possession still!) I love the idea of buying jewellery as a memento, and it is something I now do myself. It doesn't have to be expensive; it just needs to mean something to you.

My family and I go to Costa Rica a lot as we have friends there, and my kids and I always buy a bracelet each from the street markets. We wear them until they literally fall off (they are made of string and usually last for a few months) as it's always a nice reminder when it's freezing cold and horrible in New York that we have this special piece from a beautiful place where we had fun together.

That said, when I am picking jewellery for myself, I am pretty careful. I don't buy anything impulsively, as my taste is quite specific and I like to think about something a lot before I commit. My day-to-day uniform consists of black trousers and navy sweaters. This is genuinely what I wear all the time! Then with that I add a few Monica Vinader bracelets, my wedding ring (I never take mine off), a pinkie ring and a long Cartier pendant necklace. I bought that necklace at duty free, as I had worked with it a few times with clients, tried it on many, many times, and just felt really connected to it. Each piece personalizes my quiet uniform. For evenings out, you can never go wrong with one big piece. I have a giant Elsa Peretti bean necklace, and big cuffs from Sidney Garber, both of which I wear a lot. And I love a really fun statement cocktail ring. My top tip, if you are a jewellery lover, is to start with your jewellery and build the rest of your outfit around it. Jewellery can tell a story, often more than clothes can. The next time you see someone in a piece you admire, it may be worth finding out what the story is.

THE FINISHING TOUCH

Nothing I have ever worn gets more compliments than a gold ring I wear on the middle finger of my left hand. It is a contemporary take on a signet ring, with black onyx surrounded by tiny, and I must emphasize *tiny*, diamonds. *"Where is it from?"* NET-A-PORTER. *"Who designed it?"* Anissa Kermiche. *"Who gave it to you?"* Well, I bought it for myself. And that final answer never fails to thrill me. Yup, I bought myself a diamond ring—regardless of how tiny the diamonds are, diamonds they still are. I also bought myself the small diamond stud in my right ear, the small diamond hoop in my left and the delicate diamond necklace that I never take off.

Regardless of how that sounds, it is not a brag. I bought them at different times over my forty-plus years, when I could, and I am very proud of myself for that. Each piece represents a time or event in my life, and I get to carry them with me every day. I didn't wait for someone to buy them for me; I bought them for myself, and I think that is pretty bloody marvellous.

Often more so than clothing, jewellery is completely personal, as is our attachment to it. The relationship we have to each piece is emotional. It represents something different to each of us, even if it is the same piece bought from the same store. I'm not talking department store jewellery, though that does definitely have a time and place. I'm talking heirlooms, vintage finds, investments and gifts. "I've always said that there is something spiritual about jewellery and that it holds energy," Erin Wasson told me. "When you become a collector, you realize that jewellery holds power and that you can own things, like rings or a bracelet, that when you put them on it's almost like you're Wonder Woman. 'I've got my superpowers, now let's go!'"

Jewellery that you have inherited from loved ones is the most precious, even if none of the jewellery is precious at all. When I was a kid, I liked to play with my granny's jewellery that she left on her dressing table, and long after she has gone, when I think of her clip-on earrings and her string of pearls, they evoke memories of her, times we were together and even her scent. Clothes don't often do that. Though I did love a red leather jacket she had, and often wonder what became of it. None of her jewellery would mean anything to anyone outside my family, and none of it was expensive, but to my mum, my siblings and my cousins, those pieces of jewellery will conjure up different memories to mine. That is the power of jewellery. It doesn't matter what it cost, it's what it represents. We all have special connections to the tiny—or large—pieces that we often wear every day, or to the pieces that only come out for special occasions, and the importance of that connection is known only to the wearer.

Everyone has a different approach to how they wear jewellery. Some like the minimalist approach and wear only a few key delicate pieces, while others like to pile it on. Both are correct. As Kate Young told me, "One person's epitome of classic might be Audrey Hepburn, but another person's classic is Rihanna." But what they can agree on is that jewellery can instantly transform anything you are wearing. It can take an outfit from work to date, from casual to event, and it gives whatever you are wearing the personal touch, without taking huge risks. You don't even have to spend too much money, if any at all.

Now, telling someone exactly what jewellery to buy is futile, as we are all drawn to different things, but I can suggest how you buy it, what to look for and how to wear it.

You just need to know what you like, where and when you want to wear it, and most importantly, for you, when is less more, and more better?

BUYING JEWELLERY

Buying jewellery for yourself is empowering and, if you can afford it, you shouldn't wait to be gifted it. Especially as it is incredibly difficult to choose jewellery for someone else because it is so individual.

If you want to treat yourself to something special—and special doesn't mean expensive or laden in precious stones, it simply means special to you—you need to know what you are looking for. Ask yourself the following questions and do your research. Are you looking for something you want to wear all the time? Is it more of a special-occasion piece? How much wear and tear will it be subjected to? But most importantly, what is the category—ring, earrings, necklace, bracelet, etc.? Going shopping for "jewellery" is as overwhelming as shopping for "clothes," so you need to pinpoint what it is you would like and focus. If you are looking for vintage, find out all the best vintage stores in your neighbourhood, or further afield if you are willing to travel. Look online at pieces you like, find out the era or designer and build your search around that. Online marketplaces are jewellery meccas, but you must have the patience to discover and to bid.

Try pieces on so you can get a sense of weight and size, and learn your ring size! You can download a ring-sizer app to measure your existing rings, or of course there is the paper trick: wrap a strip of paper around your finger and then measure it flat. I have never been able to make that little bit of paper work accurately for me, and of course your fingers aren't all the same size; it is a rough guide if you need it—though think of it as a last-best option. Don't be afraid to go into a store, try some rings on and ask a professional to measure your fingers for you. That is their skill set, so take advantage of it.

Buying designer jewellery is the same as buying designer clothes: you are often paying for the label and not the actual worth of the piece itself. However, if you are planning to spend some money and invest in jewellery, you need to understand the value of it. Solid gold is straightforward, but get to understand the difference between gold plated, vermeil and gold filled. In basic terms, gold filled means a cheaper metal like brass or copper that has been covered in gold, but it is quite resilient. Vermeil is similar, but the base metal is always sterling silver. Gold plated is very similar to gold filled, but the difference is the way the gold is attached, and it will tarnish faster and expose the metal beneath. While silver jewellery is cheaper, you need to ensure that you are getting the best-value silver that will last. Sterling silver is more durable and harder-wearing than silver, and look for the 925 marking that will confirm that the silver is 92.5 percent pure. Silver is a softer metal than gold, so may take on the dents and reshaping of everyday wear, but I think that makes it all the more personal!

If you clean your jewellery regularly, it shouldn't give you much of an issue; however, the longer it is left unworn and exposed to the elements, the quicker it will tarnish. Do store it away from direct light, and a jewellery box is worth the investment if you have invested in a couple of pieces. Velvet lining will help prevent scratches, but even plastic boxes that keep the pieces separate and tangle-free are beneficial.

However, there are some metals that you should probably avoid, even if you love, love, love the piece: 1970s brass, I am looking at you. Vintage costume jewellery can look fantastic, but treat them as occasional-wear items only, for the metal will oxidize when in contact with sweat. Wearing necklaces and bracelets for short periods of time should be OK, but best to avoid the rings for any length of time or you may end up with green fingers.

JEWELLERY CAPSULE WARDROBE

If you are a maximalist, I'm assuming that you already know what you like and how to wear it. Pile it on with pleasure. But for minimalists, or for jewellery novices, where to start can be more difficult. So, my suggestion would be to start small and build on it once you have more confidence in your approach. There are a few items that we should all have when experimenting with jewellery, and whether they become your special finishing touch or pieces you never take off, that is always your prerogative.

CHAIN NECKLACE

Chain necklaces, like blue jeans, are a perennial. They suit everyone and work with everything. Necklaces are designed to highlight and draw attention up to the face. Or down if that is your intention—no judgement here. Although a chunkier chain necklace can serve to pull focus itself. I wear one thin chain daily but will add shorter ones when on vacation in the evening to add layers, and I like to upscale to a couple of chunkier styles in the winter so they aren't swallowed by knitwear. I used to like wearing them over black turtlenecks, but that was no more when it was pointed out that I looked like The Rock meme. If you don't know it, google it.

Ideally the chain you wear regularly should sit just below or on your collarbone, and the ones you add for layering should sit either above like a loose choker, or longer to hang below.

How to wear: Necklaces make the biggest impact when seen against skin, rather than fabric. Wear with a shirt or blouse that is opened to where you can bear to bare, and let the necklaces fall into that. It doesn't matter if you can't see the end of the necklace or the pendant, as sometimes the idea that the necklace is concealed in your clothing makes it more interesting, and seductive.

STATEMENT BRACELET

I find that either you are a bracelet person or you aren't. And if you are, you go all out. Quite right too. I discuss the art of stacking a little later, but there is something to be said for the power of one single eye-catching bracelet. Or maybe two. I have a brilliant friend with a very successful career, and after one bumper year and bumper bonus, she rightfully treated herself to a tennis bracelet. Now for those of us who don't own such an item, it is a narrow bracelet formed of diamonds or gems, real or otherwise, all of the same size, set in gold, silver or platinum. They are timeless, classic and just one has the ability to upgrade the simplest of outfits. My friend wears hers every day, and it really adds a certain something-something to her dog-walking outfits. But if you aren't in the market for diamonds (any day now) yet fancy the idea of a bracelet, then look to gold cuffs. Something a little weightier, perhaps quite sculptural, that wraps around your wrist or upper forearm, and instantly gives tired workwear a new lease on life.

How to wear: For day-to-day, team with something simple. In winter, a knit with the sleeves pushed up to reveal a stack of bracelets or one statement cuff is perfection. In summer, swap the knit for a silk shirt or cotton T-shirt. If the clothing is a neutral color, mix your metals for more interest. If the clothing is colored or printed, gold works best with warm colors, while silver shines with cooler tones.

COCKTAIL RING

The ultimate dinner-party finishing touch, practically designed for, or to encourage, expressive gesticulation. The beauty of the cocktail ring is that you only need one. The bigger, the bolder, the better. Play with colored gems—real or fake—to enhance an outfit, and be free with proportions. I love one large ring worn on the middle finger that is permitted to dominate the hand. Not clown big, but weighty enough to draw attention and start a conversation. They are perfect for evening but will also serve to transform a casual off-duty look too.

How to wear: For evening, a bit of color in the ring, or rings, will sparkle brighter in candlelight as you elegantly gesticulate when telling your fascinating story. And colored stones look more expensive in low lighting than in daylight.

COCKTAIL EARRINGS

Cocktail earrings are flamboyant, spectacular and confident. They can drop from ears to shoulders—or beyond if you so desire—or they can extend out from your lobe like a burst of sunrays. They frame your face while furbishing your look and adding an element of drama. But the best thing about cocktail earrings is that the most interesting ones are often costume jewellery and can be discovered in vintage stores for a bargain.

Picking statement earrings you like is much like how you are drawn to trinkets or ornaments for your home: they have to speak to you and charm you as much, or more so, as you expect them to charm others. Look at colored stones and how they would complement your regular clothing go-to pieces, and step out of your comfort zone in terms of size and shape. After all, what is the worst that could happen? You decide you hate them? Just take them off and pass them back to a vintage store for someone else to fall in love with.

Sure, cocktail earrings will look good with a cocktail dress, but as always, they will look better with the unexpected: a suit, double denim or of course the simplicity of a tank or T-shirt. You don't need to be dressed up from head to toe for an event; sometimes from the shoulders up makes the biggest impression. I love a chunky knit, some big earrings and a red lip. Cozy yet comely.

Allow them to dominate your outfit, rather than combining with dramatic prints, loads of textures and clashing colors, as they can all quickly overwhelm. And finally, lots of cocktail earrings, both old and new, have a clip-on fastening. This is great if you have never succumbed to a piercing; however, a heavy clip-on earring squeezing your poor earlobes will be unbearable after minutes of wear. So literally weigh up the options before committing, and if the fastening feels too tight, you can gently loosen the tension bar (bottom of the clip) to relax the intense grip on the earlobe.

How to wear: The beauty of cocktail earrings is that they work with damn near anything. If I am heading out to meet friends and can't quite figure out how dressy I want to be, or am expected to be, I will add some cocktail earrings to a low-key look of top and jeans—they instantly make me look like I have made far more effort than I actually have. The simpler the outfit, the more over the top you can go with the earrings. A neutral top with drop sparklers is fabulous. And for evening, bare shoulders benefit from shoulder-grazing earrings (and no necklace), whereas if your dress is more covered up and high-necked, keep the earrings shorter so they aren't competing with the neckline.

HOOP EARRINGS

If you have pierced ears, you can't go wrong with classic hoops. Large and theatrical, or tiny ones that cuddle your ear, and all diameters in between, I would encourage you to have several sizes in your arsenal. They are an instant pick-me-up, and they pull you together, even when you feel anything but.

How to wear: Hoop earrings are my go-to office look on a Monday, as they soften the sharp structure of a blazer, but can make a basic shirt or sweater feel more elevated. I think the ideal everyday size is 3cm (about 1.2 inches) in diameter, but by all means go bigger for evening or events.

STYLING JEWELLERY

Once you have bought, found or sourced the pieces, you then need to decide how, where and when you want to wear them.

EAR PARTY

I first had my ears pierced, after much parental begging, when I was fifteen. I went through the hell of wearing massive and ugly training studs (ages me, doesn't it), until finally one day I could remove them and wear whatever dangly nonsense I wanted. And I did. Until it became apparent that my by now swollen and constantly throbbing and bleeding ears were sensitive souls which rejected every piece of tin I tried to insert in them. Eventually I gave up and locked the tarnished earrings away, and the ear holes closed. Then, in my thirties, on a work trip to New York I met with a jeweller I knew, and with the aid of a shot of vodka I decided to have my ears re-pierced and added several new punctures on both sides. Now, piercing techniques were much improved by that point, and I must add that it was one of the industry's greats who created the holes. However, it is not ideal to have multiple piercings done at the same time on both sides of your head, as you can't lie down or sleep properly for days. Once the inevitable infections had passed (please, as your piercer will instruct, clean your new wounds with saline all the time—I did not, and I paid for it), I filled those holes with a couple of permanent hoops, and then constantly mixed and matched the rest. Sometimes I wore six earrings at once, sometimes just the one, but rarely did I wear a matching pair.

As I write this, one tiny hoop and one stud remain, but currently I have fallen out of love with wearing multiple earrings and instead choose one favorite larger sculptural piece in my left ear to dress up a work look, and I have an asymmetrical set of oversized gold drop earrings to wear for events. They always attract attention, regardless of how many times I have worn them before. Personally, I feel more like me when I wear just one statement piece and don't match. It's a small detail that is simple to achieve, but effective. Though you will need to get over people constantly asking if you are aware that you are wearing just one earring, or if you have lost the other. Just smile and nod.

But when I see the small works of art that people create in their ears—which start at the top with small studs or teeny hoops, then perhaps a stack of matching hoops sitting close to each other, before the earrings get slightly bigger towards the lobe—I know that one day I shall also return to my box of hoops and studs, ready for my ear-party resurgence. For, regardless of age, there is something about multiple piercings that hints at a sense of rebellion, like a tattoo, but one you can change or erase quickly. With that rebellion comes a youthfulness, and we should always hold on to that spirit. Personally, I plan to be an eighty-something-year-old wearing multiple earrings, in a gorgeous clash of different stones, in my no doubt deaf ears. That will get people talking, even if I can't hear them.

STACKING

When stacking rings and bracelets, there are no rules for how much is too much, nor is there a perfect stacking equation. Instead, it is about layering on the pieces, big and small, that mean something to you and make you happy.

When it comes to rings, some like to pile several on a single finger while others favor a horizontal stack across one hand, or they spread them out over left and right to create a sense of balance. The rings can all be the same, or there can be cocktail styles amongst skinny nondescript bands, and a chaos of everything and anything else. All are permitted and correct.

A stack of bracelets benefits from a mix of metals and suggested sentiment. A homemade friendship bracelet, favorite turquoise bits if that's your thing, or some cheap beads from childhood, your own children or a vacation, sitting among a watch and blend of silver and gold, will create a far more interesting tale than the metals alone.

I like the ritual of adding jewellery to an outfit before I leave the house, so take some time to curate and enjoy creating your own little unique masterpiece. Although, consider the results of the stack, especially if the combination of bracelets creates a cacophony of sounds. After all, for Jo Ellison in the Workwear chapter, it was the distracting noise of someone's bracelets that cost them a role in her team. Take note, as the cling-clanging of metal on metal might be charming to you but beyond irritating to others. Like whistling.

NECKMESS

There is a very stylish woman I know who has a knot of necklaces that give me anxiety every time I see her. Over the years she has regularly added narrow chains or pendants around her neck, and never taken them off. They have woven themselves together, it seems never to be parted, regardless of how much patience or how many tools could be applied. And while this is something my embedded tidiness couldn't bear, every time I see her I am drawn to the clutter of charms and talismans that she has collected, and I try to spot the most recent additions. Every other part of her outfit is almost uniform in its simplicity, a contrast to the neckmess, but because it is personal to her, it all makes sense.

To clarify, if not immediately clear, a neckmess is simply a stack of necklaces. But by their nature, and unlike most rings and bracelets, they are likely to coil and bond together. So, if you are a more relaxed individual than me, by all means go ahead and tangle, but forgive me if I approach you with tweezers or a safety pin and attempt to unravel them.

MIXING METALS

The days of picking your metal and sticking to it are long gone. And while cool skin tones may suit silver, white gold and platinum, and warmer tones make yellow and rose gold pop, that doesn't mean you can't mix your metals. I am not loyal to any of them. I wear a mix of gold, silver and rose gold on a daily basis, sometimes in one ear alone. The "rule" to never mix gold and silver is nonsense, and up there with "never wear blue and black." A stack of rings or bracelets in a mix of colors and textures adds depth and modernity.

WHAT TO INVEST IN

If you are looking to spend some money on an item of jewellery and don't know where to start, let me just say congratulations. Buying yourself something special will give you a thrill like nothing else, especially if you are looking to invest in a piece that you will have forever.

In one of my first jobs, when I was at the bottom of the career ladder, a group of colleagues and I were discussing ear piercings around our desks. When I lamented that my piercings had closed and I refused to have to wear training studs again, my then boss, a beautiful and sophisticated fashion director, said, "Why not just buy some beautiful diamond studs?" I think my debit card had been refused that day when trying to buy a sandwich. I didn't get diamond studs in that job, or my next three jobs, but eventually I bought one for my ear stack, and it turns out that my old fashion director was right. She was just several years too early. Diamond stud earrings will never go out of fashion. However, regardless of budget, smaller studs are always the better and forever option over larger studs.

A gold chain with a small pendant or precious stone is also a good investment. If you are spending serious money, then, if you are like me, you will want to get your wear out of it—ideally every day. So, subtle is the way to go to ensure that it works with everything. If it is a precious stone you are after, think about the colors you wear, and which stones mean something to you. I have always been drawn to emeralds and rubies, for no better reason than I love green and red. Your decision for what you like doesn't need to be any more sophisticated than that.

When I was a teenage bridesmaid, the bride very kindly gifted me a pearl necklace, as was tradition. The string was slightly too long for me, so I had it shortened so that the necklace sat closer to my throat, though not quite a choker. I wore it regularly into my late twenties, and then put it back in its box for the future. Because, for me, pearls are great when you are young, and they are great when you are older, but there is something about pearls and mid-thirties to mid-sixties that makes you look a bit, well, prim. Of course you can mix them as part of a neckmess and they can work perfectly, and look youthful, but if buying as an investment, I would think about how and when you will wear them.

HAVE A CARE

When it comes to storing jewellery, I need to take my own advice here as I have been guilty of throwing lesser-worn items into boxes at the back of drawers or piling up my go-to pieces on a small plate on my dressing table. I then wonder why the long-forgotten pieces are tarnished and unrecognizable, though I never take the time to clean them, and why my necklaces are knotted together. Nothing is more frustrating in the morning than trying to untangle a necklace that you know will bring your look together. So, this section is as much for me as it is for you.

I wear most of my jewellery all the time, only removing my rings and larger earrings at night. I am guilty of swimming (both pool and ocean) in my jewellery, washing up with rings on and spraying perfume directly on to it all. These are massive no-nos, and hugely frowned upon, so don't do as I do.

Storage is key, and ideally each piece of jewellery should have its own small compartment in a tray or box and be kept away from direct sunlight. I've already failed here so shall search for a jewellery box immediately. If you wear a lot of necklaces, it is worth hanging them when not wearing them to avoid them getting tangled. Also, if like me you prefer to wear single earrings, do store them as a pair, as I often lose one or the other for weeks at a time before it resurfaces.

Even with perfect storage, tarnishing and dulling will still happen, but there are easy ways to clean and buff. To bring the pieces back to life, I have a small pot of fine jewellery cleaner I bought online. I soak them for thirty seconds and they come up shiny and new. But you can make home remedies too, using a very small amount of dish soap, warm water and a soft cloth or soft toothbrush. Be very gentle when cleaning, and don't soak costume jewellery as it might make it worse rather than better, especially if there are any stones fixed with glue.

If you have gold-plated items and the plating has started to rub off, there are replating services available, and not at huge cost. Check if the place you bought it from offers to replate; if not, search locally, but make sure they are certified goldsmiths. While wear and tear of plating is to be expected, you can help protect your pieces by not wearing them at night, avoiding contact with water, moisturizers and beauty products, and by not wearing them in hot temperatures when your skin will inevitably sweat.

Disclaimer: If you have invested in pieces, please follow the cleaning and care instructions before you do it yourself. If unsure, please contact the brand or store you bought it from for advice, or if the piece is inherited, take it into a local jewellery store and they can evaluate it and advise.

THE FINISHING TOUCH
IN BRIEF

1   Changing your jewellery is as effective as changing your outfit.

2   Precious jewellery doesn't mean expensive.

3   Buying yourself jewellery is hugely empowering.

4   There is no such thing as jewellery rules.

5   Get to know your metals, and what they are worth.

6   Cocktail earrings are a facelift.

7   Don't be afraid to add OTT jewellery to OTT outfits.

8   Sometimes more is indeed better.

9   Storing your jewellery properly will prolong its life.

10 If you see someone wearing a piece of jewellery, or a stack of it, that you are drawn to, ask them about it. The story will always be worth hearing.

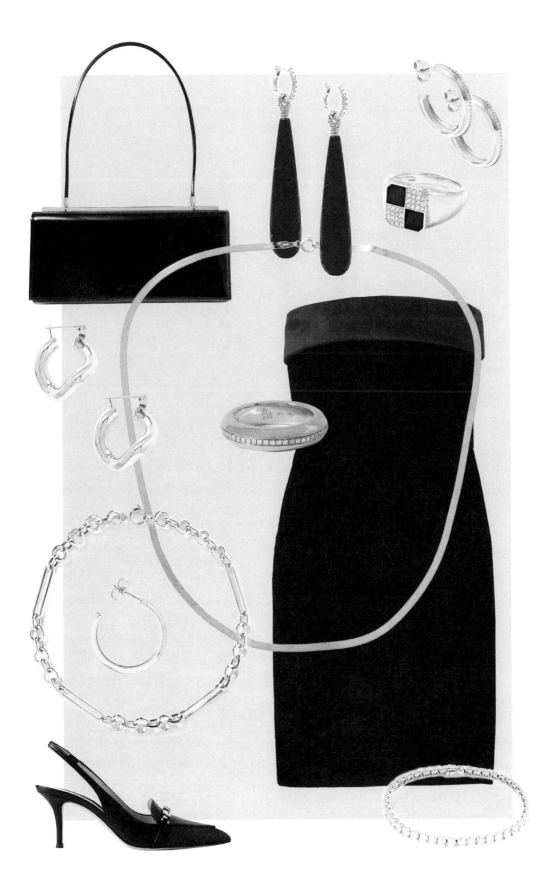

SIZE NOTE

I feel we need to talk about size. Mainly because for a long, long time, no one liked to talk about size. For many years there was only one size in fashion, and that was sample. If you fell out of that box, either smaller or larger, you were not discussed and were left to fend for yourself when it came to getting dressed. While things have moved on, and many brands in the industry are now catering for, and casting, women of every size, there is still a lot to be done, including using fit models of different sizes and shapes and not just sizing up on the sample girl. I mean, come on!

When I wrote this chapter I had a few friends question if I should mention my own sizing. "I feel it will undermine everything you have said in the book when you reveal that you are a size 6," said my most honest critic. When I took that comment to my editor for her opinion she said, "But you *are* a size 6, and there is no reason to hide that." When writing this book I wanted to ensure that it is for everyone, no matter age or size, and I have had a team of great editors make sure that it reads that way. For deciding what to wear can be overwhelming enough, and that is before we add our own personal body issues into the mix.

For the sake of transparency, I am 5'4" (and a half). I am a UK size 6, US 0, IT 38, FR 34, DK 32 and usually an XS if that is the sizing option. In jeans I am size 24, or 25 if I want them a little bit looser. I have a 32B bra size, and in shoes I am a UK 5, US 7 and European 38. I am usually bigger in more affordable store sizes than I am in designer brands. Not that that really means much. I have also been a size 23 and 28 in jeans, a UK 8, an IT 40, an FR 38, and a 5.5 and 6 in shoes, and sometimes smaller in the bra department. Alas, never bigger.

A friend of mine was once momentarily thrilled that she managed to secure a pair of shoes—in her size—from a much-in-demand designer who had just launched a new label. When the package duly arrived at her house she pulled it open, immediately tried the shoes on and, while they felt a bit tight, she was confident that they would give enough. On their first wear out, one foot became so swollen from the tight strap that she had to abandon the shoes under the restaurant table for the entire meal, which she spent berating herself for having one foot fatter than the other. The next day, she examined the shoes and discovered that one shoe was about half a size smaller than the other. You see, it is *never* about your body, it is always the size of the item— whether the sizes come up large or small, or just completely wrong.

You remain the same size after you try on clothes as you were before. Your measurements are the same size when you walk into a store as they are when you walk out. Clothing sizes are not standardized, because what exactly is standard? I'm certainly not standard. Are you?

You just need to know your body, have a rough idea of the sizing spectrum you hit, and not take it at all personally when you are a size bigger in one brand in the same way that you shouldn't become too jubilant when you are a size smaller in another. Take multiple sizes into the changing room, try not to look at the sizes when you try them on, and select the winner that fits.

If buying online, retailers will have measured every item by hand to help you choose the best fit. I realize you might be sceptical about this, but I know that this does indeed happen, as many, many years ago I was one of those employed to measure. Retail returns have a huge environmental impact, and the wrong size accounts for a significant number of them. So do yourself, the retailer and the environment a favor and get to know your own measurements. Once you have them, take time to read the measurements of the piece that you have in your basket and compare them to your own before completing your purchase. Is this time-consuming? Only a little, but it takes far less time to do this than it does to return a package. It will also save you from panic purchases, make you thoughtfully consider everything you buy, and help to avoid those horror moments when you wonder if you are going to have to cut yourself out of a brand-new dress or be stuck in it forever.

Of course our bodies change as we get older, and even if our size doesn't fluctuate, the distribution of weight will. It's a journey that every single one of us will go through, and while it might change the relationship we have with some clothes, it should not affect the way we feel about getting dressed.

Size does matter, but only *your* literal measurements matter, not the size that a dress, a pair of jeans or a bra tells you that you are.

ACKNOWLEDGEMENTS

To the smart, funny, extraordinary and, at times, brutal (if you think I am "no-nonsense" you should meet this lot) Barron family—original, extended and honorary—especially to my forever-chic mum; and to my dad, who instilled in me a love and appreciation of excellent clothes, bloody lovely things, and the power of great books. He would have got such a kick out of this.

A huge thanks to the entire NET-A-PORTER team, but especially to the fashion team, who are not only the best in the business, but every single one of them inspired this book with their own enviable personal style. A very special shout out to my NaP Golden Girls, Alice and Chiara, who are life's ultimate cheerleaders, and to Helen for being so effortlessly cool and stylish (being Scottish obviously helps). Also, Maya, Connie and Michael for their help, speed and perfect taste.

The always exceptional Robert for sitting across from me at lunch and asking, "Why haven't you written that book yet?" and for all the jokes I stole from him that feature in these pages. To Andy/Owen who cuts the best fringe, is the most connected man in all of London, and who made all of this happen with one text message. To the influential Caroline Wood, who received that message, took me on board at Felicity Bryan, and gently led me on the proposal-writing journey, knowing that if I knew from the start how much work goes into them, I would have bolted. Plus, she introduced me to the super-stylish and super-smart Jillian Taylor and the incredible team at Penguin Michael Joseph, who believed in this from the start, and who wrote me such an amazing seduction letter that my friend said I should have it etched on to my bathroom mirror to read every morning. I might still do that.

To Jo Ratcliffe for her glorious illustrations that truly brought the book to life and who managed to interpret my ramblings better than I could have imagined.

Seonaid for reading every chapter before anyone else, as even though we are related, she sugarcoats *nothing*. Cara for her thoughtful edits. Clare and all at Reluxe. Virginia, Ben, Ben, Ben, Alistair, Hywel, Jesper, Hattie, Anthony, Rossa, Jess, Fiona, Eva and Ajesh for all advice, opinions and "You are writing a book and have a full-time job, how aren't you mad yet?" therapy. I was a bit mad.

To Annabel for being wrangler-in-chief, but, of course, to all the strong, empowering, and inspiring contributors, who I am thrilled agreed to do this—thank you for believing in this book, and for understanding and articulating what clothes mean to us all. For those who have asked, "How did you get Oprah?!" I just asked, and she said yes. Which is a lesson in itself.

And, finally, to my brilliant and beautiful Giancarlo, for giving me the direct and indirect confidence to do this. Not to mention the distance and time. Who knew that book-writing was a benefit of long-distance relationships! I highly recommend.

First published in the United States of America in 2024
by Chronicle Books LLC.

Originally published in the United Kingdom in 2024
by Penguin Michael Joseph.

Library of Congress Cataloging-in-Publication Data available.

ISBN 978-1-7972-3262-1

Manufactured in China.

MIX
Paper | Supporting
responsible forestry
FSC™ C008047

Design by Dan Prescott-Bennett.
Typeset in Noah Grotesque.
Illustrations by Jo Ratcliffe.

10 9 8 7 6 5 4 3 2 1

Chronicle books and gifts are available at special quantity discounts to
corporations, professional associations, literacy programs, and other organizations.
For details and discount information, please contact our premiums department
at corporatesales@chroniclebooks.com or at 1-800-759-0190.

CHRONICLE PRISM

Chronicle Prism is an imprint of
Chronicle Books LLC, 680 Second Street,
San Francisco, California 94107
chronicleprism.com